THE BASQUE SERIES

BASQUE NATIONALISM

Basque Nationalism

Stanley G. Payne

UNIVERSITY OF NEVADA PRESS

RENO, NEVADA

1975

Library of Congress Cataloging in Publication Data

Payne, Stanley G
    Basque nationalism.

    (The Basque series)
    Bibliography: p.
    Includes index.
    1. Basque Provinces—History—Autonomy and
independence movements. 2. Nationalism—Basque
Provinces. I. Title.
DP302.B53P38   946'.6   75-15698
ISBN 0-87417-042-7

Basque Series editor, William A. Douglass
University of Nevada Press, Reno, Nevada 89507
Printed in the United States of America
Designed by Dave Comstock

To the Memory of
Joaquín Maurín Juliá
1897 — 1973

Contents

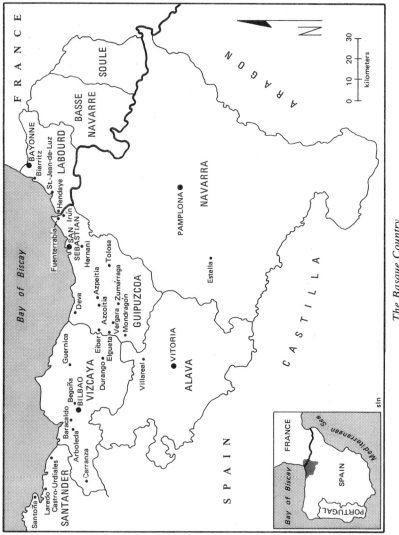

The Basque Country.

Preface

This volume is designed to present a historical account of Basque nationalism, together with an analysis and interpretation of some of the main factors involved. I hope that it may serve to dispel at least a portion of the confusion and misunderstanding surrounding the Basque problem, and that it may also stimulate more thorough monographic research in some of the main topics of modern Basque history.

The study owes a great deal to the assistance and encouragement of Professors Jon Bilbao and William A. Douglass of the Basque Studies Program at the University of Nevada. I have benefitted from the cooperation of a number of the leading figures in the Basque Nationalist Party, whose specific assistance is acknowledged in the footnotes. Professor Juan J. Linz of Yale University has helped to correct a number of errors and offered many suggestions for the expansion and improvement of the volume, not all of which I have been able to pursue. The research and writing has been made possible through generous assistance from the Graduate School of the University of Wisconsin and the American Council of Learned Societies.

This book is dedicated to the memory of Joaquín Maurín, one of the oldest and best of the many Spanish friends I have claimed in twenty years as a Hispanist. The words with which Germán Arciniegas began his own commemorative article on Maurín—"Entre las muchas cosas buenas que han ocurrido en mi vida pondré siempre entre las mejores haber conocido a Maurín"—exactly

express my own feelings. His generosity, warmth, encouragement
and personal assistance were of especial importance to me in my
early work but were never wanting even in the final years of his life.
He was a rare friend, whose memory many of us will long treasure.
Madison, Wisconsin   STANLEY G. PAYNE
May 1974

Introduction

REGIONAL IDENTITY IN
SPANISH HISTORY

for most of Spanish history "Spain" has been a fundamentally geographical expression referring to the landmass named by the Romans the Hispanic peninsula, or "Hispania."[1] During the Middle Ages the peninsula was ultimately divided between four Christian kingdoms, which were, in descending order of size, Castilla-León, Portugal, Aragón-Catalonia, and Navarra. Between 1479 and 1512 all save Portugal were dynastically united under the Trastamara-Habsburg dynasty, creating the "Spanish crown" but not establishing a unified "Spanish nation." The Spanish Habsburg state of the sixteenth and seventeenth centuries was a pluralistic royal confederation composed of the kingdom of Castilla and the Basque provinces or seigneuries associated with it, the kingdoms of Aragón, Navarra, and Valencia, and the principalities of Catalonia and the Balearic islands. A unified state system first emerged under the new Bourbon dynasty of the early eighteenth century.[2]

The historic Spanish kingdoms and principalities had their roots, not in Roman or Visigothic origins, but in the defense reaction against the Muslims in the early Middle Ages that led to the process known as the Reconquest. During the course of the eighth century the independent and/or Christian population of the mountainous regions in the extreme north of the peninsula began to coalesce around seven regional nuclei. Reading from west to east they were:

> Galicia
> Asturias
> Cantabria-Castilla
> The western Basque region
> Navarra (the southeastern Basque region)
> Aragón
> The Catalan counties

This coalescence was determined by three main factors: geography, ethnic identity (though this was of major importance only in the case of the Basques), and prevailing politico-military pressures.

In the west the most important nucleus was that of Asturias, which in little more than a generation after the Muslim conquest of most of the peninsula emerged with the title of "kingdom." By the end of the eighth century it had come to identify itself with the vanished Visigothic kingdom and claimed the latter's inheritance. The reasons why Asturias became the center of native Hispanic *révanchisme* were primarily geographic and politico-cultural; it was the most Romanized (i.e., civilized) of the high northwest mountain areas. The large, damp region of Galicia, occupying the extreme northwest corner of the peninsula, was both culturally more sophisticated and also more heavily populated, but its terrain was for the most part gentler and more difficult to defend. The high Cantabrian region east of Asturias was even more inaccessible but less Romanized and acculturated. The nascent Asturian monarchy rested on an amalgam of native semi-Romanized (or semi-Hispanized) Asturians and immigrant upper-class Visigoths. It soon established sovereignty over Galicia and also exercised dominion, though more tenuously, over the Cantabrian-Castilian region to the east.

The southward expansion of Asturias gave rise to the greater kingdom of León, but the militant eastern frontier district of Castilla later split off to become a separate kingdom that gave its name to the entire realm of Castilla-León when the two crowns were definitively reunited early in the thirteenth century. Galicia was defined as a distinct "kingdom" (*reino*) under the sovereignty of the Leonese crown yet never formed a separate state save for one brief ten-year period. On the other hand, the southern districts of the greater Galician-Portuguese cultural region in the west split off early in the twelfth century to form the independent kingdom of Portugal, never to be effectively reunited with the realms of León and Castilla.

Originally at least three different tongues were spoken in the northwest: Galician-Portuguese, which was for long the best developed and literarily the most sophisticated, the Asturian-Leonese dialect to the east of it, and finally the nascent Castilian language of the eastern Cantabrian region. Galician was for long the courtly language and chief literary medium for the high cultures of Castilla-León. However, the Castilian tongue originated in the very center of the northern sector of the peninsula and developed as the popular medium of a vigorous and expansive warrior-peasant society that ultimately extended its sway over the greater part of the peninsula. In the process, its linguistic influence extended more and more over Asturias-León, while spreading eastward among the foothills of the western Pyrenees and into Aragón.

The establishment of the independent Hispanic states of the northwest was the completely independent and spontaneous work of the local population, isolated both from the rest of western Christendom and from Muslim Al-Andalus. By contrast, the Christian counties of the central and eastern Pyrenees were established through the intervention of the powerful Frankish state at the end of the eighth century. The Catalan counties of the eastern Pyrenees were originally organized as dominions of the Frankish crown, from which they did not claim formal independence for nearly two centuries. Similarly, the county of Aragón was first established as a dependency of the duchy of Toulouse, though it was quicker to achieve its de jure independence. In part this was because the county of Aragón lay south of the main Pyrenean barrier, with its back to France and its face turned southward toward the peninsula. There were also notable linguistic differences between its vernacular and that of the eastern Pyrenees or southwestern France.

The Catalan counties, however, formed part of a trans-Pyrenean cultural, economic, and political continuum that extended northward into Rosselló and Cerdanya (later Gallicized as Roussillon and Cerdagne) and beyond to Languedoc, Provence, and the world of greater "Occitania." The broader trans-Pyrenean Catalan-Provençal culture composed a distinct unit that at first seemed as different from the "French" society and culture of the northern Carolingian monarchy as it did from the "Spanish" society and culture of Castilla-León. The peoples of Catalonia-Occitania retained greater residues of the Mediterranean Roman world than did any other part of Europe west of the Italian peninsula. They were quicker to rebuild an urban economy and commerce; they also retained Roman norms of private property in an age when feudalism and manorialism held sway in France and in a different form began to make inroads in Castilla-León.

As the power of the Carolingian crown declined in the tenth century, the Catalan counties of the southeastern Pyrenean region comprised a congeries of separate local jurisdictions as decentralized and complex as that of much of "feudal" France. A unified Catalan principality was slowly built during the tenth and eleventh centuries, and new forms of feudal dependence were established, though on a more explicit, codified basis than in most of "feudal" Europe. Catalonia remained a small principality in the northeastern corner of the peninsula, but its strength and influence was greatly enhanced by dynastic union with the "kingdom" of independent Aragón in 1137. Emergence of the confederated monarchy of Aragón-Catalonia in the northeast coincided with and paralleled the emergence of an independent Portugal in the southwest in 1128, counterbalancing the power of the enlarged kingdom of Castilla-León, which already occupied most of the north and center of the peninsula. During the twelfth century the Aragonese crown held sovereignty over the territories of Languedoc and Provence beyond the Pyrenees that were linguistically and culturally related to Catalonia but lost nearly all these lands to the crown of France at the battle of Muret in 1213. While Castilla completed the reconquest of the entire southern third of the peninsula during the later Middle Ages, Aragón-Catalonia conquered and established the new kingdom of Valencia, confederated under the Aragonese crown, together with the island principality of the Balearics. From there Catalonia expanded into the central Mediterranean and the Italian states, creating one of the two most extraordinary thalassocratic empires of medieval Europe that at one time extended as far eastward as the duchy of Athens.

The social structure of medieval Castilla notably differed from that of much of western Europe because of the high degree of individual and collective freedom and initiative in the early centuries of Castilian history. Originating as a rather egalitarian, battle-oriented frontier society, Castilla provided opportunity for direct freeholds by individual peasants or more commonly by peasant villages. Though the insecurity of Castilian life made a system of peasant sociopolitical independence impractical, strong and precise local autonomies developed throughout Castilla as it expanded southward. Some peasant communities at first enjoyed almost complete local autonomy; more common, however, was the system of *behetría* which gave local peasant villages the right to choose their own overlord and also regulated his power and their obligations. Local rights and privileges were explicitly recognized by the Castilian crown from the eleventh century on by the granting or codification of *fueros* (local laws or privileges). In some cases the formalized *fueros* merely recognized local customs or privileges, but in others the crown created new rights or privileges as rewards or incentives for local groups. As Castilla expanded into the center of the peninsula during the second half of the eleventh century, new communities were organized in the Tajo basin and elsewhere as locally autonomous *concejos* (municipal districts), their rights and responsibilities codified by local *fueros*.

There was never any genuine serfdom in Castilla, though such conditions did exist in early medieval Galicia. Generally speaking, the period from the ninth through the thirteenth centuries was a period of slowly increasing emancipation for those sectors of the north Hispanic population bound to social or legal servitude. The main conditioning element was the opportunity of the frontier, together with increasing population and slowly improving economic conditions, all of which helped to relieve pressure against the lowest sectors of society.

At the same time, however, a counter process was at work in

the expansion of the aristocratic class and the formation of increasingly seigneurial domains. The first sectors of an aristocratic elite began to emerge almost immediately during the first generation or two after the establishment of the Hispano-Christian principalities in the north. During the early generations, however, in all areas save the Catalan counties the nominal nobility functioned at least in theory as a functional "service aristocracy." At first most of its members did not enjoy hereditary privileges nor land grants in perpetuity. A powerful hereditary landed aristocracy did begin to take form in León and Galicia during the ninth century and in Castilla and Aragón during the eleventh. The extent and power of aristocratic domain over the peasantry in most areas slowly increased, accelerating from the twelfth century on. By the close of the Middle Ages, most peasant villages throughout the expanded kingdom of Castile had lost their semiautonomous status and were regulated in varying degrees by seigneurial domain—which covered approximately 50 percent of the kingdom—or the ecclesiastical domain of church lands. Yet vestiges of local *fueros* persisted, especially in the northern regions of Castilla and León, together with sizable tracts still held as common land by villages and *concejos*. This was somewhat less frequent in the small landlocked kingdom of Aragón, where subjugation of the peasantry eventually reached a greater extent than anywhere else in the peninsula.

In the development of representative civic institutions the medieval Hispanic kingdoms at first preceded all of Europe. The first regular three-estate medieval parliament in any state was that of León, which first met in 1188. Similar assemblies soon were called in Castilla and during the thirteenth century were summoned in all other Hispanic kingdoms. Yet, though the Cortes of Castilla-León were historically the oldest in Europe, they did not become the most strongly institutionalized or effective. The root of this failure lay in the structure and values of Castilian society, which was composed of aristocrats and peasants with an ethos of honor and military expansion. At no time during the Castilian expansion of the late Middle Ages did Castilian society develop a productive urban economy or an economic middle class proportionate to the kingdom's size or military significance. Castilian society enjoyed an elaborate network of laws and local *fueros* (though in many cases steadily diminished in practice), and to that extent nourished a clear-cut tradition of Castilian liberties, but these functioned within a rural society under strong overarching royal sovereignty. The towns and diversified interests to be found in some other west European kingdoms were inadequate in Castilla to develop an overall system of constitutional representative government—even for the upper classes—as distinct from the network of local privileges and exemptions guaranteed by royal law as *fueros*.

Full constitutional development went much farther in the principalities of the Aragonese confederation. The most elaborate and effective of all medieval constitutions was that of Catalonia, which in the fourteenth and fifteenth centuries achieved one of the most complete frameworks of legal guarantees and individual freedoms to be found in western Europe. By the thirteenth century Catalan society was more fully developed than that of Castilla and by the early fourteenth century was one of the two major mercantile and industrial powers of the western Mediterranean. Growth of a powerful, wealthy, and numerous middle class solidified and extended a well-articulated representative system. The Catalan Corts established and retained an almost complete power of the purse and of fiscal apportionment. They also developed a permanent executive board for the parliament, known as the *Generalitat*, and established the principle of judicial review. The Catalan system was largely reproduced in the separate but confederated structure of the kingdom of Valencia, originally organized in the second half of the thirteenth century.

The Cortes of the kingdom of Aragón also wielded great authority, though on a somewhat different basis from that of Catalonia. Whereas the latter rested on the interests of the upper middle class and the aristocracy, the Aragonese Cortes was dominated by the nobility, which were represented by two separate chambers of upper and lower aristocracy. The Catalan Corts often strongly supported a constituionally delimited royal authority in the interests of expanding Catalan-Aragonese power and prosperity, whereas the Aragonese aristocracy used the Aragonese parliament strictly as a means of nullifying royal power so as to guarantee the local social, economic, and juridical predominance of the nobility, leaving the Aragonese lower classes probably the most downtrodden in the peninsula. In Castilla, parliamentary power was much weaker by the fifteenth century, but royal authority was sometimes used more in the interests of the lower than of the upper classes.

By the late Middle Ages the Hispanic kingdoms had developed elaborate legal systems of constitutional pluralism, though overarching public sovereignty had become concentrated in the Trastamara-Habsburg crown of Castilla. The regional constitutional systems did not finally succumb until the new centralizing Bourbon dynasty took over in the early eighteenth century. Even then the Basque principalities largely retained their special constitutional structures. This preserved the uniqueness of Basque civic institutions, which became the last surviving vestiges of the historic Hispanic constitutional systems in their traditional form. In that sense, they represented what had once been the common tradition of the peninsula as well as exceptional Basque conditions.

NOTES

1. The standard study of this topic is José Antonio Maravall, *El concepto de España en la Edad Media* (Madrid, 1954).

2. For an overview of regional and constitutional pluralism in Spanish history, see Luis Carretero y Nieva, *Las nacionalidades españolas* (Mexico City, 1952).

1

EVOLUTION OF THE
BASQUE PRINCIPALITIES

Though modern Basque nationalists have postulated that *Euskera*-speaking people originally inhabited a broad stretch of territory reaching from Bordeaux in the north to Zaragoza and Burgos in the south and to Santander in the west,[1] there is no clear evidence to support this. From the time of the earliest historical records, there is no direct indication that an *Euskera*-speaking population inhabited much more territory than that pertaining to the modern "seven provinces."

The question of Basque "origins" has puzzled ethnologists for two centuries and is probably insoluble. In terms of either biology or historical anthropology, there is no scientific support for the concept of a Basque "race" as vaguely employed by the fin-de-siècle ideologues of Basque nationalism. The historic Basque people are evidently an amalgam of several early ethnic groups in the western Pyrenees area; their unity is based on language and culture rather than biology, even though they exhibit certain somewhat distinct physical characteristics.[2] Nonetheless, in terms of formally recorded history, the Basque population must be considered fully autochthonous, since neither it nor its language[3] can be traced to any other region or ethnic group. The exact relationship of the Basques to other pre-Roman populations in the peninsula will have to remain an open question.

At the dawn of history, the Basque population was organized in very small tribal units inhabiting the valleys of the western Pyrenees. They originally formed no single civic unit and spoke a wide variety of tribal dialects of *Euskera* whose diversity—in some cases extending to mutual unintelligibility—has persisted to the present day. Most of the original Basque region was never directly occupied by Roman arms, but this does not mean, as some Basque historians have tried to establish, that the Basque region remained independent of Rome.[4] Rather, the Basque tribes seem to have come to terms with an overarching Roman sovereignty rather more easily than did some other ethnic groups of the northern and western sectors of the peninsula. Their relations with Rome were generally amicable, and they apparently accepted the theory of overall Roman sovereignty in return for general local autonomy in most individual districts of the region. Romans were not generally interested in the Basque territory because of its remoteness and the intractable character of the population. The imperial government did, however, establish an administrative center in Pamplona, the first city in the Basque region, which became known in *Euskera* as "Iruña"—the "city," by definition. While by no means totally uninfluenced by Roman culture and technology, the Basque tribes remained less conditioned by these factors than any other sector of the peninsula, with the possible exception of the Cantabrian tribes in the higher mountains directly to the west of them.[5] Similarly, the Christian religion was introduced into the Basque region in Roman times, but apparently scarcely spread beyond the southern fringes of the Basque area (lower Alava and Navarra).

South of the Pyrenees, the Basque population in early Roman times was limited to the area of the modern province of Navarra, the eastern parts of Guipúzcoa, Logroño, and perhaps Alava, and the northwestern corner of Aragón. Vizcaya, northern Alava, and much of Guipúzcoa were inhabited by the tribes of the Caristios and Várdulos, whose relationship to the Basques is uncertain. It has been conjectured that the latter were in fact a separate Basque group, apart from the main sector of tribes. With the breakdown of order in the late Roman period, the Basque population apparently expanded to the west and also to the north, moving out from the Pyrenees into a larger corner of what would later be southwestern France. This created an entire trans-Pyrenean Basque domain, later known to the French as Gascony (from *gascon* or *vascón*,[6] the earliest Romance vernacular terms for "Basque"). In the west, Caristios and Várdulos ultimately lost their identity amid the expanded Basque population.

Relations of the Basque tribes with the Visigothic crown were much more turbulent than with Rome, paralleling the general—though never complete—breakdown in civic structure throughout the peninsula during the post-Roman period. The Visigothic crown never established full sovereignty over the Basque territory, though it did occupy and hold Pamplona. The persistence of Basque military resistance through the seventh and eighth centuries indicates that some kind of civic unity may have been established among a number of tribes. During this period, the expansion of Christianity made slow progress, mainly among the southernmost and northernmost tribes.

Hispano-Basque history, like that of Christian Spain as a whole, essentially began in the aftermath of the Muslim conquest with the initiation of that historical process that has become known as the Reconquest. At no time did the Muslim invaders, who were at first very few in number, make a serious effort to occupy the northern mountain districts of the peninsula. The only Basque territory over which they established a tenuous hegemony was that of the southeastern clans (in southern Navarra and northeastern Logroño provinces). On the other hand, part of the southwestern section of Basque-inhabited territory, comprising a portion of modern Alava and adjacent districts to the west, was occupied by forces under the nominal jurisdiction of the Asturian crown during the first major Asturian expansion under Alfonso I (739−756). At that time one of the two foci of Basque Christianity was located in Alava, and this district was one of the most Romanized parts of the Basque territory. We know almost nothing of the exact relationship between the Asturian crown and the Alavese clans during the eighth and ninth centuries. It does not appear that the sections associated with Asturias were conquered by force of arms alone, but however that may have been, relations between the Asturian crown and Alavese Basques were intermittently stormy and were marked by not infrequent rebellions among the latter, over whom the crown lost all control by the tenth century.

Insofar as there was a center in the Basque territory during the early Middle Ages, it lay in the city of Pamplona and the nucleus of independent Navarrese-Basque territory to the north and northeast. Northern Navarra may have had organized military leadership and an incipient civic structure as early as the seventh century. It was never fully conquered or occupied by the Muslims. The latter did take Pamplona, intermittently holding it during the eighth century, though they were driven out several times, most notably in the great revolt of 755. The independent nucleus of northern Navarra, which contained in the Leire district one of the two principal foci of Christianity within the Basque territory,[7] strove desperately to maintain its freedom both from the Muslims and from the expanding Frankish empire to the north. Forces from northern Navarra fell on the rear guard of Charlemagne's army as it retreated through Roncesvalles after an unsuccessful expedition to seize the key Muslim-controlled city of Zaragoza on the lower Ebro in 778. This Navarrese attack became immortalized in the *Chanson de Roland*.

As Muslim Al-Andalus became institutionalized, the region of the upper Ebro (the modern districts of Logroño and southern Navarra) formed an autonomous principality under the Banu Qasi dynasty, descended from a local Visigothic overlord, Cassius or Casio, who adopted Islam in 714. This power was a "local," rather than a foreign or Cordoban, Muslim regime, and relations with the still partially pagan Basques of northern Navarra were generally amicable for nearly two centuries. A Banu Qasi governor ruled Pamplona in the late eighth century, possibly as a result of the Cordoban Muslim conquest of part of Navarra in 781, but the Banu Qasi and Navarrese usually tended to cooperate to preserve their mutual autonomy.

Banu Qasi rule in Pamplona was overthrown at the close of the eighth century by a pro-Frankish party in Navarra, but the latter was in turn defeated by the partisans of independence, led by the strongest of the Navarrese oligarchs, Iñigo Aritza. After years of complicated maneuvering and fighting between Cordoban Muslims, Frankish expeditions, and internal competition, Iñigo Aritza founded the independent principality of Pamplona early in the ninth century. This was the first organized state in Basque history. For several generations it retained generally harmonious relations with the Banu Qasi, strengthened by a number of inter-dynastic marriages.

The dominant sectors of Navarrese society were nonetheless Christian, and their principality was increasingly influenced by the religion and culture of Carolingian France to the north, while the Banu Qasi territory was more and more conditioned by Muslim Al-Andalus. A new sense of identity and goals was present in Navarra by the early tenth century. In 905 a new dynasty took power under Sancho Garcés I (905–25), who wanted to make his principality a fully sovereign Christian state equal in form and pretensions to France or Asturias-León. He took the title king of Pamplona (transformed by the twelfth century into king of Navarra) and permanently ended the long alliance with the Banu Qasi. Inaugurating a policy of Christian Navarrese expansionism, he incorporated the districts of Estella (southwest Navarra) and also temporarily that of Nájera (in modern Logroño province). Sancho Garcés I then adopted for himself the term "emperor," and his successors made of small but unified Navarra a genuine power factor during the middle of the tenth century when León was crippled by internal strife.

The apogee of Navarrese history occurred during the reign of Sancho III el Mayor (999–1035), who before his death became nominal overlord of all Christian Hispania save the Catalan counties. The full reasons for this dramatic expansion of Navarrese power are still not entirely clear. It has been hypothesized that at the beginning of the eleventh century Navarra was comparatively the most "modern" of the Hispano-Christian states, due above all to its capacity for absorbing new trans-Pyrenean influences. The latter apparently affected many aspects of Navarrese life: political ideas and structure; commercial and administrative technique; military technology; and religious policy. Navarra may have been the principal channel for the entry of Cluniac and other new Catholic reform currents into Hispania, even though at that time part of the Navarrese population may still have been at least marginally pagan. Sancho el Mayor accepted all the new Roman rites and structures, replacing the old Visigothic forms earlier than in any other Christian principality save the Catalan counties. He also adopted the new French definition of royal sovereignty "by the grace of God," which differed in emphasis from the Asturian-Leonese doctrine of the autonomous institutionalized legitimacy of the state. Sancho, like his recent predecessors, also accepted the French-modeled concept of imperial expansion and unification on the basis of the feudalization of public power. The term *vasallo* was now applied to the previously modest sectors of the Navarrese nobility who swore loyalty to the crown and were confirmed in their possession of local lands and honors, many of which were recognized as *feudos*. The economy expanded, and Navarra evidently became the first Hispano-Christian state to develop the new trans-Pyrenean form of heavy armored cavalry, which had a novel effect in peninsular warfare equivalent to the later introduction of the armored tank.

Through marriage alliances and an astute policy of submission, Navarra was the only major part of the Christian north not ravaged by the last great Muslim offensives of the late tenth and early eleventh centuries. When Córdoba suddenly began to collapse, Navarra was in a position to expand its power east, south, and west. The three "Aragonese" counties to the east, Aragón, Sobrarbe, and Ribagorza, were annexed, and perhaps all the more easily because of the Basque population in western Aragón. When Sancho's father-in-law, the count of autonomous Castilla to the west, died in 1017 leaving only an infant son as heir, Sancho established himself as "protector" of the county of Castilla. After the nephew was murdered in 1028, Sancho incorporated all Castilla under his personal sovereignty. The western or "new" Basque territory—roughly the modern "Basque country" or provinces of Vizcaya, Guipúzcoa and Alava—had for some time been associated with the crown of León, and then independent Castilla. In 1029 Sancho detached the "Castilian" Basque territory and directly incorporated it into the kingdom of Navarra. For the next few years all Basque-inhabited territory south of the Pyrenees recognized a single Basque political sovereignty for the first and last time in history. North of the Pyrenees, where the Gascon region had long recognized French suzerainty, Sancho temporarily incorporated some *Euskera*-speaking territory as well.

In 1034 Sancho laid claim to the crown of León and entered the Leonese capital in triumph, theoretically establishing a "Navarrese empire" over all the northern part of the peninsula save the Catalan counties, but this tenuous feudal sovereignty did not survive his death a year later. Sancho divided his realms among his three sons, as kings of Navarra, Castilla, and Aragón respectively, thus establishing the new royal dynasties that ultimately reigned over all the peninsula except Portugal. The new crowns of Castilla and Aragón quickly threw off any bonds of sovereignty tying them to Navarra. Their southward expansion during the eleventh and twelfth centuries completely preempted any territorial growth by Navarra, leaving the small Basque kingdom a rustic backwater during the late Middle Ages. The extent to which the identity of Navarra was Basque and regional rather than pan-Hispanic and absorptive or collaborative, like Castilla and Aragón, may have contributed to the isolation of Navarra after the early eleventh century. The Navarrese crown was assumed by a French dynasty from Champagne in the thirteenth century, and the kingdom later briefly owed sovereignty to the crown of France. Nevertheless Navarra retained its separate identity and constitution, together with its own Cortes (parliament) and system of *fueros*. Full independence was regained in 1329 and was held until cis-Pyrenean Navarra was incorporated by the united Spanish crown in 1512.[8]

Whereas Navarra formed a single political unit from the early ninth century, the history of the western parts of the Basque territory was more complicated. As mentioned earlier, the Asturian crown established a tenuous sovereignty over a portion of Alava in the 750s. Later, during the long reign of Alfonso II (791–842), some sort of association was also made with the northwestern district, Vizcaya, and later an attempt was made to establish sovereignty over Guipúzcoa in the north-center. By the end of the ninth century most of these efforts had come to naught. After successive revolts against the crown, the Vizcayans completely defeated a Leonese army under king Ordoño in 870.

By the tenth century each of these districts had achieved some sort of organization as a locally autonomous entity and, under pressure of power politics, wavered back and forth between association with the new county (later kingdom) of Castilla and the kingdom of Navarra. Vizcaya took the form of a *señorío* (seigneury), in which the clan and valley leaders selected a military overlord to provide leadership and protection. The first *señor de Vizcaya* who can be identified is Iñigo López, a Navarrese knight and courtier, who was chosen at the time of Navarrese hegemony under Sancho el Mayor. His second son, Lope, later supported the Castilian crown in the struggle with Navarra, beginning the long association of Vizcaya with Castilla. In 1076 the López family helped temporarily to bring Alava and Guipúzcoa into the Castilian orbit. They were rewarded with the propertied Castilian seigneury of Haro and, henceforth known as López de Haro, retained the position of *señores de Vizcaya* for most of the next three centuries. Throughout that period the López de Haro constituted one of the most powerful and active aristocratic dynasties in all Castilla. However, the *señorío de Vizcaya* was not a typical west European seigneury, for the seigneur held no "dominical" power of property possession. His rights were restricted to the perquisites pertaining to political and military leadership. Vizcaya never became a dependency of Castilla, but was merely associated with the Castilian crown. Even after the *señorío* was inherited by the king of Castilla in 1379, Vizcaya remained independent of the kingdom of Castilla, recognizing only the personal leadership of the crown within its own local structure of laws, rights, and customs. It remained constitutionally *tierra apartada*.[9]

Navarrese hegemony was soon restored over Alava and Guipúzcoa, and under García the Restorer the Navarrese crown temporarily became *señor de Vizcaya* in 1144. After García's death that position reverted to the López de Haro family and Castilian hegemony over all three western districts was permanently established by the end of the twelfth century. In 1188 most of Alava was conquered by force of arms, the siege of its capital, Vitoria, being led by the *señor* of Vizcaya in the service of the Castilian crown while its nominal sovereign, the king of Navarra, vainly sought aid from Muslim power in the south. Even so, the establishment of Castilian sovereignty over Alava was made conditional on respect for the rights and laws of the province, terms freely recognized by the crown.[10] Guipúzcoa was apparently not conquered at all but seems to have reached an agreement with the Castilian crown, passing from Navarrese hegemony to that of Castilla in return for the recognition of local *fueros* of autonomy. It has been suggested by recent scholars that the Guipuzcoan villagers and fishermen may have preferred the freedom of Castilian laws to the feudalizing tendencies of Navarra. At any rate, Guipúzcoa emerged in 1200 as a local autonomous "province" of Castilla under royal sovereignty. Henceforth all the Basque territory south of the Pyrenees save Navarra remained in the Castilian orbit.

The legal and administrative structure of the historic Basque districts was based upon an elaborate series of *fueros*, which in general originated in two different ways. The first historical definition of a *fuero* was made by the Castilian king Alfonso el Sabio in his legal guidebook, *Las Siete Partidas*, which defined it as a custom that became recognized by law. In addition, many of the most important *fueros* originated as specific agreements with or grants by the crown, conceding privileges or regulating local rights and responsibilities. Though the Basque provinces retained their historic *fueros* longer than any other region, the system of local laws, privileges, and exemptions involved was common to most of western Europe during the Middle Ages, and particularly in the case of the Hispanic kingdoms. In the peninsula, *fueros* were developed earliest and most broadly in Castilla, and it was in large measure the Castilian system that was established and expanded in the Basque territory.[11] Nonetheless, Basque *fueros* were unique in being established at least in part on the provincial level. In most of Castilla (and Portugal and Aragón), *fueros* were limited almost exclusively to local towns, villages, and districts, and thus did not serve in the long run to foster broader regional or provincial identities. Despite the multiplicity of individual and local Castilian liberties, these never crystallized effectively in a broader dimension. Thus Castilla in general became a kingdom of personalist subjects who enjoyed numerous privileges but overall were politically subordinate to an authoritarian monarchy. That the Basque territories developed *fueros* partially on a provincial level was due not merely to geography but to some extent to their ethno-cultural, or at least linguistic, distinctiveness, which set them apart from the Castilian population as a whole.

Sets of general provincial civic regulations were not really developed, however, until the close of the Middle Ages. Of the three Castilian Basque provinces, Vizcaya was the most unified, with both local and provincial *fueros* recognized on the province level from the eleventh century under the general dominion of *señorío*. However, the medieval *señorío* did not include all the modern province of Vizcaya. The westernmost district, known as the "Encartaciones" and including fourteen local municipal areas, had been originally populated and organized under Alfonso I of Asturias, and its affairs were regulated by a local *junta* (or council) throughout the Middle Ages.[12] The Durango district in the southeast was also separate, and remained longer under Navarrese sovereignty.

Guipúzcoa came to be administered by two different provincial councils, a *junta de villas* (representing the new seaports and towns founded mostly from the twelfth century on, in some cases partially at the initiative of the crown itself) and a *junta de merindades* (for rural districts). The internal situation of the county of Alava was even more diverse, particularly in the thirteenth century. Vitoria was under direct royal domain, like nearly all major towns of Castilla, while much of the province was governed under local seigneurial or church domain. In this respect, Alava remained more similar to Navarra than to Vizcaya and Guipúzcoa, where local aristocratic control was somewhat less extensive.

The western Basque region entered a more advanced phase of development during the eleventh and twelfth centuries, with the growth of towns and of maritime and commercial activities. The nominal Christianization of the entire population is supposed to have been completed by the eleventh century,[13] bringing Basques more fully into the orbit of western medieval culture. Growth of new economic interests sparked intense conflicts between the towns and villas on the one hand and the *anteiglesias*, or rural villages, then almost entirely under the dominion of local *jaunchos*, or aristocrats. Specific new *fueros* for the establishment of new towns or district jurisdictions after the twelfth century were in most cases patterned on royal grants in Castilla. The new Basque seaports participated in cooperative associations with non-Basque towns, especially in the famous *Hermandad de las villas de la Marina de Castilla*. At several points during the fourteenth and fifteenth centuries naval pacts were signed with the English crown by major Basque ports, but this was not so unique as modern Basque ideologists have claimed. During the Middle Ages the north Castilian seaports were sometimes authorized by the crown to undertake specific naval negotiations on their own initiative to simplify diplomatic relations.

From the thirteenth through the fifteenth centuries, Basque *jaunchos* remained turbulent and oppressive. The entire region was persistently wracked by bloody, extended aristocratic clan feuds, the *guerras de linajes* or *guerras de banderías*. In the western Basque country the principal *banderías* were those of the Oñacinos and Gamboínos. In Navarra they were the *agramonteses* and *beaumonteses* (the former pro-French and the latter pro-Castilian); while farther east, in Catalan Rosselló, there were later feuding bands of *nyerres* and *cadells*. In the Basque country such feuds were aristocratic power struggles pure and simple; their destructiveness retarded the development and modernization of the region. All told, the Basque country suffered as much from the depredations of its own aristocratic class as did most parts of Castilla. In the late fifteenth century the united Spanish crown, supported by the Basque towns, played a major role in putting down the *banderías* and in bringing law and order to the three provinces of the Basque country.[14] It was in this process that the functioning of regional government was finally regularized, and the main agent was the crown itself.

Maximiano García Venero has observed that the principal factors in Basque regional government under the Castilian crown were the provincial *Juntas Generales*, the royal *corregidores*, and the *pase foral*, or right of review of royal legislation.[15] A central feature of late medieval Castilian administration, the *corregidores* were royal appointees named to supervise the affairs of local districts. The first *corregidor* in the Basque country, Gonzalo Moro, was appointed to Vizcaya in 1394 at the behest of local spokesmen to restrain the feuding *jaunchos*. Moro proved a popular and effective administrator; his brief tenure helped to formalize and codify regional government. A *cuaderno*, or set of regulations, was drawn up for Vizcaya that same year and represented an expansion and clarification of the first codification of Vizcayan law a half-century earlier. There had also been a codification of

Guipuzcoan laws and regulations in mid-century, but a revised *cuaderno* for the *Hermandad General Guipuzcoana*, based in part on the recent revision in Vizcaya, was drawn up under Moro's supervision in 1397. Whereas the original Guipuzcoan *Hermandad* had been a loose union of the larger towns against the depredations of the aristocracy, the *cuaderno nuevo* was broadened to include all villages and districts not directly under seigneurial control. This formed the initial substance of the historic *Juntas generales de la Hermandad de Guipúzcoa*; the *cuaderno nuevo* was officially ratified by the crown as provincial *fuero* in 1455.[16] In Vizcaya the so-called *Fuero Viejo* was recodified in 1452 to give the aristocrat-dominated *anteiglesias* unified representation apart from the villas, with their royal privileges. This legislation was further elaborated in the *Fuero nuevo* of 1526.[17] The first general codification of Alavese laws and regulations was made in 1417 and then extended to the royal recodification of 1463, which established what was to become the modern Alavese foral system.

The *Juntas Generales* were always presided over by the royal *corregidor*. Representation was uneven, indirect, and restricted, varying greatly from one local district to another.[18] Votes were normally weighted according to the tax contributions of each town or district represented, and small local regions sometimes banded together, choosing district group delegations. In 1472 it was established that the *Juntas* would meet twice each year, though this was eventually reduced to annual meetings in 1745, by which time their powers were becoming increasingly restricted.

The *Juntas* never had a direct legislative function but were empowered to advise royal administration, ratify royal decrees, and apportion local taxes, whose level they were always successful in holding below that of Castilla. Their right of *pase foral* was officially granted by the Castilian crown for Alava in 1417, Vizcaya in 1452, and Guipúzcoa in 1473.

The fifteenth century was a time of notable economic development for Vizcaya and Guipúzcoa. By that time the waters off their coast had become known to western Europe as the Bay of Biscay, and Vizcayan shipping dominated the peninsula's main carrying trade with northern ports. Vizcayan merchants and seamen served as middlemen and freighters for Castilian wool, while developing a major fishing and whaling industry. The *pinaza vasca* (Basque pinnace) was a local variant of the new, faster ocean-going vessels whose technological development culminated in the Portuguese caravel. Inland the production of iron expanded, and its operations moved down into the river valleys where transport made larger operations possible. In some districts, particularly in Vizcaya, the *jaunchos* began to settle down and go into commerce and manufacturing.[19]

The sixteenth century was a period of social change and of relative emancipation for the lower classes in Vizcaya and Guipúzcoa. An expanding economy brought freedom for virtually all those still restricted by the residues of peasant servitude, until the two leading Basque provinces became the socially freest and juridically most egalitarian areas in Spain. By that time, strict peasant servitude in the legal sense only persisted in the rigidly institutionalized societies of Aragón and Valencia, but throughout most of Castilla a juridically free peasantry was by the end of the century being ground down by crushing taxes and also by the overweening social and economic predominance of the aristocracy. Conversely, Vizcaya (1526) and Guipúzcoa (1610) won implicit royal recognition of the "noble" status of all their native inhabitants; in the traditional Spanish system such social status was the only way of recognizing relative equality before the law and freedom from most common taxes.

The situation of the peasantry in Navarra and Alava—and also in Catalonia—was somewhere in between that of Vizcaya and Guipúzcoa on the one hand and of most of Castilla on the other. Rural property in Navarra and Alava remained more comprehensively under seigneurial and ecclesiastical jurisdiction than in the two advanced provinces, but terms were generally better than in Castilla, not to speak of Aragón. Under the protection of the *fueros*, a large minority of the Alavese population—at least one-eighth— also attained *hidalgo* status, and a process of peasant emancipation and social mobility continued in much of Navarra and Alava through the seventeenth century. A not inconsiderable number of peasant communities won or purchased their freedom from seigneurial domination.

In general, during the imperial age of Habsburg Spain the

interests of the greater Basque region easily harmonized with those of the Spanish crown. Rumblings of discontent were rare, and the classical structure of the *fueros* was perfected. Though Basque society remained in some respects culturally archaic and did not participate to any notable extent in the intellectual and esthetic culture of the Spanish Golden Age, this was the period in which formal Basque historiography was initiated, in which the first formal defenses of the value and continuing use of *Euskera* were published, and in which the historic myths of primeval Basque liberties were formulated.[20]

While the three small provinces of the French Basque country were becoming an insignificant and almost isolated corner of the French realm, Basques had played and were continuing to play major roles in nearly all the significant enterprises of greater Castilian and Spanish affairs.[21] Basque culture and customs were only minimally altered by this interaction. *Euskera* was still spoken almost universally save in parts of Alava, though Castilian had long been the language of government. Basque law and property rights had been little influenced by the advance of individualistic Roman law since the late Middle Ages. Property was still based on broad family ownership, with condominium between husbands and wives.[22]

If Basque society remained the most traditionalistic—and also in many respects the freest—in the peninsula, that of Catalonia had always tended to be the most "modern" and "European." Traditional Catalan society had been wracked with civil war and social revolt in the fifteenth century and, though the historic Catalan constitutional system had been fully preserved by the Habsburg crown, there was always much more conflict with Spanish government. The Basque country was closely associated with the main Castilian economy; Catalonia occupied a far corner of the peninsula and lived in a separate west Mediterranean economic world. A not insignificant number of Basques volunteered for the royal Spanish army and navy; Catalan volunteers were rarer. The Basque country, for all its *fueros* and autonomy, recognized the specific sovereignty of the Castilian crown; to Catalans a Castilian-based government and monarchy was always viewed with a degree of resentment and suspicion. Basque autonomy was primarily restricted to the protection of local legal and economic interests; Catalonia had a fully developed representative constitutional system that was politically and juridically more advanced than that of Castilla. Basque society remained in some respects archaic; that of Catalonia was more fully articulated and in some ways resembled that of southern France more than it did that of much of Castilla. Both areas contributed much less per capita in taxes than did the people of Castilla, but the Basques accepted their lesser share with little resistance while the Catalans haggled endlessly about paying anything.

The great Catalan revolt of 1640–52 against the Spanish crown also turned into a social struggle within Catalonia, if not to the same extent as the conflict of the 1470s. As in the earlier instance, Catalans in rebellion against the crown were unable to stand by themselves and had to invoke French assistance, which simply created a new master whose yoke they found even heavier. The pattern of the fifteenth and seventeenth centuries in some respects foreshadowed the fate of Catalanism in the twentieth century, when the all-Spanish revolutionary left took the place of France as an ally.[23]

Within Spain the revolt of the Catalans was settled on the basis of the status quo ante bellum. Thus the second half of the seventeenth century constituted the golden twilight of the historic pluralistic Spanish constitutional system. Regional particularism was if anything even more meticulously respected than before.

In general the second half of the seventeenth century witnessed the nadir of the economic decline of imperial Spain, but the recovery began on the eastern and northern peripheries during the last three or four decades of the period. Thus it was that as early as the dismal reign of Carlos II the fundamental economic imbalance of modern Spain first began to manifest itself. While most of Castilla stagnated, there were marked signs of recovery and expansion in Catalonia, followed by Valencia and to a lesser extent by Vizcaya and Guipúzcoa.

The faint Spanish recovery of the late seventeenth century was temporarily wiped out by the heavy costs of the War of the Spanish Succession (1702–13). Navarra and the Basque provinces followed the lead of Castilla in accepting the legal inheritance of the

Spanish crown by a junior branch of the French Bourbon dynasty, as provided for in the testament of the decadent, successionless Carlos II. This was only natural in view of the close and essentially harmonious association of the Basque principalities with the civic structure of Castilla, and of the relative integration of their economies. Despite the centralizing thrust of Bourbon government in France, the heir, crowned as Felipe V, swore to uphold the pluralistic legal structure of the Hispanic system.

The Aragonese principalities, however, soon foreswore allegiance to the Bourbon monarchy and embraced the cause of the Austrian Habsburg pretender, Archduke Karl. The causes for this were complex: Felipe V showed little interest in the Aragonese principalities and failed to visit them all in person; pluralistic autonomy was associated with the policies of the Habsburg crown, but the reverse was true of the Bourbons; anti-French feeling was strong in Aragón and Catalonia; revival of the Catalan economy and Catalan overseas trade, still largely excluded from Spanish America, created stronger extrapeninsular interests and was less integrated with the Castilian economy; and, finally, the countryside of Aragón and Valencia, where seigneurial domination was stronger than in most other parts of the peninsula, rose in rebellion against the local Bourbon-identified aristocracy. Aragón and Valencia were defeated and occupied within five years, but Barcelona, the center of Catalan resistance, held out to the bitter end. The siege of isolated Barcelona, cut off from the outside world and deserted by all foreign allies, was the wonder of Europe in 1713–14 and was buoyed up by the obdurate resistance of its lower classes to outside domination.

Yet the resulting defeat was as total as the resistance had been glorious. The Bourbon triumph in Spain marked the death of the traditional constitutional systems of the Aragonese principalities. All their regional parliaments were suppressed and their legal, financial, and administrative systems, together with organs of self-government, were absorbed by the centralized structure of the eighteenth-century Spanish monarchy. All that was left of regional particularism were parts of the traditional Catalan legal codes, administered from that time forward by the central apparatus of the Spanish state.

Economic resurgence grew out of the ashes of civic incorporation, at least for Catalonia and Valencia. From the 1740s onward the Catalan economy expanded more rapidly than did that of any other part of the peninsula. Eighteenth-century growth was originally based upon a versatile rural and small-town economy, whose surplus created the margin for a process of regional preindustrialization.[24] Later in the century, the opening of the Spanish American trade to all parts of the peninsula provided a great stimulus to Catalan commerce and exports. Textile production expanded rapidly; by the close of the century Barcelona comprised one of the largest protoindustrial complexes in western Europe outside England. The advantages of economic opportunity and growth, together with more rational and enlightened administration, won Catalan acceptance of the new centralized polity. With a few minor exceptions,[25] Catalonia was politically as peaceful during the second half of the eighteenth century as it had been disturbed during the first half of the seventeenth or early eighteenth centuries.

The only major exception to the centralization of eighteenth-century Spanish government and administration was retention of the traditional legal and administrative structure of the Basque principalities. As the decades passed, however, this tended to become more apparent than real. The fiscal exemptions guaranteed by *fuero* were in several respects overridden by Felipe V during the succession war, and in 1717 a royal decree to include Basque imports within the common Spanish tarriff system provoked the *machinada*, a brief but broadly supported fiscal revolt in Vizcaya and Guipúzcoa that was bloodily suppressed.[26] The traditional tariff regulations were restored in 1722, but only at the sufferance of the crown, not in recognition of the validity of traditional law. The reformist reign of Carlos III (1759–88) brought notable reduction of Basque privileges; legal exemptions in commerce were reduced, and fiscal pressures mounted. At times the crown intervened to regulate selection of representatives to the provincial *juntas*. By the 1780s it seemed that the traditional system that had operated in the two preceding centuries was on the verge of becoming a dead letter, even though nearly all the formal usages remained.

There was notable economic expansion during the second half

of the century. Agricultural output increased in all the Basque territory, and shipping and iron production grew markedly in Vizcaya and Catalonia. Basques from all four regions remained active in the affairs of the Spanish empire,[27] and in Vizcaya and Guipúzcoa there emerged a new "enlightened" upper-middle class of progressivist priests and landowners, seconded by merchants and shippers. In those two provinces there seemed to be more civic consciousness and more interest in the study and promotion of modern political economy than in Catalonia. The outstanding expression of this concern was the formation of Spain's first *Sociedad de Amigos del País* in Azcoitia (Guipúzcoa) in 1766. This was the first of a series of more than sixty local academies and study groups in various parts of Spain devoted to technical education and modern development. The Azcoitia technical academy was the first genuine private, secular school in modern Spain. It has been conjectured that the Castilian-speaking sector of the Basque population may have had the highest literacy rate in Spain by the close of the century.

The eighteenth century produced a new flowering of Basque historiography, particularly in Vizcaya and Guipúzcoa. Resistance to pressures from Madrid, coupled with concern to preserve Basque identities in a more complex and demanding world, resulted in the expansion of earlier myths about Basque history, especially those concerning the preservation of civic identity and foral liberties from time immemorial. The myth of a common, unsullied ethnic or racial unity was given its first expression by a Guipuzcoan Jesuit, Manuel de Larramendi, who maintained that Basques were the direct descendants of the ancient personage Tubal, recorded in the Book of Genesis.[28] Larramendi also produced the first regular *Euskera* grammar, and the difficulty of the achievement is indicated by its title, *El imposible vencido* (The impossible vanquished). In this connection, it might be noted that one of the goals of the *Sociedad de Amigos del País* in the Basque region was to bring closer unity and cooperation between the three western provinces, who had for several centuries been known simply as the "Basque country," in distinction from Navarra.

Yet, despite the example of Basque initiative in several aspects of the Spanish enlightenment, the structure of Basque society was in general rather little altered by the end of the eighteenth century. For nearly a millennium the Basques had shown a remarkable ability to accept technical improvements from the outside world without completely altering the foundations of their own culture. In large measure because of the advances already made in terms of local freedoms, relative civic equality, and widespread property distribution, Basque values were in many respects more conservative than in other parts of Spain. Catholic religiosity, despite some pagan residues, more thoroughly permeated Basque society, customs, and family relations than was true in most other parts of Spain. By the late eighteenth century the paradox of the modern Basque region was already being formed: it was at the same time one of the most progressive and most conservative areas of southwestern Europe. It is true that the progressive elements were disproportionately concentrated in the towns of Vizcaya and Guipúzcoa, while conservatism dominated the countryside, but occasionally the two orientations would coincide in the same personalities.

Though the greater *Euskera*-speaking region on both sides of the Pyrenees had never formed a single political system, the modern centralized state had the effect of separating the southern and northern regions even more. Each of the three provinces of the French Basque area had a distinct social and juridical structure. During the Middle Ages the westernmost province of Labourd (Lapurdi) on the coast owed sovereignty to a viscount (roughly similar to the *señor* of Vizcaya) and had temporarily passed to the English crown in the fourteenth century. However, the full system of feudal relationships had never developed and by the close of the Middle Ages the comparatively weak local aristocracy may have controlled no more than 5 percent of the land. The middle province, Basse-Navarre (Benaparroa), lived entirely under royal domain after the late twelfth century. Only the easternmost province, Soule (Zuberoa), tucked into the Pyrenees, had a more or less feudal structure.

After their final incorporation by the French monarchy in the fifteenth and sixteenth centuries the northern provinces retained their local privileges to almost as great a degree as did the southern states. All three had limited representative assemblies; that of

Labourd, the *Biltzar*, was composed of mayors of towns and village districts, excluding the weak local nobility. The Estates of Soule and Basse-Navarre, where the aristocracy held more land, were traditional three-estate corporate assemblies as in the Cortes of Navarra. During the sixteenth and seventeenth centuries the *fors* and customary laws and privileges of the three provinces were codified. However, royal administration soon began to intervene more directly in the French provinces than in Spain. Political and fiscal pressures mounted during the eighteenth century, and the crown arbitrarily increased the power of the aristocracy in Soule.

Until the late nineteenth century, French Basques were proportionately more active culturally than were those on the peninsular side. Possibly stimulated by association with a more vigorous and developed Romance-language culture, one of them had published the first book in *Euskera* in Bordeaux in 1545, and their rate of publication remained distinctly greater.

The attitude of French Basques toward the French revolution was at first passive, save for the desire of peasants in Soule to abolish aristocratic privileges. However, Basque religiosity soon led to hostility against Jacobin radicalism, and a number of Labourd villagers were deported by the revolutionary Terror. Administrative reorganization combined the three provinces into the large southwestern department of Basses-Pyrénées. Despite the new centralism, the traditional agreements, or *faceries*, among Basques on both sides of the frontier governing mutual use of water and pastures in the international boundary districts were continued down to the early twentieth century and, in some instances, to the present.

In general, the French government paid little attention to the French Basque territory, deeming it a small, remote, and backward area. In total contrast to the prominent role of Basques in Spanish affairs, their northern kinsmen were inconspicuous in the national affairs of France.[29]

NOTES

1. One of the most extreme statements is that of Fernando Sarrailh de Ihartza (pseud. of Federico Krutwig Sagredo), in his *Vasconia* (Buenos Aires, 1962).

2. In one blood-type study, 28.2 percent of the Basques sampled were found to be Rh negative, versus a standard norm of 19.6 percent. Those having type O blood exceeded the norm by 6 percent, those having type B blood fell 50 percent short of the norm. Dr. J. L. Goti Iturriaga, "Los grupos sanguíneos en los vascos," *La Gran Enciclopedia Vasca*, I, 39−62.

Other studies revealed an even lower proportion of type-B blood, and a slightly higher percentage of Rh negatives. Morton H. Levine, "The Basques," *Natural History* 76, No. 4 (Apr. 1967), 44−51.

In another seroanthropological study, Miguel Angel Etcheverry found 33 percent Rh negatives among a sample of the Basque population in Argentina. Federico Arteaga, *E.T.A. y el proceso de Burgos* (Madrid, 1971), 55. Further studies providing still more confirmation are cited in Léon Boussard, *L'Irrintzina, ou le destin des Basques* (Paris, 1969), 56−57.

3. The best philological introduction is Antonio Tovar, *The Basque Language* (Philadelphia, 1957).

4. As for example, Ramón Ortiz de Zárate, *Jamás los romanos conquistaron completamente a los vascongados y nunca estos belicosos pueblos formaron parte integrante del imperio de los Césares* (Vitoria, 1866).

5. Joaquín Gonzalez Echegaray, *Los Cántabros* (Santander, 1966).

6. A name apparently derived from the notion of "mountain people" or the "high" or "haughty." The Basques' own name for themselves in *Euskera* is *Euskaldunak*.

7. The clearest brief treatment of the problem of the Christianization of the Basque territory is José Ma. Lacarra's "La cristianización del País Vasco," in his *Estudios de historia navarra* (Pamplona, 1971), 1−31.

8. The clearest brief account of medieval Basque history is Federico de Zabala, *Historia del Pueblo Vasco* (San Sebastián, 1971), 2 vols. Joaquín Arbeloa, *Los orígenes del Reino de Navarra* (San Sebastián, 1969), 3 vols., offers an interesting recent reinterpretation. The early classic work on the origins of Navarra was José de Yanguas y Miranda, *Diccionario de antigüedades del Reino de Navarra* (Pamplona, 1840−43), 3 vols., followed by T. Ximénez de Embrun, *Ensayo histórico acerca de los orígenes de Aragón y Navarra* (Zaragoza, 1878). Antonio Ubieto Arteta, a leading exponent of the "Navarrese" theory of medieval Hispanic development, gives a sketch of medieval Navarrese history in his *Ciclos económicos en la Edad Media española* (Valencia, 1969), 55−62. There is a summary of the Navarrese foral system in R. R. Bard "The Medieval Fueros of Navarre" (master's thesis University of Washington, 1971).

9. See Francisco Elías de Tejada, *El Señorío de Vizcaya (hasta 1812)*

(Madrid, 1963), and more broadly on the medieval Basque territory in general, Julio Caro Baroja, *Los vascos* (Madrid, 1958), 21–114.

10. The official relationship of the county of Alava to the Castilian crown was codified by Alfonso XI in 1332.

11. That Basque civic institutions were structurally derived from foreign (i.e., non-Basque) models was admitted by Manuel de Irujo, *Instituciones jurídicas vascas* (Buenos Aires, 1945), 30.

12. P. Eduardo de Escarzaga, *Avellaneda y la Junta General de las Encartaciones* (Bilbao, 1927). In turn, some towns in the Burgos region also enjoyed the privileges of the *fuero de Vizcaya*. Darío de Areitio y Mediola, *Temas históricos vascos* (Bilbao, 1969), 89–129.

13. According to Z. García Villada, *Organización y fisionomía de la Iglesia española* (Madrid, 1935), I, 18.

14. On the *guerras de linajes*, see *Las bienandanzas e fortunas* of Lope García de Salazar, written in 1476 and published in a new annotated edition in Bilbao in 1955; Julio Caro Baroja, *Vasconiana* (Madrid, 1957), 19–61; Juan Carlos de Guerra, *Oñacinos y gamboínos* (San Sebastián, 1930); Ignacio Arocena, *Oñacinos y gamboínos* (Pamplona, 1959); and Carmelo de Echegaray, *Las provincias vascongadas a fines de la Edad Media* (San Sebastián, 1895).

15. *Historia del nacionalismo vasco* (Madrid, 1968), 86.

16. Carmelo de Echegaray, *Compendio de las instituciones forales de Guipúzcoa* (San Sebastián, 1924); Fausto de Arocena, *Guipúzcoa en la historia* (Madrid, 1964); and F. Elías de Tejada, *La Provincia de Guipúzcoa* (Madrid, 1965), 10–36.

17. In addition to Tejada's *Señorío de Vizcaya*, see J. M. Martín de Retana, "Orígenes, evolución y bibliografía del Fuero de Vizcaya," *La Gran Enciclopedia Vasca*, I, 221–29.

18. The "democratic myth" about historic Basque institutions is an invention of the nineteenth and twentieth centuries. Basic statements of this myth are Benito Jamar, *La cuestión vascongada* (San Sebastián, 1891), 52; J. de Urkina, *La democracia en Euzkadi* (San Sebastián, 1935); and especially José de Ariztimuño ("Aitzol"), *La democracia en Euzkadi* (San Sebastián, 1934).

19. See J. A. García de Cortázar, *Vizcaya en el siglo XV* (Bilbao, 1966).

20. On constitutional and historical doctrines of the period, see Elías de Tejada's *Señorío de Vizcaya*, 73–165, and *Provincia de Guipúzcoa*, 52–133.

21. Cf. the vignettes in Darío de Areitio's *Los Vascos en la historia de España* (Bilbao, 1959) and A. Lafarga Lozano, *Los Vascos en el descubrimiento y colonización de América* (Bilbao, 1973).

22. On traditional Basque social and family structure and its legal norms, see Antonio de Trueba, *Bosquejo de la organización social de Vizcaya* (Bilbao, 1870); Miguel de Unamuno, *Derecho consuetudinario en Vizcaya* (1896), in his *Obras completas* (Madrid, 1958), VI, 232–66; and brief analyses by Ramón de Madariaga, *El derecho foral de Vizcaya en relación con la organización familiar* (Bilbao, 1932), and Luis Chalbaud y Errazquin, *La familia como forma típica y trascendental de la constitución social vasca* (Bilbao, 1919).

23. The final outcome was the partition of historic Catalonia, for in the peace treaty of 1659 the French crown exacted as its price the cession of the two trans-Pyrenean Catalan provinces, Rosselló and Cerdanya. For years, these two Catalan speaking provinces put up stiff internal resistance to political and cultural incorporation in France. See Josep Sanabre, *Resistencia del Rosselló a incorporarse a França* (Barcelona, 1970).

24. The classic study is Pierre Vilar, *La Catalogne dans l'Espagne moderne* (Paris, 1963), 3 vols.

25. A few limited examples of protest against centralization are recorded by Ernest Lluch, "La Catalunya del segle XVIII i la lluita contra l'absolutisme centralista," *Recerques* (Barcelona, 1970), I, 33–50.

26. A sketch of this incident is given in Adolfo Lafarga, *Aportación a la historia social y política de Vizcaya* (Siglos XVI a XIX) (Bilbao, 1971), 61–73.

27. Julio Caro Baroja, *La hora navarra del siglo XVIII* (Pamplona, 1969), narrates the activities of Navarrese merchants, financiers, and administrators in Madrid during the first half of the eighteenth century. These personages came in large measure from the overpopulated Valle de Baztán.

28. On Basque historiography and historico-political ideas in this period, see Andrés E. de Mañaricúa, *Historiografía de Vizcaya* (Bilbao, 1971), 205–69; and Elías de Tejada. *Señorío de Vizcaya*, 166–240, and *Provincia de Guipúzcoa*, 135–200.

29. On the history of the French Basque country, see Philippe Veyrin, *Les Basques de Labourd, Soule et Basse-Navarre* (Paris, 1955), Joseph Nogaret, *Petite histoire du Pays Basque Français* (Bayonne, 1928); G. Bernoville, M. Etcheverry, P. Veyrin and J. Ithurriague, *Pays Basque* (Strasbourg, 1964); and M. Sacx, *Bayonne et le Pays Basque* (Bayonne, 1968).

2

LIBERALISM AND REGIONALISM
1793 – 1876

T he first instance of political separatism in the history of modern Spain occurred in the wake of the French military advance into Guipúzcoa during the French revolutionary war of 1793−95. Weak Spanish forces were ill prepared to resist the determined and massive French assault, and after the occupation of San Sebastián the Republican government in Paris was eager to detach Guipúzcoa and annex it to France as a protectorate. They apparently found a small group of willing collaborators, in the persons of a triumvirate leading the *Diputación General* of the *Junta General* of the province and the mayor of San Sebastián, Michelena. The exact intentions of the latter have never been clarified.

In general, the French Revolution aroused less sympathy in Spain than in any other major part of Western Europe, and Jacobin anti-Catholicism and political terror turned this aversion into extreme antagonism. It is true that by the 1790s there existed in Spain a small body of "preliberal" opinion, concentrated among the numerically meager pro-enlightenment sectors of the Spanish intelligentsia. Yet the Spanish enlightenment of the second half of the eighteenth century was overwhelmingly Catholic and royalist and

had little to do with philosophical or political radicalism. Small
groups of anticlerical, prorevolutionary radicals did begin to meet
in several Spanish cities during the mid-1790s but constituted tiny
islands of opinion, not to be noticed in Spain as a whole. The
several small semiclandestine groups of freethinkers formed in San
Sebastián, Irún, and Bilbao in 1794–95 were isolated amid the
Basque country's otherwise unanimously Catholic society.

Sectors of the Vizcayan and Guipuzcoan upper-middle class
may have been more influenced by late eighteenth-century French
culture than any other part of peninsular society, save for a small
circle of esthetes and intellectuals. It was not uncommon for sons to
be sent to complete their education in French universities, while the
first modern secular school in Spain was the Royal Seminary or
Academy of Vergara, established in 1767. In San Sebastián there
seems to have been some sympathy among the small upper-middle
class for the moderate Girondist phase of the Revolution. Even so,
this would never have assumed the form of political treason had it
not been for the Spanish military collapse and the occupation of
northern Guipúzcoa by French troops. The Guipuzcoan leaders
who tried to negotiate with the French were strongly influenced by
the mythical historiography developed in Vizcaya and Guipúzcoa
during the past three centuries that hammered on the theme of
ancient independence and the unsullied maintenance of foral autonomy. These collaborationists did not think of themselves as
traitors but retained vague semifeudal ideas about the independent
legal right to *desnaturarse*, or change allegiance. They originally
proposed association with France as an autonomous federal state,
but that was overruled by Republican authorities. Instead the latter
permitted the cooperative Guipuzcoan *Diputación* to continue to
function under French authority.[1]

The attitude of the San Sebastián collaborationists was profoundly unrepresentative of the greater Basque territory and even
of the Guipuzcoan population as a whole. In September 1794, one
month after the formation of the French protectorate, representatives of eighteen Guipuzcoan *concejos* (council-districts) met to
organize a new provincial *Junta General* in unremitting opposition
to the French invasion.

The Guipuzcoan defection, limited though it was, together

with the general lack of preparedness of the small Basque militia, sharply increased the suspicion and hostility with which the royal government viewed the separate constitutional structures of the four territories. After the French were expelled, immediate reprisals were limited, but pressure against the Basque *fueros* and Navarrese constitution, which had been building throughout the century, reached a climax in the course of the reign of Carlos IV. This inept sovereign had made the customary gesture of swearing to uphold Basque laws, but his *valido*, Manuel Godoy, who dominated government during most of his reign, endeavored to continue the work of the centralized monarchist state, in the process eliminating the foral immunities of the Basque territories. In 1796 a special commission was authorized to study the origins and purposes of the *fueros* but never actually took up its work. At almost the same time, a royal decree arbitrarily suppressed the Navarrese *juicio de sobrecarta*, Navarra's version of the *pase foral*, which had already become inoperative de facto in the Basque territories.

A juridical and historiographic assault was launched against the historic origins and validity of the foral system. Its main expressions were the first two (and only) volumes of the *Real Academia de la Historia*'s *Diccionario geográfico-histórico de España* (1802), devoted to the four Basque territories, and P. Juan Antonio Llorente's *Noticias históricas de las tres provincias vascongadas* (1806–08) 5 vols. Formidable works for their time, these two accounts undeniably advanced the state of Basque historiography, but their polemical bias was so strong that they distorted almost as much as they clarified and were met by several counterpolemics on Basque and foral history from writers in Alava and Guipúzcoa.[2]

Between 1799 and 1806 the Spanish government issued a series of drastic new tax and draft levies in Navarra and the Basque provinces. It was, of course, perfectly legal for the crown to request special grants of money and men in emergencies, but when the Basque territories resisted, their protests were largely swept aside. Though royal demands were in some instances reduced, the right of *pase foral* and ratification had in fact been virtually done away with. On the eve of the Spanish War of Independence, Basque foral liberties seemed about to become a dead letter. The weight of these

pressures fell most heavily on Navarra, since more was demanded
of it due to its greater size and population.[3] Moreover, the bypass-
ing of legal forms was also more severe, since Navarra had a fully
articulated medieval constitution, with an executive administration
(though not independent sovereignty), its own judiciary, and a
Cortes of limited legislative power, however nominal and in practice nearly defunct.

Nonetheless, the only violent resistance occurred in Vizcaya,
and that was touched off only indirectly. Vizcaya was internally
divided because of the tension between its prosperous chief port
and commercial center, Bilbao, and the poorer small towns and
rural areas. This tension was a common phenomenon in Vizcayan
history but had been building again during the past half century
with the renewed growth of Bilbao. A small town notary, Simón
Bernardo de Zamácola, proposed to the crown that permission be
granted for the establishment of a second major free port, reducing
Bilbao's commercial advantage. He proposed to win approval by
gaining support among the Vizcayan *Junta General* for a sort of
local militia that could be added to the royal forces in moments of
danger. In the existing state of internal and external tensions, this
touched off an explosion, for it seemed to threaten the end of foral
military exemptions. Several Vizcayan notables who were close to
Madrid politics and eager for the downfall of Godoy may have
encouraged a broad-based riot, called the *zamacolada*, which
drove the notary from the province and brought thousands of
Vizcayans out in opposition to royal interference. This was quelled
by the entry of several thousand royal troops. A number of
ringleaders were shipped to colonial penal institutions, and the
notables who were involved were banished from Vizcaya. In the
aftermath the office of separate royal *corregidor* as chief administrative officer of Vizcaya was abolished and was replaced by that of
a new district military commander.[4] This marked another major
step in the reduction of the foral structure.

When the young prince Fernando briefly assumed the throne
on the eve of the French invasion (1808), he decreed full restoration
of the *fueros*, but they were entirely negated by the advent of
Spanish liberalism in the Constitution of 1812. The Basque territories altogether sent eight of the nominally 300 representatives

that appeared in the Cortes of Cádiz—though one-third of the latter attended rarely or not at all. The Basque delegation was not totally disproportionate to their approximately 4 percent of the total Spanish population. Of the 184 deputies who actually signed the new constitution, the heaviest proportions came from the liberal periphery as distinct from inland Castilla.[5] The new constitution was thus the work of a small minority of upper- and middle-class liberals. It abolished all *fueros* and special jurisdictions, prescribing a uniform structure of provincial government, law, and administration for all Spain. On the local level, however, the 1812 constitution provided for a considerable degree of municipal autonomy. The representatives of the three western Basque provinces endorsed the liberal constitution. They were products of the late eighteenth-century Basque enlightenment and believed that liberal constitutionalism would expand the freedom of all, while municipal autonomy would give the rest of Spain most of the essential privileges previously enjoyed by Basques.[6] In this they reflected the opinions of the most politically active elements in the western provinces, but not those of Basques as a whole. The Navarrese representatives, on the other hand, faced the loss of a complete constitutional structure and staunchly resisted the dissolution of the Navarrese system into a central Spanish state.

When the despotic Fernando VII returned to the throne in 1814, he needed little encouragement to overthrow the new charter and return to virtual absolutism. It may, however, have been more than coincidental that Francisco Javier de Elío, the captain general who incited the royal coup, was a Navarrese, and that Francisco Eguía, the army commander at Madrid who closed the Cortes, was a Vizcayan.

In restoring the system of government that had obtained prior to 1808, Fernando VII specifically reaffirmed Basque *fueros* and the Navarrese constitutional system. Nonetheless, his monarchy did not rest upon unalloyed tradition but was the heir of the largely centralized and increasingly interventionist regime of the eighteenth century. Pressures from Madrid were soon resumed. A royal order of 1817 that upheld the *fueros* of Vizcaya made them contingent upon the "unity, order, and royal rights" of the crown,[7] thus leaving the way open for their systematic reduction. A royal decree of 1818 established that all the Basque territories would henceforth be responsible for regular manpower contributions to the Spanish army, from which they had hitherto been exempt. This was renegotiated to take the form of new financial subsidies proportionate to the number of men that would have been requested, but one of the cornerstones of foralism was displaced in the process.

The Basque area had nothing to do with the collapse of royal government and the beginning of the liberal triennium of 1820−23. The *pronunciamiento* of Riego was a political process developed mainly in Andalusia and Castilla. Nevertheless, the Basque territories, like all the rest of Spain, initially accepted the restoration of liberal constitutionalism with scarcely a protest, despite all the dangers of antiforal centralization that were involved. The region most hostile to liberalism was the kingdom of Navarra, whose status of autonomy was more complete than that of the western provinces, and whose economy and society were less involved with northern and central Spain than were those of Vizcaya and Guipúzcoa. Thus the first conservative royalist revolt against liberalism broke out in rural Navarra at the close of 1821. The royalist Supreme Junta that was formed soon after had its seat at the Seo de Urgel, in the conservative mountain country of northwest Catalonia, an area whose social structure was not very different from most of Navarra.

After the liberal regime was overthrown with the assistance of a major French military invasion in 1823, authoritarian monarchy was restored. Indeed the decade 1823−33 was in some ways the closest thing to absolute monarchy that Spain ever experienced, since Fernando's standard of government was to avoid as much as possible any check on royal power. This time the Inquisition was not restored by the crown, and a national police system was established in its stead that even included the Basque territories, though somewhat tenuously. Fernando's restoration of traditional government did include renewed recognition of Basque *fueros* and the Navarrese constitution—which enjoyed their Indian summer during the following decade—but stressed that "*fueros* and privileges were concessions of royal grace and hence subject to modification."[8]

The predominant attitude in the Basque provinces after 1823

became increasingly concerned with preserving local rights and hence was conservative, but it was not at all identical with the new ultra right-wing *apostólico* faction in Spanish politics. The *apostólicos* had developed among the church hierarchy and hyperconservatives of the court and aristocracy represented in the royal Council of State. They criticized the Fernandine restoration for being too secular and opportunist, and insufficiently doctrinaire and clerical. *Apostólicos* demanded restoration of the Inquisition, an even more complete purge of government personnel than had been carried out in 1823–24, greater authority for the conservative rural militia, the Royal Volunteers, that had been formed to supplement (and virtually replace) the semiliberal regular army, and in general the appointment of *apostólicos* to all important positions. As Fernando resisted efforts at *apostólico* domination of his regime, they began to transfer their loyalties to his extremely clerical, traditionalist younger brother, Don Carlos María Isidro.

In their zeal to purify government, the *apostólicos* stressed the absolute sovereignty of the crown, and this was specifically denounced by conservative royalist Navarrese constitutionalists and Basque foralists. The Basque territories played no role in the first pre-Carlist revolt, the *Guerra dels Malcontents*, or *Guerra de los Agraviados*, in rural Catalonia during 1827. The revolt of the *Malcontents* broke out in the spring of 1827 and gathered momentum, until by September of that year most of the principality of Catalonia was more or less dominated by it. Within another month or two, after the bulk of the Spanish regular army was committed to the region, it collapsed even more quickly than it had begun.

The *Malcontent* movement was apparently at least partly fomented from the outside by certain church leaders and *apostólico* personalities at court. Its base was rural middle Catalonia, drawing on a peasantry and village artisan class threatened by new economic change and the postwar depression.[9] The larger towns and coastal area of Catalonia were by that time one of the most liberal parts of Spain, while the semi-isolated Pyrenean foothill districts of northern Catalonia were more self-sufficient and less easily mobilized. The peasants of the Basque territories were perhaps better off economically, thanks to slightly better land distribution and lower taxes.

The final meeting of the traditional Navarrese Cortes was held in 1828–29. Only a few weeks after its sessions ended, a royal decree of May 14, 1829, declared that all royal laws and ordinances in effect in other parts of Spain would also be valid for Navarra and the Basque provinces until the *junta* to investigate and validate all *fueros* originally named in 1796 should finally carry out its function. This was the death knell of foralism and the traditional Navarrese constitution, but just as the Spanish viceroy in sixteenth-century Naples hoped that death would come to him from Madrid since all dispatches of the Spanish government were so slow to take effect, so the new *junta* was never actually put into operation amid the confusion and internal conflict that attended the last years of Fernando VII (1830–33). Throughout that time the *diputaciones* of the Basque territories fought a determined delaying action to try to retain as much of the foral structure as possible.[10]

A new era began with the death of Fernando VII in September 1833 and the subsequent outbreak of the seven-year-long First Carlist War. The nominal issue at stake in the Carlist struggle was the succession to the Spanish throne. A moribund Fernando VII had left the throne to his eldest offspring, the three-year-old princess Isabel, annulling the French Salic law originally established in Spain by the Bourbon dynasty. The right of succession by eldest legitimate child, whether male or female, was previously the historic succession law of the Spanish crown. The supporters of the pretender Don Carlos made the inviolability of the Salic law (succession through the male line only) their chief legal argument, but obviously much more than that was at stake. The issue in the Carlist War was the continuation of traditional Spanish institutions—governmental, social, and religious—or their replacement by centralized parliamentary constitutional monarchy and an individualistic, capitalistic society. The queen regent, María Cristina of Naples, could not hope to retain the Fernandine system of semiabsolutism for her daughter without alteration. During the last eight years of his life the ailing despot had already made too many initial concessions to modernization in the sphere of law and economics—though not in politics—for the supporters of traditionalism and *apostólico* clericalism to accept his three-year-old heiress as distinct from his rigidly narrow and piously clerical younger brother. The queen regent and her supporters, in their uncertain control of the crown, had ineluctably to seek the support of moderate liberalism against the Carlists. This took the form of the *Estatuto Real* of 1834, a limited constitution granted unilaterally, and the issue was joined.

The first Carlist revolts actually began in January 1833 in north-central and southern Spain and were quickly suppressed. The first official group to announce its adherence to the Carlist cause immediately after the death of the king in September was part of the membership of the provincial *diputación* of Vizcaya, which may be taken as an indication not merely of the religious fervor of Vizcayans and the extent to which some Vizcayan notables were impressed by the Carlist legal argument, but also as a token that it was believed that foral liberties were much more likely to be preserved by a traditionalist monarchy. Small Carlist bands soon formed in rural districts throughout the Basque territories, and Bilbao and Vitoria (the capital of Alava) immediately fell under Carlist control. The liberal stronghold, San Sebastián, however, proclaimed the succession of Isabel II, and government troops easily reoccupied Bilbao and Vitoria within two months.

In the first weeks the main scene of conflict among small bands was the provinces of Alava and Vizcaya, where the Spanish government decreed martial law (*estado de guerra*) and on November 30, 1833, temporarily suspended the *fueros*. Political opinion among notables in the Basque territories was sharply divided, and between more than two simple attitudes. All the *diputaciones* split between *carlistas* and *isabelinos*, and only the larger towns remained generally liberal in their orientation. Sympathy in the rural districts—that is, among the overwhelming majority of the population—was generally in favor of Don Carlos.

There were risings by small peasant bands in every major Spanish region during the autumn and winter of 1833−34, but only in the Basque territories did the revolt slowly begin to acquire importance. This eventually led some commentators to assume that the main base of Carlist support was derived from the defense of regional foralism. Such an interpretation was, however, immediately disputed by a not inconsiderable number of contemporary observers and participants, and the controversy has persisted in the historiography of the Carlist wars down to the present.[11] What may be concluded from this debate is that the majoritarian Basque support for Carlism may not be attributed to foralism pure and simple but cannot be explained without taking foralism into account.

Sources of support for the Carlist cause were complex. Nothing was more important than the issue of "true religion" and church norms in opposition to "the enemies of God," as liberals were not infrequently referred to. To some commentators[12] this has seemed paradoxical, since the roles of church and state were more nearly separated in historical Basque institutions than anywhere else in the peninsula. Clerics had never been allowed to hold secular office in the western provinces, and even the mighty Inquisition had to some extent been held at bay. Be that as it may, the political assault of liberal anticlericals roused more intense opposition in the Basque territory than elsewhere because there it was perceived as part of a general onslaught against the institutions and values of local society. In other regions of Spain the anticlerical issue seemed much more distinct from broader civic concerns. In the Basque territory it became synonymous with the entire local way of life, to the extent that Salvador de Madariaga has denounced the Basque clergy as being from that time onward "the heart, brains, and root of intolerance and the hard line"[13] within Spanish Catholicism. That trend was not fully reversed until the 1960s.

This was accompanied by the defense of regional rights and identity, which became associated with Carlism. To the foralist issue per se was added the fact that in regions where traditional legal norms were revered more than in most parts of Spain, the purely dynastic argument of legitimacy was taken more seriously. Moreover, complex social and economic factors were apparently involved, and these have been little studied. Carlism was a rural movement, and seems to have been supported by specific elements of rural and small-town society that felt threatened by modern liberal capitalist and urban society.

These motivations serve to explain why a cause termed "absolutist" by its enemies was embraced by most of a people whom a highly perceptive contemporary English visitor termed as proud as any on earth. George Borrow claimed that the Basques had in fact "a kind of republican pride . . . and no one will acknowledge a superior. The poorest car man is as proud as the governor of Tolosa."[14] Basque Carlists were not fighting to uphold monarchist or aristocratic privilege, but their own rights, their values, and their way of life.

Several environmental factors have also to be kept in mind. The First Carlist War began, ended, and in large part was conducted by the Carlists as a *guerra de partidas* or *guerrilla*, that is, a "guerrilla war." Such operations are possible only in forests, jungles or mountain areas. Since Spain had no jungles and scant forests, operations had perforce to be concentrated in hill country. That the Basque and, specifically, the Navarrese hill country became the main focus was due, in addition to the combination of aforementioned factors, to several specific conditions. Among these were the emergence of the only fully charismatic and effective military leader, the redoubtable Guipuzcoan commander Tomás de Zumalacárregui,[15] who took charge of operations in Navarra early in 1834 and managed to rally a broad base of support. Navarrese and some other Basques more easily took to arms because of the tradition of guerrilla war and military adventure already established in the recent conflicts of 1808−12 and 1821−23, which had already mobilized a higher proportion of Navarrese society than was the norm in most other parts of Spain. In Guipúzcoa and to some extent in Vizcaya there existed significant liberal urban elites, but in Navarra even the majority of the city council of its largest city, Pamplona, was at first pro-Carlist.

Throughout the war there existed a major current of what might be called "liberal foralism," that is, of notables in the four districts who were willing to accept the Isabeline monarchy but hoped that it would still be possible to preserve regional privileges. The first major blow came on November 30, 1833, when the civic administration of Spain was reshaped in its modern form of fifty-one provinces that includes the entire country without exception. Meanwhile, the Carlist *Junta Gubernativa* in Navarra carefully observed most foral procedures in districts that it controlled during 1834, yet made no major statement placing the preservation of foral structure among the chief goals of the war. As mentioned earlier, there was a potential conflict between the kind of absolute royal sovereignty sought by some *apostólicos* and the conservative ideas of Basque constitutionalism, and at first the main Carlist political leaders seemed unaware of (or perhaps unconcerned about) the political potential that might be derived from the foralist issue.

The promulgation of the new royal statute in early 1834 in effect completely did away with the Basque legal systems and constitutional autonomy, establishing uniform structures for all fifty-one provinces. Nevertheless, strong voices were persistently raised in Madrid about the need to conciliate the Basques through some sort of compromise on the issue of *fueros*, which many now believed was at the root of the conflict there. The Marqués de las Amarillas, a member of the regency council appointed by the will of Fernando VII, declared in November 1834 that "At the present time the war in Navarra is for its inhabitants a national war, and with scant difference such is the case in the three exempt [Basque] provinces."[16]

For the next five years Spanish government policy remained ambivalent, or rather practice contradicted theory. Government and military figures continued to recognize in principle the importance of achieving some compromise on the issue of foralism, and a number of semisecret missions were dispatched to negotiate with "moderate" or "practical" sectors of Carlists on that issue. In practice, however, the *fueros* were from 1834 on almost completely obliterated. New liberal city administrations were appointed and new liberal provincial administrations created. More important was that all sections of the Basque territories under government control were ruled by martial law, involving arbitrary arrests, confiscations, and the execution of prisoners. This policy, adopted by government commanders from the middle of 1834 on, gave the war a viciously sanguinary quality, with no quarter offered on either side.

It was partly as a result of this that the year 1834 witnessed a dramatic growth of Carlist strength in Navarra and the other Basque provinces. Zumalacárregui's prestige began to reach its height as he occupied and won over the semi-isolated valleys of northern Navarra that had previously been unmobilized and vaguely proliberal. Don Carlos himself crossed the French border in July and joined his determined supporters. One of his first royal orders on

July 17 specifically recognized the validity of the Navarrese and Basque legal systems.

During 1835 Carlist strength increased until by June of that year it occupied nearly all the four Basque areas, and Bilbao itself was under siege. That siege, undertaken against the advice of Zumalacárregui, who wanted to launch a mobile campaign into central Spain—for which the Carlist forces were better suited—marked a crucial turning point, for it ended in failure and cost the life of Zumalacárregui. Though the Guipuzcoan *caudillo* had managed to convert a few petty guerrilla bands into a greatly expanded and disciplined force that approximated the structure of a regular army, he had no successor able to provide brilliant military leadership combined with political unity.

In the aftermath of the crucial loss of Zumalacárregui, the Carlist leadership began to emphasize more strongly than ever the foral issue as a base of support. The regional *Junta de Navarra* that was in charge of governing Carlist Navarra stressed strict adherence to the traditional constitution in all its usages. The Madrid government at length replied by naming in April 1836 the secret Olivarría commission to try to reach a foralist compromise with moderate Carlists. After two months, it failed completely.

In August 1836 Spanish liberal politics moved sharply to the left with the successful sergeants' revolt at La Granja, and the ultimate result was the much more liberal constitution of 1837 that completed the work of centralization and the civic integration of the Basque territories. Whenever liberal spokesmen raised their voices to suggest publicly that accommodation on the foralist issue would be necessary to end the civil war, they were shouted down by the radicals, for whom absolute uniformity and centralization was the only way to achieve civic justice and quality. Another mission dispatched at the end of 1837 to seek a foralist compromise with moderate Carlists also ended in failure.

In 1837 the military directly assumed functions of government in Pamplona—the only *cristino* (liberal) stronghold in Navarra—when the provincial government of Navarrese liberals declared themselves unable and unwilling to squeeze more tax money and military support out of the Navarrese, who were being ground down by the long war. In August 1837 there occurred an insurrection by the *Tiradores de Isabel II*, a unit of liberal Navarrese volunteers that demanded better treatment for the troops and, somewhat more vaguely, more attention to the forces of Navarrese liberalism. Internal control in Pamplona rested on an uneasy balance for the remainder of the year.

Meanwhile the Carlist cause passed its highwater mark with the failure of the Carlist expedition against Madrid in the summer of 1837. The spectacle of Don Carlos's own indecisive leadership, increasingly severe internal division, and general exhaustion from a grueling and endless civil war were taking their toll.

By 1838 severe hostility had developed between moderate and *apostólico* Carlists. The military arm of the *apostólicos* were the so-called *brutos*, guerrilla volunteers from the peasant and lower-middle classes, in most cases Navarrese, who had been promoted to high military commands for which they were unprepared. Most of the professional officers in the Carlist camp, who tended to be moderates, had no use for them and applied the term *bruto* to designate their lack of training, technical preparation, inability to plan and coordinate, and in some cases their actual illiteracy. But the *brutos* were strongly supported by the *apostólicos*, who controlled the Carlist court. In May 1838 they engineered the courtmartial and imprisonment of two leading Navarrese professional commanders on a charge of dereliction of duty. This led to a minor insurrection that was suppressed, but thenceforth the Carlists were severely divided.

This situation was ably exploited by a small group of liberal spies and agents serving as provocateurs. Their first effort in April 1838 to bring Basque units out in revolt under the banner of "Peace and *Fueros*" was a failure, but it further weakened and discredited the Carlist cause. Foreign governments, never very active in support of Don Carlos, began to lose interest altogether, since it appeared more and more that in the main theater of action what was at stake was not a popular contest over the structure of Spanish government per se but merely the preservation of regional privileges.

The main Carlist army in the Basque area received better leadership when the professional (and Murcian) General Rafael Maroto was named to its command in June 1838. Maroto was an able technician and a careful commander, and a moderate in Carlist politics. Hostility of the *apostólicos* toward him was intense. He seems to have believed that Carlism was becoming hopelessly identified with despotic absolutism and that Don Carlos must emphasize a program of traditionalist constitutionalism, associating it with a sort of representative government, in order to overcome the image of reactionary absolutism that he projected. Maroto became the natural leader of the moderates by the end of 1838. At that point he may still have hoped for the victory of reformed Carlism, since the liberal forces, though much more numerous and better equipped, had little offensive spirit and were losing large numbers of reluctant draftees as deserters. Carlist forces had been reorganized and greatly expanded in Catalonia and in southern Aragón, so that the greater part of the northeastern Spanish countryside was in their hands. There was danger of a Carlist rebellion by peasants in La Mancha, and the government, which doubted its ability to finance the war through 1840, made contingency plans to withdraw to Andalusia should the Carlist forces in Aragón descend on Madrid.

The real clues to the situation were, however, extreme war-weariness in the Basque territories, inept leadership by Don Carlos himself, and severe internal division of the Carlists in the north. The main fighting in 1834–37 had occurred in and around Vizcaya, and perhaps as a result the proportion of volunteers from the Vizcayan and Guipuzcoan peasantry had been greater than from Navarra. However, these battalions were now exhausted and eager for an end to the war. Many Carlist notables had become disillusioned with the incompetent leadership of Don Carlos himself and doubted that he was worth further sacrifice. The internal strife between Maroto and the *apostólicos* reached a climax in February 1839 when Maroto arrested and arbitrarily executed five *bruto* commanders and then won approval from the vacillating pretender for the banishment of sixty-four *apostólico* personalities to France. This did not restore unity but made internal distrust more severe. Carlist forces in the Basque area were now worn by five years of attrition; they were outnumbered at least three to one by well-organized units that possessed much greater firepower. The Vizcayan and Guipuzcoan contingents, particularly, lacked the will to go on, and it was the Vizcayan commander, Latorre, who initiated the terms of a compromise capitulation with the liberal general Espartero. Maroto saw the ground cut out from under him, and on August 31, 1839, tacitly accepted the Compromise of Vergara, by which Carlist forces that surrendered were to be incorporated into the regular Spanish army and retention of Basque *fueros* recommended to the Madrid parliament.[17] The remaining Navarrese and Alavese battalions took no part in the capitulation, though their homelands were severely wracked by the liberal government's scorched-earth policy in 1838−39. After the capitulation, however, they had no choice but to lay down their arms, and the Carlist contingents in Aragón and Catalonia were then forced to disband in the following year.

On October 25, 1839, the Madrid Cortes approved a law that confirmed the *fueros* of Navarra and the Basque provinces insofar as they did not infringe the principle of Spanish constitutional unity under "a single monarch with a single Cortes for the entire nation." It authorized the government, after discussions with representatives of the four districts, to present to the Cortes whatever modifications in the *fueros* that might be required to adjust them to the liberal system. In the meantime, a subsequent royal decree directed that the regular *Juntas Generales* of the western provinces could reconvene and that in Navarra a new provincial *diputación* would be chosen by elections and would for the time being enjoy the "same powers that belonged by right of *fuero* to the *diputación* of the old kingdom of Navarra."[18] Basque leaders in the western provinces eagerly seized on the reconvening of the oligarchic *juntas* and ignored the directive to renegotiate the structure of foral institutions. Thus the latter survived with little modification until 1876.

The Navarrese case was different, for it involved not the continuation of provincial foral institutions but the conversion of a constitutionally separate kingdom into a forally autonomous province. This reorganization was skillfully negotiated by the upper and upper-middle class liberal leadership of Navarra and was officially established by the Pact Law of August 16, 1841. The Navarrese Cortes and royal council were replaced by an elective provincial *diputación* that in fact was allowed to exercise a greater degree of administrative autonomy than under the preceding system in which local administration, at least on the provincial level, had been dominated by royal administrators.

Retention of most foral rights meant the preservation of the main usages of Basque law on the intraprovincial level. In all matters pertaining to interprovincial and national regulations, the Basque territories had generally to conform to Spanish law and administration, and their population was represented in both houses of the Spanish legislature on the same basis as all other inhabitants of Spain. While the Basque provinces were henceforth included in the general Spanish fiscal and tariff system, their tax liability was limited to special provincial quotas (called a *concierto* for the three western provinces and a *convenio* for the more independent Navarra)[19] at a rate distinctly below the Spanish norm, distribution and collection of which was left up to autonomous intraprovincial administration. The provinces had also to accept liability to the Spanish military draft but were allowed to discharge this through their own administrative program, with the right to substitute bounty payments altogether.

In the mid-nineteenth century the centers of Spanish political life were the provincial capitals of eastern and southern Spain, whose political intelligentsia was in most cases distinctly more radical than those of most of the Basque towns. In general, the Basque provinces were quiet and orderly by comparison. Basque politics were dominated by an upper-middle-class liberal elite, as elsewhere, but most Basque liberals remained staunch upholders of foralism. The constitutional structure that they worked out with Madrid—largely integrating the Basque territories into the greater Spanish structure while retaining key foral differences in taxes and certain local institutions—endured for nearly a century.

By the 1840s the key region in Spain was Catalonia, and it held this eminence for the next hundred years.[20] Barcelona province was the only genuine industrial center in Spain and the only area which at that time had generated a modern bourgeoisie. Catalan business leaders were active in lobbying for an increased tariff to protect and foster their production, but throughout the nineteenth century they had at least some tendency to think in terms of developing a broad Spanish policy of economic development.

Their own base was comparatively narrow, however, and they did not achieve a full and close relationship with the main political base of the country, which was "Castilian." Despite its economic and political importance, Catalonia thus remained merely a special and more modernized region, not the spearhead of Spanish development as a whole.

Moreover, Catalonia has always been highly diversified politically, economically, and socially. From 1833 to 1874 it was a political microcosm of all Spain; its political activists ranged from ultra-Carlists to radical republicans and utopian socialists. The radical, legalistic, but dissociative individualism of Catalan politics had come to the fore by the mid-1830s. Throughout the decade 1835–44 Barcelona led all other European cities in urban rioting and intermittent wholesale insurrections against central authority. Not without reason did Friedrich Engels later observe that "Barcelona is the city whose history records more struggles on the barricades than that of any other city in the world."[21]

The mid-nineteenth century was a time of new discovery of regional cultures. In the Basque region this stimulated new work in historiography but had much less effect[22] than did the new cultural romanticism in Catalonia and Galicia. Catalan culture was more affected by the European romantic stress on cultural *volksgeist* than was that of any other part of Spain. Catalan poetry, virtually extinct, was suddenly revived. The New Testament was finally published in Catalan for the first time in 1832, albeit in London. (A Basque New Testament had originally appeared in 1571.) A romantic Catalan historiography developed, but its implications were more radical than nineteenth-century Basque foralist historiography. Whereas the latter was essentially conservative, the new Catalan historiography emphasized the centuries of Catalan-Aragonese independence and by implication criticised the present civic structure of Spain as a whole. The first short-lived weekly newspaper in Catalan appeared in 1841. The second, *Lo Verdader Català* (Barcelona, 1843–44), has been called the first organ of cultural Catalanism and the earliest standard bearer of the literary *Renaixença*. It was the first to coin the slogan that "Spain is the nation and Catalonia is the fatherland [patria]." However, the *Renaixença* merely produced a culture of the elite and failed for nearly half a century to establish a regular Catalan-language press or a Catalan theater. Though *Lo Verdader Català* protested lack of government protection for Catalan industry, the cultural revival remained primarily esthetic for nearly forty years.[23]

The first overt question mark about the future of Catalonia as a regional political entity was posed by Juan Illas Vidal in his pamphlet, *Cataluña en España* (1855), which asserted that the centralized Spanish state abused Catalan interests. He proposed that this be remedied by a change in economic policy and a greater degree of local self-government. Nearly five years later there appeared a series of newspaper articles by Juan Cortada, published in book form as *Cataluña y los catalanes* in 1860. Cortada cited the medieval glories and current achievements of Catalans to demonstrate that they "are not like other Spaniards." He believed that the task of forming a single modern nationality in Spain was more difficult than in any other existing nation-state of contemporary Europe, due to the great cultural, social, and economic diversity of its regions. Cortada stressed the fundamental point that state building had been much easier than the formation of a modern nation would be. Yet Cortada offered no concept of political particularism but only asked for greater accommodation of Catalan interests within the Spanish liberal state. If Catalans were "different," people of all regions were still "Spanish."

Despite a growing sense of Catalan culture and of regional interests,[24] there was greater enthusiasm in Catalonia than in the Basque territory for modern national Spanish undertakings. A special battalion of Catalan volunteers played a prominent role as shock troops in the Hispano-Moroccan war of 1859–60. At that time dynamic Catalan society was seeking modern goals with which to identify; its economy had now become more fully interconnected with that of Spain as a whole than was the case with the Basque country, and Catalan society thought in terms of expansion and even of *españolismo*. Basque society in the 1850s and 1860s was less modernized, economically less dynamic, and politically more conservative. Thanks to the partial preservation of *fueros*, it was also more autonomous and, contrary to the situation that had existed prior to the late eighteenth century, more alienated from general Spanish government and culture than was Catalonia.[25]

In contrast to the relative Catalan enthusiasm, the Basque provincial *diputaciones* proved so obdurate in negotiating new contributions for war expenditures that in 1860 the current Spanish government forbade them to meet without approval from their respective provincial governors. Later, in 1864, Basque parliamentary representatives reintroduced their periodic proposals for full restoration of all foral privileges. When the senator for Alava referred to Basques as a "nationality"—one of the first uses of that term—he drew a heated rebuke from the prime minister, who declared there was only one nationality in Spain.[26]

Vizcaya, and especially Bilbao, did begin to grow rapidly in the 1850s and 1860s. Up to mid-century the main entrepôt of the north Spanish coast had been Santander, and Bilbao ranked only fifteenth in import traffic among all Spanish ports.[27] However, Bilbao prospered more than did any other north coast town from the railway-building boom of the fifties and sixties. Thanks in part to the enterprise of a small number of Vizcayan businessmen, Bilbao played a significant role in the importation of railroad materials. Its trade increased slowly but steadily during the 1850s, then rose rapidly from 5.5 percent of all Spanish foreign trade in 1860 to 11.8 percent in 1865.[28] In the spurt of new limited-liability banking and credit institutions that followed liberalization of state regulations, Bilbao and Santander both formed the relatively modest number of three each, whereas by 1865 Madrid had twelve banking corporations, Barcelona seven, Valencia five, and Valladolid four. The new Banco de Bilbao and Banco de Santander were among the most soundly organized, however, and were among the very few to underwrite industrial as well as commercial and financial activity. Thus they have survived to the present day whereas nearly all their original contemporaries have long since disappeared. Modern industrialization was just beginning to get underway in Vizcaya and Guipúzcoa after mid-century. Several new metallurgical factories were founded; though total production remained very small, Vizcayan output of cast iron increased 500 percent between 1856 and 1871.[29] Development of the leading Basque province was attested by Vizcaya's increase in population from 112,000 in 1840 to 190,000 in 1868,[30] a growth record proportionate, though not equal, to Barcelona's.

When a new democratic monarchist system was introduced in Spain after 1868, the response in Catalonia and the Basque region was quite dissimilar. Catalonia became Spain's leading stronghold of democratic progressivism and of the burgeoning new federal republican movement.[31] Under the short-lived Federal Republic of 1873–74, two-thirds of Spain's provincial governors at one point were Catalan.

The bulk of the Basque population viewed the new democratic regimes with suspicion. In the five elections held in Spain between 1869 and 1873, voting in Catalonia varied from moderate liberal to extremely liberal or radical, depending in large measure on which parties were in power. During the first three elections, all four Basque provinces (with the partial exception of Alava) voted heavily for Carlist candidates. The last two elections, in 1872–73, were won by liberals, but these contests were nearly meaningless since most of the Basque population boycotted them under conditions of civil war.

The new democratic regime soon resulted in a major new wave of anticlericalism. The expansion of liberalism and further measures of centralization produced a revival of Carlism in nearly all the regions of the northeast where it had been strong in the 1830s, though the first attempt at a Carlist revolt in the Basque region in 1872 was smothered. What fanned the flame into a major blaze was the collapse of the democratic monarchy in 1873 and its replacement by a radical, anticlerical federal republic. This led to the second major Carlist civil war, whose main phase lasted three and a half years until the close of 1876. In some of the eastern regions Carlist bands were little more than bandit groups; the main theater of war was once more the Basque region.

Nonetheless, Basque support for Carlism was more limited and somewhat different in nature than in the 1830s. It was perhaps more ideological and less foralist, for the *jaunchos*, or notables, who had earlier supported Carlism mainly out of concern for local privileges held more aloof. Vizcayans and Guipuzcoans were proportionately less involved, and the main effort was made by the Navarrese. Nonetheless the Carlist banner was still popular and able to recruit widely throughout the Basque country among the threatened and the displaced, as well as among the ultraclerical. In

Navarra and Alava it drew considerable support from the urban population, as well.[32]

By this time Carlism was developing a more modern right-wing ideology, though it involved new contradictions. The current pretender, Don Carlos "VII," was in a sense one of the first modern Spanish nationalists. He stood for a new sense of Spanish purpose and unity, though on the basis of the distinct interests of the regions. Basque concern for foralism was clear; in his 1872 proclamation to the Catalans, Aragonese, and Valencians, Don Carlos announced that to these regions also he was restoring original *fueros*, and even went so far as to promise a restored Catalan Cortes.[33] Many of the leading figures of Carlism, however, had little interest in foralism. Increasingly they stressed the doctrinaire principles of religious unity and national union under authoritarian and corporative monarchy. The idea of semiautonomous provinces and town governments based on corporative organization began to replace foralism.

Militarily, the civil war of 1873–76 was a much more circumscribed repetition of the conflict of the 1830s, as Basque Carlists and the other *partidas* were worn down by attrition. For the Basque region, the outcome threatened to be more disastrous. A new Spanish law of July 21, 1876, declared that any changes in the foral system of the western provinces that were "required . . . for the proper government and security of the nation"[34] would be immediately effected. Yet, though Navarra had been the chief bastion of Carlist strength, the government did not feel empowered to abrogate the Navarrese Pact-Law of 1841, which had been negotiated by the representatives of a separate constitutional system rather than an exempt province. Navarra retained its administrative and fiscal autonomy[35] while the remaining foral rights of the other three provinces were about to be abolished. This accentuated what during the next two generations would become a growing difference between Navarra and the western Basque provinces, a difference especially marked by the much more rapid rate of social and economic development in Vizcaya and Guipúzcoa.

The architect of the new Spanish constitutional monarchy, Antonio Cánovas del Castillo, was seen by the majority of Basque opinion as the incarnation of centralist iniquity, but in fact Cánovas was a wise and experienced politician who had considerable respect for the functional efficiency of Basque institutions. He proposed reducing the scope of Basque exemptions and bringing local institutions into closer harmony with the Spanish state, but not the total abolition of foral rights. He even wrote that, properly adjusted, "far from desiring the disappearance of such institutions, I should like to extend them if possible to the rest of Spain."[35] After stipulating that the Basque provinces must take their full share of Spanish tax and military service responsibilities, the law of July 21 authorized the government, while arranging all necessary reforms of the foral system, to consult with the three western provinces directly if that were judged to be opportune.

The attitude of the three Basque provincial *juntas* was one of complete intransigence and noncooperation. The Vizcayan *junta* was the most rigid and outspoken, and so was soon dissolved by the Spanish government. The Guipuzcoan and Alavese *juntas* were eventually dissolved in November 1877, and all three were replaced by regular provincial governments.

The elimination of foral rights led to the formation of two new ad hoc *neofuerista* groups whose principal base was Vizcaya, which had the most important economic interests to protect. The majority of Basque liberals and business representatives, however, worked effectively within the new system to retain the most important of their privileges—fiscal autonomy. In May 1877 the three western provinces were officially incorporated into the regular legal-administrative structure of the Spanish state, but the key issue of taxes was safeguarded. In February 1878 the Spanish parliament approved a new *concierto económico* for the three provinces, limiting their tax liabilities to a fixed quota calculated on the basis of their contributions under the Isabeline regime. Moreover, the method of raising and apportioning taxes was left to the new Basque provincial governments, whose assemblies, like those of all other provinces, were directly elective under the new 1876 constitution. Thus, despite the loss of most foral rights, Basque economic privilege remained triumphant. In the first regular elections held under the restricted suffrage system of the restored monarchy (1879), the progovernment Liberal Conservatives— with the assistance of considerable abstention and also of electoral manipulation—defeated the intransigent neoforalist candidates by a wide margin.

NOTES

1. There has been considerable controversy over just what occurred during this episode. See Fermín de Lasala, *La separación de Guipúzcoa y la Paz de Basilea* (Madrid, 1895); García Venero, 100−112; and from a twentieth-century nationalist viewpoint, José de Aralar, *Los adversarios de la libertad vasca* (Buenos Aires, 1944), 1−39.

2. For an evaluation of both sets of writing, see Mañaricúa, 273−335.

3. The new demands made of Navarra are briefly narrated in Rodrigo Rodríguez Garraza, *Navarra de Reino a provincia (1828−1841)* (Pamplona, 1968, 16−27.

4. On the *zamacolada*, see García Venero, 120−27, and Tejada, *Señorío de Vizcaya* 284−35, but above all, Fidel de Sagarmínaga, *El gobierno y el régimen foral de Vizcaya*, (Bilbao, 1892), VI.

5. According to José Luis Comellas, the largest number of signatures by peripheral region was as follows:

Catalonia 15
Valencia 15
Galicia 15
Asturias 7
Murcia 6

"Las Cortes de Cádiz y la Constitución de 1812," *Revista de Estudios Políticos*, no. 126 (Nov.-Dec., 1963), 80.

These figures are heavily disproportionate to the region's percentage of total population only in the cases of Valencia and Murcia. See the booklet by Manuel Ardit, *Els valencians de les Corts de Cadis* (Barcelona, 1968).

6. This attitude is explained in Gregorio de Balparda's *La crisis de la nacionalidad y la tradición vascongada*, quoted in García Venero (1945 edition), 62−63. (All other references to García Venero are to the 1968 edition, unless otherwise indicated).

7. García Venero, 146.

8. According to a government pronouncement quoted in Ibid., 151−52.

9. See Jaume Torras, *La guerra de los Agriviados* (Barcelona, 1967), and, on the question of social composition, his article, "Societat rural i moviments absolutistes," *Recerques*, I (1970), 123−30. Torras' statis-

tics, admittedly quite limited, indicate that in certain districts as many as one-third of the *malcontents* came from the village artisanry.

10. On the Navarrese reaction, see Rodríguez Garraza, 98–146.

11. The classic exposition of the foralist thesis is E. Echave-Sustaeta, *El partido carlista y los fueros* (Pamplona, 1914). For brief summaries of and speculations about the antiforalist argument, see Rodríguez Garraza, 154–160; García Venero, 163–74; and Julio Aróstegui Sánchez, *El Carlismo alavés y la guerra civil de 1870–1876* (Vitoria, 1970), 237–312.

The literature on Carlism and the Carlist wars is enormous. Most of it is narrative, uncritical, and often hagiographic. Students may begin with the five-volume bibliography edited by Jaime del Burgo (Pamplona, 1953–66). The most extensive collection of material is the thirty-volume collection of pro-Carlist writings, *Historia del Tradicionalismo español* (Sevilla, 1930–59), edited by Melchor Ferrer et al. The best one-volume narrative is Roman Oyarzun's *Historia del carlismo español* (Madrid, 1940).

One of those who liked to dwell on the regional liberties aspect of Carlism was Karl Marx. In one of his articles for the *New York Daily Tribune* in 1854 he wrote: "Carlism is not a simple, retrograde dynastic movement as mendacious and well-paid liberal historians have tried to say. It is a free and popular movement for the defense of traditions more liberal and regionalist than the official all-devouring liberalism. . . . Carlist traditionalism possessed an authentically popular and national basis in the peasants, small proprietors and clergy. . . ." Quoted in Patxi Isaba, *Euzkadi socialiste* (Paris, 1971), 152.

12. Gregorio de Balparda, *Relaciones entre el Estado y la Iglesia en Vizcaya* (Bilbao, 1908), presents the clearest statement.

13. Madariaga, *Memorias de un federalista* (Buenos Aires, 1967), 172.

14. George Borrow, *The Bible in Spain* (London, 1906), 341–42.

15. The two principal biographies are J. Azcona y Díaz, *Zumalacárregui* (Madrid, 1946), and J. A. Zariátegui, *Vida y hechos de D. Tomás Zumalacárregui* (San Sebastián, 1946). Zumalacárregui's elder brother, the moderate liberal jurist Miguel Antonio, was a nonelected parliamentary representative and a secretary of the Cortes of Cádiz.

16. Rodríguez Garraza, 189.

This aspect was sometimes heavily emphasized by foreign commentators, especially W. Walton, *The Revolutions of Spain from 1808 to the End of 1836* (London, 1837), 2 volumes, and *A Reply to the Anglo-Christino Pamphlet Entitled "The Policy of England towards Spain"*

(London, 1837). Cf. Manuel de Irujo, *Inglaterra y los vascos* (Buenos Aires, 1946).

17. On Maroto and the end of the war in the Basque region, see Stanton W. Gould, "General Rafael Maroto and the Carlist War of 1833−40" (Ph.D. diss., University of Chicago, 1953).

18. Jaime Ignacio del Burgo, *Origen y fundamento del régimen foral de Navarra* (Pamplona, 1968), 341. Del Burgo's work presents an exhaustive politico-juridical account of the establishment of the new autonomous system in Navarra.

19. The evolution of the Navarrese *convenio* is described in Jaime Ignacio del Burgo's *Régimen fiscal de Navarra* (Pamplona, 1971). Del Burgo has published a brief synopsis of the Navarrese arrangement, *El Pacto foral de Navarra* (Pamplona, 1966).

20. The basic introduction to nineteenth-century Catalonia is Jaime Vicens Vives, *Cataluña en el siglo XIX* (Madrid, 1961).

21. Quoted in Angel Carmona, *Dues Catalunyes* (Barcelona, 1967), 130. On the intermittent Catalan tendency toward *arrauxement*, or passionate extremism, see Vicens Vives, *Noticia de Cataluña* (Barcelona, 1954), 117−159; and Rodolf Llorens, *Com han estat i com som els catalans* (Barcelona, 1968).

22. It was, however, in 1854 that the patriotic song "Guernikako Arbola" (Tree of Gernika), was composed by the Guipuzcoan balladier and former Carlist soldier, Iparraguirre. It subsequently became the anthem of Basque, or at least Vizcayan, regionalism. On its composer, see José M. Salaverría, *Iparraguirre, el último bardo* (Madrid, 1932).

23. For a brief introduction, see Rafael Tasis, *La renaixença catalana* (Barcelona, 1967), and J. M. Poblet, *Els precursors de la renaixença* (Barcelona, 1968).

24. The early development of Catalan regionalism is described by Maximiano García Venero, *Historia del nacionalismo catalán* (Barcelona, 1967), 1, 1−305.

25. Eduardo Tarrero has tried to analyze differences between Basque and Catalan society by categorizing Catalans as "viscerotonic," digestive, less active but more culturally inclined, individualistic and influenced by the equal separation of goods under their marriage laws. He finds Basques "somatotonic," more physical and more directly achievement-oriented, not contemplative but cooperative, more family and association-oriented and influenced by community property norms in marriage. "Analogía y diferencias vasco-catalanas," *Gran Enciclopedia Vasca*, IV, 705−8.

There is some truth to this, but historic changes in structural-functional relationships must always be taken into account.

26. García Venero, *Nacionalismo vasco* (1945 edition), 212.

27. Santander handled the bulk of the wheat and other agrarian exports of north-central Spain and since the eighteenth century had developed a modest shipbuilding industry that rivaled that of Bilbao. In 1848 Santander imported nearly twice as much as Bilbao and exported three and a half times as much. Bilbao did not even figure among the larger towns of the peninsula, having only 17,000 inhabitants compared with Santander's 25,000 or Barcelona's 150,000.

During the year 1848 Barcelona led all Spanish ports in imports with 140,000 tons. Cádiz and Málaga were second with 84,000 and 80,000 tons respectively. Bilbao ranked ninth with less than 16,000 tons. Cádiz and Málaga, based on the wine and olive trade, led in exports, with Barcelona third. Bilbao ranked a feeble fifteenth. San Sebastián ranked fourteenth in imports but scarcely even figured in exports. These figures are taken from Laureano Figuerola's *Estadística de Barcelona en 1849* (Barcelona, 1968), 187, 229.

In general, the main ports of the east and south ranked far ahead of the north in commercial activity, and this helps to explain why the eastern and southern towns took the political lead.

28. Gabriel Tortella Casares, *Los orígenes del capitalismo en España* (Madrid, 1973), Table III−8, 101.

29. Ibid., Chapter 3.

30. See Antonio de Trueba, "Organización social de Vizcaya en la primera mitad del siglo XIX," *Gran Enciclopedia Vasca*, II, 603−25; III, 350−66.

31. For a brief description of the growth of Catalan federalism see Fèlix Cucurull, *Orígens i evolució del federalisme català* (Barcelona, 1970). The ideology of the leading Catalan federalist is treated in Antonio Jutglar's "El federalismo español de Francisco Pi y Margall" (Ph.D. diss. University of Barcelona, 1966), and in his book *Federalismo y revolución* (Barcelona, 1966).

32. Aróstegui Sánchez has given a clearer picture of Carlist recruitment in Alava than is available for the other three provinces. In Alava nearly all Carlist officers came from the urban middle classes, and one-third of all Carlist recruits were of urban backgrounds. Indeed there seems to have been more support for Carlism among the threatened artisan sector of the lowest middle class (though not among the very poor) in the towns than in the countryside, for the urban third of Carlist recruits were all volunteers, whereas part of the peasant majority were draftees. In the Alavese countryside, support was strongest among the *labradores* or small independent farmers. Among the larger landowners "a majority professed liberal

ideas," according to Antonio Pirala, *Historia contemporánea* (Madrid, 1879), VI, 380.

Middle-class liberals in Alava as throughout the Basque country were just as interested in foralism as were the Carlists. In fact, foralism was more important to them, since they often concentrated on that issue and were not diverted by religious or dynastic issues. The low-lying Rioja and Ebro regions of Alava and Navarra were the main liberal redoubt in the southern part of the Basque country. There social and economic interests were more typically middle class and more integrated with other parts of Spain. A small fraction of liberal foralists in the Basque region split off to support federal republicanism.

33. Though a minority of rural Catalans remained Carlist, the forefront of Catalan politics in 1873–74 was completely dominated by federal republicans, who stimulated a distinctive sense of modernist, secular Catalanism. Yet in Barcelona there was great apathy; only 17,500 of the 60,000 eligible voters participated in the 1873 republican elections. See Miguel González Sugranes, *La República en Barcelona* (Barcelona, 1896).

34. García Venero, *Nacionalismo vasco*, 228. The Spanish liberal position was clearly stated by Francisco Calatrava, *La abolición de los fueros vasco-narvarros* (Madrid, 1876). There is a description of these developments by Fermín de Lasala y Collado, *La última etapa de la unidad nacional. Los Fueros vascongados en 1876*. (Madrid, 1924).

35. The minor modifications in the Navarrese law are listed in Jaime Ignacio del Burgo, *Ciento veinticinco años de vigencia del Pacto-Ley de 16 de agosto de 1841* (Pamplona, 1866).

36. In Cánovas's prologue to Rodríguez Ferrer's *Los vascongados*, quoted by Jaime Ignacio del Burgo, "Descentralización foral," *El Europeo* (Madrid-Barcelona), March 24, 1972.

3

SABINO DE ARANA Y GOIRI AND THE CREATION OF BASQUE NATIONALIST IDEOLOGY

Contrary to what has sometimes been asserted, the Spanish Restoration era of 1876–98 was not a time of suffering or depression for the Basque region as a whole. In the two leading provinces it was the period in which the basis of a modern industrial economy was developed. During the two decades 1875–95 Vizcayan iron production increased twenty times over.[1] By the end of the century Spain was producing 21.5 percent of the world's iron ore, and most of this came from Vizcaya. The great bulk was for export, but from that basis commercial profits, sound management, foreign investment, and judicious association with Spanish national policy were combined to lay the foundation of the first significant heavy industry complex in modern Spain.

In Alava and Navarra, by contrast, the aftermath of the final Carlist war was one of relative social and economic stagnation. Whereas a new dynamic upper-middle-class elite seized the direction of affairs in the industrializing provinces, the two exclusively rural provinces were led by rural notables and wealthy landowners. Conditions for the peasant majority throughout the Basque region did not change very rapidly in the later nineteenth century. Traditionalist sentiment remained strong, and there was still widespread support for Carlism. On the provincial level, Carlism retained great strength even in Vizcaya, winning eight of twenty seats in the elections for the provincial *diputación* in 1880 and seven in 1882.[2]

Though some of the new Vizcayan and Guipuzcoan elite was coming to terms with the ruling Conservative party of Cánovas del Castillo, liberal upper-middle-class foralists in general remained intensely hostile and by the time of the 1881 elections united with the nascent Spanish Liberal party led by Sagasta. With the Liberals temporarily in power in Madrid, they swept the 1881 elections in the Basque country as elsewhere. This antipathy to the Conservatives was due almost solely to the fact that it had fallen to Cánovas and his party to reorganize the chaotic Spanish polity in 1875–76 and curtail the *fueros*. The Liberals were in principle decidedly more centralistic in orientation than the Conservatives. Moreover, after the experience of the democratic interlude and with the spread of industrialization, the beginnings of a radical political clientele were developing in Bilbao. As a consequence of these circumstances the difference between "Liberals" and "Conservatives," especially in the Bilbao region, began to blur. In the 1884 national elections, they put up a joint ticket, though it was dominated by Conservatives.

The 1880s were the heyday of *caciquismo*—of boss rule and elections manipulated from Madrid. The only region able persistently to buck the dominant national political alignments was the Basque territory. In 1886 the Liberals in power in Madrid swept the national elections but got only one of two seats in Alava, three of six in Navarra and two of five in Vizcaya, where the Conservatives won the majority. In 1887 the Liberals forced a 50 percent increase in the Basque tax quotas under the *concierto*, but the rate was still lower than in the rest of Spain. In 1888 the expanding Vizcayan shipyards won their first big new contract from the navy,[3] and in the new tariff of 1892 the Basque metallurgical industry received strong protection. When the new Liberal government attempted a broad trade agreement with industrial Germany in 1893, the recently organized *Liga Vizcaina de Productores* mobilized a campaign to stop it. By that point the Basque (or more precisely, Vizcayan) industrial bourgeoisie was beginning to play the role of enterprising national bourgeoisie to which some Catalan business leaders had aspired in mid-century. The Vizcayan group encouraged formation of a *Liga Nacional de Productores*, which was functioning by 1894. Meanwhile a realignment of the liberal industrial bourgeoisie was completed when Victor de Chávarri, the outstanding entrepreneur in Vizcayan heavy industry, went over to Cánovas's Conservative party in 1893. By that time the Carlist vote was declining in Vizcaya, though a sizable republican vote persisted in Bilbao, where the Socialists were also organizing by the end of the century.

The industrialization of Vizcaya, and to some extent of Guipúzcoa, was producing a closer association of Basque interests with other parts of Spain, particularly with Madrid and the political-financial superstructure. Basques were showing more concern for Spanish national endeavors, the first of the late nineteenth-century Spanish Africanist societies being Manuel Iradier's *Asociación Eúskara para la Exploración y Civilización del Africa Central*.[4] At the same time, Vizcaya was becoming highly differentiated structurally from the rest of Spain. Along with Barcelona, it was one of only two industrial provinces in a rural, agrarian country. The process of development and differentiation placed heavy strain on the old structure of Vizcayan society, threatening traditional values and identity.

It was in this environment of a rapidly changing and industrializing Vizcaya—or more properly of the greater Bilbao district and adjoining estuary—that modern Basque nationalism was born. Despite extensive attention, the whole question of the genesis and motivation of modern European nationalism has never been resolved. Various partial explanations have been attempted, ranging from that of reaction to national oppression through the economic needs of the rising middle classes to the problems of identity and value of a nascent intelligentsia and on to the marginality thesis, according to which backward or marginal regions, bypassed by modernization or feeling acute pressures from two different phases of development or cultural/civic identities, are most likely to respond with movements of acute national self-affirmation. Regional

nationalism and separatism have in modern times normally developed in the more backward parts of developing countries as a
response to modernization—the American South, Quebec, Flan-
ders, Brittany, Slovakia, Macedonia, and the Mezzogiorno. All
these explanations are at best partial. Exceptions may be found to
each of them, and some are directly contradicted by the conditions
of most nationalist movements. Indeed, so prominent an analyst as
Carleton Hayes concluded that "we really do not know what has
given vogue to nationalism in modern times."[5]

The origins of Basque nationalism can best be explained by a
peculiar variation of the thesis of modernization marginality and
the crisis of the intelligentsia. The Basque country was obviously
not being left behind in Spanish development. In strictly economic
terms, Vizcaya was beginning to lead it, but the process of development began to produce a unique combination of pressures.
The Basque country had never been a "normal" or "regular" part
of Spain in the way that Castilla, León, or La Mancha had been. On
the other hand, neither had it ever been oppressed. Even after 1876
it enjoyed greater privilege than any other part of the peninsula.

The very process of economic and social modernization was a
challenge to Basque identity, institutions, and values, for it brought
industry, major urbanization, large-scale non-Basque immigration
(at least into Vizcaya), and growing atomization of society. The
existing situation was excellent for Vizcayan economic interests,
but it disconcerted a few elements of the younger intelligentsia
searching for identity and meaning after the shipwreck of royalist-
apostolicist foralism.

This was hardly anomalous, for nearly all nationalist movements, like all modern ideologies, are creations of elements of the
intelligentsia. Indeed, in an acute recent study of the ideas of
nationalism, Anthony D. Smith goes so far as to say that "really,
nationalism's primary function is the resolution of the crisis of the
intelligentsia."[6] This is no exaggeration insofar as the first stage of
the development of nationalist ideology is concerned.

In a general way, nationalism is born of the intersecting of
traditionalism and modernization, and of the need to adjust to and
achieve the latter while preserving as much as possible of the
former.[7] The final defeat of Carlism and traditional foralism was

followed in Vizcaya by the onset of full-scale industrialization, which required a drastic adjustment of particularism in order to adapt it to modern circumstances.

Sabino de Arana y Goiri, the creator of Basque nationalist ideology and the founder of the movement, was the product of both traditionalism and industrialization. His father—both a major Bilbao shipbuilder and fervent Carlist—became a leading financier of the traditionalist military forces in Vizcaya between 1872 and 1876. Though the elder Arana regained much of his shipyard investments under the liberal Restoration system, the Carlist collapse dealt him a psychological and emotional blow from which he never recovered. After 1876 he went into a deep depression that at one point bordered on psychosis and finally died in 1883.

Young Sabino grew up in an atmosphere of great moral seriousness, profound *apostólico* Catholic piety and, after 1876, deep gloom. Moreover, his health was poor, reinforcing a personal psychological pattern that tended toward great inner intensity, an emphasis on suffering and, particularly in moments of crisis, religious mysticism. As an adolescent, Sabino shared the family's *apostólico* sense of Carlism and its complete rejection of modern Spain's civic structure. Yet the very hopelessness of their Carlist and *apostólico* ideals, together with the rapid adjustment of the Vizcayan elite to modified liberalism, deprived them of viable expectations for the future.

The first new direction in the political orientation of the Arana family was taken by Sabino's brother Luis, three years his senior. In 1880 he left home for a year's study at a Jesuit college in La Coruña province. While en route by train Luis de Arana wore on his suit lapel a small insignia reading *Vivan los Fueros*. A fellow traveller from Santander complained that he did not understand how Arana as a "Spaniard" could demand something that other Spaniards had no right to. According to the elder brother, this provided his first insight that Vizcayans and other Basques were intrinsically different from Spaniards. This idea took firmer root in the course of conversations with Basque Jesuits who were among his instructors in La Coruña, and whose influence foreshadowed the major role that the Basque clergy would always play in the development of the nationalist movement. In the following year

Luis de Arana moved to Madrid to study architecture, and during this period he developed firm nationalist convictions.[8]

Returning to Bilbao for the Easter vacation on Resurrection Sunday 1882, Luis announced to his younger brother that Carlism was a false banner. The problem was not primarily the antithesis between Carlism and liberalism, but that between the Basque people of Vizcaya and the Spanish as a whole, with whom the Vizcayans had little or nothing in common. Vizcaya was not part of "Spain" but was an ancient republic that had voluntarily associated itself with the Castilian crown while retaining absolute autonomy and institutional and ethnic purity. "Spain" had usurped the government and rights of Vizcaya while attempting to corrupt the mores of its people. Years later, after the nationalist movement had become a reality, Arana's disciples annually celebrated the *Aberri Eguna*—Fatherland Day—on Resurrection Sunday, in commemoration of the first clear definition of the nationalist idea among the Arana brothers.[9]

The Arana Goiri family moved to Barcelona in the autumn of 1882, apparently to permit the seventeen-year-old Sabino to begin his university education in a mild Mediterranean climate that would preserve his fragile health. The family remained there for nearly six years. This sojourn coincided with the climax of the *febre d'or*—the "gold fever," a wave of prosperity almost unparalleled in the history of Catalonia that lasted from 1876 to 1886 and in some respects through the Barcelona World Exhibition of 1888. Arana left no explicit record of the influence of Catalonia on him, but only a year in Barcelona was needed before he fully embraced his older brother's Vizcayanist thesis. The date given by his biographers is 1883, roughly coinciding with his father's death and what might be inferred to have been a youthful identity crisis.[10]

The cultural Renaixença of nineteenth-century Catalonia began to reach its climax in the Barcelona of the *febre d'or* with the emergence of major writers such as Jacint Verdaguer and Angel Guimerà. A bright flowering of new publications was crowned by the appearance of the first daily newspaper in Catalan, Valentí Almirall's short-lived *Diari Català* (1879–81). The literary Provençal movement in southwestern France, then at its height, reached across the Pyrenees to make contact with the poets of the

Renaixença.[11] New Catalan cultural societies expanded their activities beyond the merely literary in the late 1870s and afterward, far exceeding the new interest in provincial museums and antiquarian Basque culture then developing in Vizcaya and Guipúzcoa.

The Catalanist movement first began to assume clear political form in 1880. The initiative was taken by Almirall, a former federalist leader who after the collapse of the republic devoted his energies to developing a regionalist movement specifically for Catalans. His first Catalanist congress in Barcelona was attended by fifteen hundred people in 1880; two years later he formed a small *Centre Català*, the first concrete entity formed to pursue the goal of Catalan autonomy. In 1885 the *Centre Català* brought together a group of Catalan notables who prepared a public memorandum to the crown protesting the dangers of a lowered tariff and the proposed leveling of what remained of the Catalan civil code (particularly in the regulation of inheritance and partnerships). This petition, known to Catalanists as the *Memorial de Greuges*,[12] protested its loyalty to the unity of Spain, and ultimately its main goals were achieved. The tariff was raised, not lowered, and the new Spanish civil code of 1889 still included exceptions for Catalan law.

In 1886 Almirall published a collection of speeches and articles that articulated a doctrine of political Catalanism under the title, *Lo Catalanisme*. He insisted that Catalanism was based on a distinct regional culture and society whose psychology and values differed from the rest of Spain. Thus Catalonia required very broad politicoadministrative autonomy, with a regional parliament representing universal male suffrage on one level and corporative economic interests on another. Almirall's program was neither republican nor exclusivistic; he conceived of Catalonia as the first fully modern region of Spain, whose example and stimulus would help promote the modernization of the rest of the country.[13]

A different concept of Catalan regionalism was propounded by the elderly Juan Mañé y Flaquer, probably the most influential journalist of the preceding generation in Catalonia. In 1886 he also published a collection of his articles under the title *El Regionalismo*. A staunch admirer of Basque *fueros*,[14] Mañé rejected Almirall's liberal Catalanism as a radical and Satanic derivation from federalism that would destroy the harmony of Spain and Catalonia's historic institutional balance. Spain was an absolute necessity for Catalonia; it need only recognize the region's historic laws, institutions, and interests for both Spain and Catalonia to prosper harmoniously. Mañé stood for the restoration of a degree of local autonomy but rejected the drastic reordering of institutions proposed by Almirall. He has not inaccurately been called the chief spokesman of the conservative Catholic Catalan bourgeoisie, opposed to radical changes and interested in the advancement of tangible interests.

A different tonality was expressed by the Barcelona chaplain and later bishop of Vich, Josep Torras i Bages. In a series of articles he propounded autonomous regionalism from the viewpoint of its grounding in the spiritual traditions of Catalan society. Though uncertain about political structure, he advanced the curious notion that "perhaps there exists no other nation as completely and solidly Christian as was Catalonia" and held that Catalanism could reaffirm and safeguard religious values.[15]

Another zone of regionalism was beginning faintly to emerge from the Galician literary and cultural renascence of the nineteenth century. Unlike Catalanism, Galicianism scarcely went beyond the esthetic stage of cultural revival,[16] but a few spokesmen for Galician regionalism appeared. The most prominent was Alfredo Brañas, whose book *El Regionalismo*, published in Barcelona in 1889, proposed the reorganization of Spain on the basis of its major historic regions, rather than provincial federalism. In backward, rural Galicia it proved almost impossible to rally civic support for any major venture, but the gesture of Brañas and his handful of colleagues was noted in Barcelona.

In the Barcelona of these years of burgeoning Catalanist ideas the young Arana y Goiri began to conceive his own doctrine of Vizcayan-Basque nationalism. Though his ideas were not directly modeled on those of any of the prominent Catalanists, it may be reasonably inferred that the latter served as an indirect stimulus. Arana began to devote himself entirely to Basque studies in 1885. He had to start with the language, since, like nearly all upper-middle-class Vizcayan families, the Aranas spoke only Castilian. The next three years were therefore devoted to linguistics; Arana lived primarily in Barcelona but spent summers in Vizcaya, and in 1888 published in Barcelona the first part of his *Gramática elemental del Euzkera bizkaíno*. In the summer of 1888 he moved back to Bilbao permanently, ready to take up the challenge of developing an ideology and a movement of Vizcayanism that would ultimately become Basque nationalism. His first step was to present himself as a candidate for a new chair of Basque linguistics in the Secondary Institute of Bilbao. There were five other candidates, among them the young Vizcayan writer and philologist, Miguel de Unamuno, but the chair went to a priest, Resurrección Ma. de Azkue, who subsequently gained fame as the most active Basque philologist at the turn of the century.[17] Arana continued his philological studies for the remaining fifteen years of his brief life, though he never fully completed his basic Basque grammar.

Arana's first major political statement was a little book, *Bizkaya por su independencia*, published in 1892. This consisted of a fanciful interpretation of four dimly understood battles in medieval Vizcayan history, which Arana converted into the guideposts of "Vizcayan independence," something which, of course, had never existed in any organized sense at any point in Vizcayan history. The booklet attracted a certain amount of interest, and in June 1893 Arana was feted at a luncheon in Begoña (outside Bilbao) by some twenty friends and admirers. There he announced his intention to form a political movement that would work for the independence of Vizcaya, restoring its supposed original "state of liberty." This shocked even his own associates, men who represented different shades of Carlism, Integrism (a theocratic, nondynastic offshoot of apostolicist Carlism), and Vizcayan "neofuerism."

Amid the stability and revival of prosperity that accompanied the Restoration period, Basque language and culture was receiving new attention from scholars and devotees. Four new journals dealing with culture, philology, and Basque affairs were founded between 1878 and 1885, but interest and support was weaker than in Catalonia, and only one survived more than a few years.[18] These same years brought further development of historiography, especially in Vizcaya, which culminated in the appearance of the first volume of E. J. de Labayru's *Historia general del Señorío de Bizcaya* in 1895. The best achievements of this new generation of

Basque historiography reached a new height of scholarship, but nevertheless most of it was polemical and unsystematic, arguing either for or against foralism or for or against Carlism.[19] One notable variant consisted of the Basque studies and the investigations of Navarrese institutions and history by Arturo Campión,[20] which helped to create a cultural climate of non-Carlist provincialism or provincial regionalism in Navarra.

None of the new literature on the Basque region proposed anything so radical as Arana's position. The nearest thing to a precursor would have been found in the writings of Joseph Augustin Chaho half a century earlier. A French Basque from Soule, Chaho was a progressive in his general views but had defended what he interpreted to be the basic motivations of Basque Carlism. In his booklet *Paroles d'un Bizkaïen aux libéraux de la Reine Christine* and then in his *Voyage en Navarre pendant l'insurrection des Basques* (1837), Chaho posited a common identity among all the Basques—on both sides of the Pyrenees—and interpreted support for Carlism as based on the defense of Basque liberties, which he deemed the freest, most egalitarian and well-structured constitutional system in the world. He concluded that the political problem of the Basque region would never be solved unless the Basques were fully allowed to affirm their separate identity.[21]

In the development of a Vizcayan independence movement Arana faced seemingly overwhelming obstacles and lacked a genuine base of support. By contrast, the more moderate and collaborationist elements of Catalanism were beginning to build an organization. Since Almirall's political connotations were too radical for many elements associated with regionalism in Catalonia, a conservative group of intellectuals had broken away to form a *Lliga de Catalunya* in 1887. This fused with a leading Catalanist cultural group four years later to form an *Unió Catalanista*, which took up the task of giving political content to Catalanist sentiment. A congress at Manresa in 1892 drew up "Bases for a regional Catalan constitution," stipulating complete internal administrative autonomy for the region. The entire decade of the 1890s was a time of growing dissatisfaction on the local level with the inadequacy of government leadership and services. The notion of autonomy for Catalonia slowly but steadily gained adherents among the middle classes, and some went further: during the 1890s the term "nationalist" was first used with frequency to denote autonomist Catalan regionalism.

The *Unió Catalanista* produced the first complete ideologue of Catalanism in one of its most active young middle-class leaders, Enric Prat de la Riba.[22] In 1894 he published a *Compendi Nacionalista*, of which thousands of copies were printed and distributed. This was the precursor of his major work, *La Nacionalitat catalana* (1906). Prat was a clear and forthright nationalist ideologist, influenced by French conservative and historico-nationalist thought (as distinct from doctrinaire French liberalism), and by the historical school of law as practiced in Catalonia (following Savigny).[23] The distinction between the practical and historical-particular, as in the English model, and the doctrinaire, abstract-rational, and centralist French orientation, had earlier been emphasized by Almirall and always remained prominent in moderate middle-class Catalanism.

Prat defined Spain as the political state and Catalonia as the true fatherland of Catalans, who were said to constitute a distinct and fully developed nationality; hence their state must be altered to conform to their nationality. Unlike Arana's Vizcayanism, Catalan nationalism was not separatist, but demanded a regional parliament and government and a fully autonomous administration. Catalanism would thus become the vehicle of middle-class modernization and economic development, promoting social harmony. It would not rely on inorganic democratic suffrage alone but would also employ partial corporate representation. Prat held that Catalan society was being corrupted by shortsighted utilitarianism, divisive individualism, and decadent Spanish cultural and moral "gypsyism" (*flamenquisme*). Catalan nationalism would redeem Catalan cultural and social values, while modernizing the framework of Catalan life.

By contrast with the steady growth of support for Catalanism, Arana had to begin his Vizcayanist campaign almost singlehanded. In mid-1893 he founded a biweekly journal, *Bizkaitarra* (the Vizcayan), in which he began to expound his doctrines while publishing articles on Euzkeran grammar and philology, Basque history, culture, and local politics. His efforts centered on Vizcaya, for, while affirming a common identity of all Basques, he deemed it contrary to the spirit of Basque institutions for the inhabitants of one province to prescribe for those of another. In his Begoña speech, Arana noted that at least eight different political parties functioned in Vizcaya: three Catholic (Carlist, Integrist, and Foralist) and five liberal parties (Spanish Conservatives, Liberals, Radical Republicans, Federal Republicans, and Possibilist Republicans). There was no Vizcayanist group in Arana's sense, and he proposed to remedy this in July 1894 with the organization of the first *Euzkeldun Batzokija* (Basque Center) in Bilbao. During the past year a mob had harassed the Spanish prime minister in San Sebastián because of a slight increase in the Basque tax quota; the Arana brothers' first political incident occurred in August 1894 when they burned a Spanish flag after a Basque musical concert before the symbolic "foral tree" of Guernica. Their little group finally took explicit political form on July 31, 1895, with the organization of the *Bizkai-Buru-Batzar* (Vizcayan provincial council) of what was eventually termed the Basque nationalist party (PVN).

The political slogan of Arana's embryonic organization was *Jaungoikua eta lagi-zarra* (God and the Old Laws). Its original program declared:

1. Vizcaya, on organizing itself as a republican confederation, does so on the basis of the political doctrine enunciated by Sabino de Arana y Goiri under the slogan "*Jaungoikua eta lagi-zarra*," which is expressed in the following articles.

2. *JAUNGOIKUA*—Vizcaya will be Roman, apostolic and Catholic in every manifestation of its internal life and in its relations with other peoples.

3. *LAGI-ZARRA*—Vizcaya will be freely reconstituted. It will reestablish the essence of its traditional laws, called fueros, in their full integrity. It will restore the fine usages and customs of our ancestors. It will be constituted principally, if not exclusively, with families of Euzkeran race. It will establish Euzkera as the official language.

4. *ETA*—Vizcaya will establish perfect harmony and conformity between the religious and political orders, between the divine and human.

5. DISTINCTION BETWEEN *JAUNGOIKUA* AND *LAGI-ZARRA*—Vizcaya will establish a clear and marked distinction between the religious and political orders, between the ecclesiastical and the civil.

6. PRECEDENCE OF *JAUNGOIKUA* OVER *LAGI-ZARRA*—Vizcaya will establish complete and unconditional subordination of the political to the religious; of the state to the church.

7. CONFEDERATION—Being through its race, language, faith, character and customs a sister of Alava, Benabarra, Guipúzcoa, Laburdi, Navarra and Zuberoa, Vizcaya will join itself or confederate with these six peoples to form a whole called Euskalerria, without diminishing its own autonomy. This doctrine is expressed in the following principles: *Bizkaya libre en Euskeria libre.*

8. The Euskeran Confederation will constitute itself by the free and express will of each of the Basque states, with each having the same rights in the formation.

9. The necessary bases for solid and lasting national unity are: unity of race in so far as possible, and Catholic unity.

10. The essential bases that are derived from the equal rights and liberties with which the Basque states form their union are: liberty to separate, and equality of rights and duties within the Confederation.

11. Once the Confederation is established, all states will have identical rights and obligations within it.

12. The Confederation will bind them only in the social order and in their relations with foreigners; they will otherwise retain their traditional absolute independence.

13. All of these articles are irrevocable.[24]

Arana's ideology was a unique blend of nineteenth-century Spanish post-Carlist apostolicism with modern Eureopean ethnic nationalism. Instead of the Carlist slogan "God, Fatherland, and King," he affirmed a syncretistic Vizcayan republicanism that was at one and the same time culturally neotraditionalist, politically revolutionary, and radically theocratic. The norm of "subordination of the political to the religious" was a product of *apostólico*-Integrist ideology. In contrast, the Basque provinces had always had the most secular civic structure of any territory under the old Castilian crown. Monastic establishments had been held to a minimum and, unlike the situation in all other Hispanic states, church hierarchs were never allowed to hold key political or administrative positions. The Basque provinces had been the only part of the peninsula where the Inquisition did not hold direct jurisdiction. From the viewpoint of Arana's radical apostolicism, these crucial aspects of Basque tradition were ignored.

Since the Basque area in toto had never formed a single discrete political unit and did not even have a name, Arana had to invent one. His original usage of *Euskalerria* was soon shortened to *Euzkadi*, an Aranist neologism that meant approximately "Basque land." He also designed a flag, a two-cross banner on a red background, with a white cross symbolizing Christian faith and superimposed upon it the green cross of San Andrés, symbolizing the green tree of Guernica—the token of foral freedoms—and also the Saint's Day on which, according to legend, the ninth-century Vizcayans defeated Ordoño of León at the battle of Arrigorriaga and supposedly affirmed Vizcayan independence.

Second only to his belief in quasi theocracy was Arana's concept of Basque purity, both ethnically and culturally, and probably derived at least in part from the same religious source. The maintenance of Basque racial purity might have been thought almost magical, but Arana explained it by the rigor of Basque *fueros* and the integrity of Basque culture.[25] Arana was not a biological racist and recognized that not all Basque people were of Basque biological background. The important thing was to preserve values and the way of life. To maintain "purity of race" so conceived, an independent *Euzkadi* would permit foreigners who had essential business to take up temporary residence under the supervision of their consulates, but those not originally of Basque parentage would not be permitted to become naturalized.[26]

Arana was not a man of broad culture, for he cut short his education to immerse himself in obsessive, exclusivistic Basque studies. One of the main aspects of his zeal for purity was his determination to purify the Euskeran language. There are more than a socre of local dialects of *Euskera*, some of them mutually unintelligible. Arana proposed to purify and rationalize the language by giving it a systematized logical structure. The result was creation of a new hybrid literary language (with a new orthography developed to differentiate it from Castilian phonetics), but with a structure nonetheless based on Romance philology—the only sort that Arana knew. He apparently never became fluent in spoken *Euskera*.[27]

Despite his religious ultraorthodoxy and search for tradition, Arana's ideology was not conservative but a curious blending of otherwise conflicting radicalisms. His doctrine of Vizcayan and Basque independence, rather than being based on Basque political tradition as he claimed, was in some ways analogous to the quasi-anarchist theories of anticlerical federal republicans. Like the federalists, he rejected integral nation-building and ultimately based political sovereignty on the smallest local civic groups, the municipalities, whom he credited with the original creation of the Basque "republics" by having freely confederated together.[28]

Arana completely rejected the readiness to compromise shown by most of his Catalanist contemporaries, drawing an absolute and total distinction between that which was Basque and that which was Spanish, or *maketo*, as he termed it. He vehemently condemned those Vizcayans who had intermarried with "Spaniards," whom he said had "confounded themselves with the most vile and despicable race in Europe."[29] The only positive quality with which many contemporary Europeans credited the Spanish was religiosity, and Arana denied them even that. Spanish Catholicism was, he suggested, ritualism and hypocrisy. The Spanish were not Christian but pagan, "the people of blasphemy and the razor."[30] It was, he said, not necessary for Basques to become "separatists," for they had never been really joined with Spain. It was impossible to separate that which had never been united; Basques need only reassert their fundamental independence.

Thus Arana strongly denounced the "Catalanist error," which was to define the Basques as their "brothers in misfortune" and to assume that the Basques' proper aspiration was regional autonomy. The Catalans were part of "Spain" (in Arana's lexicon, "Maketania"), whereas *Euzkadi* had nothing to do with "Spain."

When we say Catalan *fueros*, Aragonese *fueros*, etc., we do not mean by the word *fueros* the same thing as when we say Basko-Nabarro *fueros*.

The former are laws obtained or maintained by concession, the latter are laws created and legitimized by people who enjoy free sovereignty. The former constitute special legislation; the latter, general legislation. The former are regional codes; the latter are national codes. In the case of the former, the Spanish state is free to reduce, abolish, amplify, or modify them; the latter cannot be legally touched except through acts of international character.[31]

Catalan politics, for example, consists in *attracting to it* [italics Arana's] other Spaniards, whereas the Vizcayan program is to *reject from itself* all Spaniards as foreigners. In Catalonia every element coming from the rest of Spain is Catalanized, and it pleases them that urban immigrants from Aragón and Castilla speak Catalan in Barcelona. Here we suffer greatly when we see the name 'Pérez' at the bottom of a poem in Euzkera, when we hear our language spoken by a *riojano* teamster or a Santander salesman, or by a gypsy, or when we find a *maketo* name among a list of seamen shipwrecked in Vizcaya. The Catalans want all Spaniards living in their region to speak Catalan; for us it would be ruin if the *maketos* resident in our territory spoke Euzkera. Why? Because purity of race is, like language, one of the bases of the Vizcayan banner. So long as there is a good grammar and a good dictionary, language can be restored even though no one speaks it [a danger that Arana realized was facing Euzkera]. Race, once lost, cannot be resuscitated.[32]

Arana had no specific social program in the modern sense but was strongly influenced by Catholic doctrines of social harmony and economic justice. He recognized the inequities of nineteenth-century society, and frequently denounced capitalists for their materialism and egotism.[33] He was equally vehement in rejecting contemporary doctrines of socialism as merely a new form of tyranny.

Though a man of independent means through his family, Arana was neither a bourgeois nor a social radical but a nationalistic populist. He was a devotee of folk customs and informal dress and loved Basque country music and dancing. His main avocational diversion, despite poor health, was to tramp across the hills of Vizcaya hunting the few wild boar remaining. His personal identification was with ordinary Vizcayan people, undefined in terms of class. Arana's position was that social justice and equality would be achieved by the full reestablishment of Basque institutions as he perceived them. According to Arana's mythicized understanding, Vizcayan society had always honored work and had never recognized serious social distinctions.

The Spanish Restoration regime of the late nineteenth century was liberal and reasonably tolerant but not democratic. Arana's all-out assault on the Spanish civic structure, together with his verbal attacks on local authorities, soon brought reprisal, even though he had no more than a few score followers. In August 1895 he was tried for subversion and sentenced to forty-one days in jail.[34] His refusal to pay a concomitant fine, combined with three other charges against him, kept him in prison for approximately three months. In September the authorities suspended *Bizkaitarra* and temporarily closed down the *Euzkeldun Batzokija*.

The years 1896−97 constituted a phase of partial withdrawal from political activity as Arana devoted himself mainly to literary endeavors. In 1897 he burned the bridges between Aranist Vizcayanism and orthodox Carlism with the publication of his pamphlet *El Partido Carlista y los Fueros Vasco-navarros*, which charged that Carlism had exploited Basque needs in the interest of all-Spanish dynastic politics.

The Spanish national and colonial disaster of 1898 was a major stimulus to Catalanism and Vizcayanism. The trauma of this catastrophe raised serious doubts as to the viability of Spain in the modern world, promoted a decade of "Regenerationist" activity in Spanish politics, and encouraged regional businessmen—primarily in Catalonia—to look for an alternative political framework in which to develop their affairs. At one point during the brief Spanish-American war Arana's home was stoned by a mob of Spanish patriots in Bilbao, but in the 1898 provincial elections he won a seat in the Vizcayan provincial assembly and became the first elected Basque nationalist representative. When municipal elections were held the following year, five nationalists were elected to the city council of Bilbao and three nationalists won seats in smaller towns. By that time Vizcayan Carlists were beginning to fear the defection of part of their youth group to the militant new nationalist movement.

Once again, however, it was the Catalans who led the way. For the national elections of 1901, Catalan business interests[35] supported the formation of a political party, the *Lliga Regionalista*, led by Prat de la Riba, the perspicacious Francesc Cambó, and other young middle-class Catalanists. With the assistance of the Republicans, it broke the virtual monopoly of the Spanish Liberal and Conservative parties,[36] winning six of the forty-four Catalan seats in the Cortes. From there the *Lliga* went on to become the major political force in Catalonia for the next two decades.[37]

Vizcayanism altogether failed to generate this kind of support. By the turn of the century Bilbao industrialists and financiers were beginning to develop a more modern structure of operations than their Catalan counterparts.[38] Though the total size of Catalan industry was still much larger than that of the Basque country,[39] Basque entrepreneurs were expanding their activities at a much more rapid rate. They had learned to use foreign credit, joint-stock financing, and industrial banking, and were closely associated with Madrid and London. Their frame of reference was neither parochial nor regional, but national[40] and international. By 1900 39 percent of the Spanish merchant marine was Vizcayan,[41] and after another decade 30 percent of Spanish banking investments were concentrated in the Basque provinces. From iron and steel, industrial development expanded into chemicals, cement, and paper, and hydroelectric projects in neighboring regions were also financed and promoted. The whole scale of operation was beginning to surpass that of Barcelona businessmen.

Another difference between Basque and Catalan society was that, aside from the industrial zone of Vizcaya, Basque society was in general less secularized than were significant portions of Catalonia. Even among the middle classes and some of the workers in the industrial region there was stronger Catholic identity. This reinforced ideological conservatism and diminished the impact of a radical new doctrine such as Arana's. As a consequence of all these obstacles, his new publishing ventures of 1899—1901 quickly folded, and in the next Vizcayan provincial elections of 1901 Basque nationalists failed to hold their single seat.

In May 1902, three days after the coronation of young Alfonso XIII in Madrid, Arana dispatched a telegram to President Theodore Roosevelt upon the passage of the Platt Amendment by the American Congress. He saluted the American federal system and hailed the United States for "liberating Cuba from slavery."[42] This telegram was intercepted, and on May 30, 1902, Arana was hauled back to prison.

Arana seemed less interested in the independence of small peoples than in diminishing Spain and praising stronger powers who had bested it in overseas competition. From jail he sent another telegram to the British prime minister, Lord Salisbury, "congratulating"[43] the British government for its conquest of the South African Boers. He expressed the hope that Britain's "yoke" over the South Africans would be "light," offering "protection rather than domination, as for equally fortunate [colonial] peoples." There was no allusion to the fact that Scots, Welshmen, and Irishmen enjoyed distinctly less autonomy than did Basques in Spain.

Even so, Arana's praise of a sort of liberal imperialism may have been related to the basic change of direction that he began to conceive during his seven weeks in jail during mid-1902. He could no longer explain away the frustration of his political efforts during the past decade, the failure of his publishing ventures, and the lack of support for the PNV. The Spanish state was proving stronger than expected and had weathered the trauma of 1898. Despite Arana's historiographic inventions, Basque people were accustomed to cooperating with the Spanish system, and the new generation of industrial entrepreneurs rejected merely regional identities. Thus he reluctantly came to the conclusion that the nascent Vizcayan movement was far too weak to combat the Spanish state on the issue of all-out intransigence aimed at Basque independence. If the movement were ever to broaden its support, it would have at least for the time being to cooperate with the Spanish system as were the Catalanists, giving up exclusivism in favor of practical regionalism.

With Arana's authorization, the weekly *La Patria*, the nationalists' only organ, published a report on June 22, 1902, that Arana

> proposed to cease exhorting his compatriots to Basque nationalism, recommending that those who have heretofore followed him recognize and respect Spanish sovereignty and asking of them a final vote of confidence to edit and expound the program of a new Basque party that is also Spanish, aspiring to the well being of the Basque country under the Spanish state without infringing established legality, offering a general plan for the reconstitution of the Spanish state with special autonomy for the Basque country . . . adjusted to the needs of modern times. . . .

On the following day Arana wrote privately to his brother Luis:

> The entire press accepts the rumor in *La Patria* as genuine. No other course was possible. Now my passion begins. . . . Past glory vanishes; my crown has faded. Yet all this can still be suffered for the Fatherland! Since I cannot explain my full intentions to anyone, there is resistance in many but others are one by one allowing themselves to be convinced. I think they will all give me a vote of confidence. Since this was the moment in my life in which I could inspire most confidence among the nationalists and most respect among the others, I had to take advantage of it.
>
> I will set out my thoughts in writing and explain them to three or four nationalists privately, in the event that God calls me before reaching the goal of this plan, so that others may continue it. The newspapers insinuate that I gave in to avoid punishment, that my will has been broken. How lovely it is to suffer for the Fatherland! My advice is this: we must become *españolistas* and work with all our soul for a program of that character. The Fatherland demands it of us. This seems a contradiction, but if people trust me, it must be accepted. It is a colossal stroke, unknown in the annals of political parties. All my reputation is tarnished and the work of many years, carried on at the cost of many sacrifices, is undone, but you will understand me.[44]

Arana subsequently told a reporter from *La Gaceta del Norte* (Bilbao) that henceforth the Basque movement must work for "the most radical degree of autonomy possible within the unity of the Spanish state,"[45] and on August 24 *La Patria* announced the formation of a new *Liga de Vascos Españolistas* for the four provinces.

On October 26 *La Patria* stated that "several thousand" Basques had declared their support for the new *Liga*. In that issue Arana announced that Basque regionalists would be as well served by a republic as by a monarchy; what was needed was a legal reordering of the Spanish constitution to provide Basque autonomy within the Spanish state. This would be the most sophisticated, effective, and "modern" formula. Arana said that he proposed "eventually to demonstrate that the Carlist, Foralist, and Integrist programs" have "lacked an historical basis" and did not know how to "adapt" Basque needs to "modern conditions."

At Arana's eventual court arraignment on November 7 he was absolved of any earlier wrongdoing, and later radical Basque nationalists claimed that Arana's change of direction was but a temporary ruse to gain breathing space.[46] There is no clear proof that Arana completely renounced his long term goal of Basque independence, but the available evidence indicates that Arana was absolutely firm in his decision that for the foreseeable future the Basque movement must develop within the legal framework of the Spanish state.[47] Controversy over Arana's exact intentions stems from the fact that by 1902 his health had gravely deteriorated due to Addison's disease and he could no longer provide active leadership. The *Liga de Vascos Españolistas* was stillborn and never became formally organized. The PNV continued without an official change of direction; its thousand or so hard-core members were in many cases more inflexible and intransigent than Arana. By the autumn of 1903, Arana was near death, though only thirty-eight years old. On September 30, 1903, he had to give up his place on the *Bizkai-Buru-Batzar* and in the following month supervised the selection of a new president, Angel de Zabala, for the PNV. He died on November 25, 1903, his final moments those of the exemplary Christian he had always been in private life. Addison's disease, which took his life, also slew his Catalan counterpart, Prat de la Riba, fourteen years later.

In concrete political terms Arana had achieved very little, yet he had created an ideology and a mythos, together with the embryo of a political movement. He had founded modern Basque nationalism.

NOTES

1. The great spurt first occurred at the end of the Carlist war, when Vizcayan iron ore output increased tenfold between 1875 and 1880, then doubled again by 1900. See F. Sánchez Ramos, *La economía siderúrgica española* (Madrid, 1945), 221–22, and on the metallurgical industry at the turn of the century, Pablo de Alzola y Minondo, *Informe relativo al estado de la industria siderúrgica en España* (Bilbao, 1904).

2. The best source on Vizcayan politics in the late nineteenth century is Javier de Ybarra, *Política nacional en Vizcaya* (Madrid, 1948).

3. The potential of the shipbuilding industry was analyzed by Benito de Alzola y Minondo, *Estudio relativo a los recursos de que la industria nacional dispone para las construcciones y armamentos navales* (Madrid, 1886). There is a general account of the Vizcayan shipping industry in the nineteenth and early twentieth centuries in Teófilo Guiard y Larrauri, *La industria naval vizcaina* (Bilbao, 1968), 203–91.

4. Manuel Iradier, *Africa: Viajes y trabajos de la Asociación Euskara "La Exploradora"* (2d ed., Vitoria, 1958), 2 vols.

5. C. J. H. Hayes, *The Historical Evolution of Modern Nationalism* (New York, 1932), 302, quoted in Milton M. da Silva "The Basque Nationalist Movement" (Ph.D. diss., University of Massachusetts, 1972), 202.

6. Anthony D. Smith, *Theories of Nationalism* (New York, 1971), 133.

7. In Smith's formulation, "nationalism is born among the intelligentsia, when the messianic 'assimilationists' [modernizers] try to realize their former vision by adopting the ethnicity solution of the defensive reforming 'revivalists'." Ibid., 255.

This formulation fits the genesis of Catalanism, but, as will be seen below, not that of Basque nationalism. The latter was the product of a radical semimodernist transformation of traditionalism, but did not involve direct fusion with a transformed radical ex-cosmpolitanist modernism. Whereas most of the elements that earlier supported a more cosmopolitan modernism in Catalonia were won over to Catalanism, this has for the most part not been the case in the Basque country and has constituted a permanent weakness of Basque nationalism.

8. Jon Bilbao, "Raíces del nacionalismo vasco en siglo XIX" (Paper presented at the annual meeting of the Society for Spanish and Portuguese Historical Studies, April 1972).

9. Cf. "Ikasta" (pseud.), "Albores del nacionalismo vasco," in the *Libro del Aberri-Eguna* (Bilbao, 1932), 17–18; and Arana's remarks as quoted in P. Bernardino de Estella, *Historia vasca* (Bilbao, 1931), 382–83.

10. The principal laudatory biographies of Arana are Ceferino de Jemein, *Biografía de Arana Goiri'tar e Historia gráfica del Nacionalismo* (Bilbao, 1935), and Pedro de Basaldúa, *El Libertador vasco* (Buenos Aires, 1953). The account in Ramón Sierra Bustamante, *Euzkadi* (San Sebastián, 1941) is hostile but perceptive. The best brief synopsis is José Ma. de Areilza's "Otro centenario: Sabino de Arana y Goiri," *Vizcaya*, no. 24 (1965).

11. This included what might be a regional variant of the pan-Latin cultural idea. See Roger Barthe, *L'Idée latine* (Toulouse, 1951–52), 2 vols.

12. There is a brief booklet by J. de Camps i Arboix, *El Memorial de Greuges*. (Barcelona, 1968).

13. On Almirall, see Antoni Rovira Virgili's *Valentín Almirall* (Barcelona, 1936). The background of these years is treated in García Venero's *Nacionalismo catalán*, I, 365–412, and Rovira Virgili's *Resum d'història del catalanisme* (Barcelona, 1936).

There is a useful chart of chronology and outline of Catalanist political parties by E. Moral Sandoval, "El nacionalismo catalán: esquema de su evolución," *Boletín Informativo de Ciencia Política*, no. 7 (Aug. 1971).

14. Finding it difficult to awaken the proper sense of regionalism among Catalans, Mañé made a prolonged trip through the Basque provinces in 1876 and was designated an official "Padre de Provincia" by the *diputaciones* of Vizcaya and Alava. His articles on the Basque region were collected in *La paz y los fueros* (Barcelona, 1876) and *El Oasis. Viaje al país de los fueros* (Barcelona, 1878–80), 3 cols.

15. Torras i Bages, *La Iglesia y el regionalismo* (Barcelona, 1887) and *La Tradició catalana* (Barcelona, 1892).

16. On the Galician cultural revival, see José Luis Varela, *Poesía y restauración cultural de Galicia en el siglo XIX* (Madrid, 1958), and Ricardo Carballo Calero, *Historia da literatura galega contemporánea* (Vigo, 1963), I. Something of the background of Galician particularism

may be learned from F. Elías de Tejada, *La tradición gallega* (Madrid, 1944) and *El Reino de Galicia hasta 1700* (Vigo, 1966).

17. Luis de Michelena, *D. Resurrección Ma. de Azkue* (Bilbao, 1966).

18. Da Silva, 100, lists the following: *Revista de las Provincias Euskaras* (Vitoria, 1878–80); *Revista Euskara* (Pamplona, 1878–83); *Euskal-erria* (San Sebastián, 1880–1907); and *Revista de Vizcaya* (Bilbao, 1885–89).

19. For an historiographical review of the more serious specimens of this literature, see Mañaricúa, 360–441. After Labayru, the most widely consulted were Arístides de Artíñano y Zuricalday's summary, *El Señorío de Bizcaya, histórico y foral* (Barcelona, 1885), which recapitulated the existing state of foralist legend and spoke of the "pueblo euskaro," and the *neofuerista* Sagarmínaga's lengthy documentary collection, *El Gobierno y el régimen foral del Señorío de Vizcaya* (Bilbao, 1892), 8 vols.

20. Campión's writings were voluminous. Full references may be found in Jon Bilbao's *Eusko Bibliographia* (San Sebastián, 1970); for a brief summary, see Campión's *Discursos políticos y literarios* (Pamplona, 1907), and the outline of his work in B. and M. Estornés Lasa, *¿Cómo son los vascos?* (San Sebastián, 1967), 19–25.

21. There is a summary of Chaho's position in F. Sarraill (pseud.), *La Cuestión vasca* (n. p., n. d. but ca. 1967). Chaho believed that there were physical differences between Basques and Spaniards, but attributed these to cultural-environmental factors, especially mountain life. A briefer, more critical synopsis of Chaho's ideas, emphasizing his dichotomistic pro-French and anti-Spanish views, is given in Jaime del Burgo, *Bibliografía de las Guerras carlistas y de las luchas políticas del siglo XIX* (Pamplona, 1966), V, "Suplemento," 501.

22. Jordi Solé Tura, *Catalanisme i revolució burgesa* (Barcelona, 1967), provides an incisive analysis of Prat's doctrines. For a brief introduction, see A. Rovira Virgili, *Prat de la Riba* (Barcelona, 1968); Rafael Olivar Bertrand, *Prat de la Riba* (Barcelona, 1966), is a descriptive biography.

23. On Manuel Duran y Bas, leader of the Catalan historical school of law, see J. J. Gil Cremades, *El reformismo español* (Barcelona, 1969), 303–22.

24. Quoted in García Venero, *Nacionalismo vasco*, 282–83.

25. The principal ideologist of Basque racism was Arana's close collaborator, Engracio de Aranzadi (Kizkitza). Aranzadi's two major political publications were *La Nación vasca* (Bilbao, 1918) and *Ereintza (Siembra de Nacionalismo Vasco)* (Zarauz, 1935), the latter constituting one of the best sources for the early history of the nationalist government.

A short-lived but more radical counterpart was the "cranial theory" of Dr. Robert, a leading fin-de-siècle Catalanist, who endeavored to prove that the native Catalan population possessed superior cranial and intellectual capacity. Cf. Salvador de Madariaga, *Memorias de un federalista* (Buenos Aires, 1967), 34.

26. Arana, "La pureza de raza," *Bizkaitarra*, 3:24 (Mar. 31, 1895). His writings have been collected in a large volume of *Obras completas* (Buenos Aires, 1965).

It might be noted that Arana's aim of severely curtailing the residence of foreigners did have certain precedents in earlier Basque history.

27. It should be recognized that any attempt at systematizing a new or improved form of a literary language becomes somewhat arbitrary. R. M. Azkue, Arana's senior philologist and fellow nationalist, soon published a major new Euskeran grammar that some complained was more *ascuence* than *vascuence* (that is, more Azkue's literary idiom than regular Basque).

28. *Bizkaitarra*, 2:11 (June 29, 1894).

29. Ibid., 2:15 (Oct. 16, 1894).

30. *Diario de la Mañana* (Bilbao), June 18, 1899.

31. Arana, *El partido carlista y los fueros vasco-navarros* (Bilbao, 1897).

32. *Bizkaitarra*, 2:16 (Oct. 31, 1894).

33. Aranzadi quotes him as saying on one occasion that "we abhor with mortal hatred the aristocracy of diplomas and of money and all this business about classes." *Ereintza*, 109.

34. The speech of his defense attorney, Daniel de Irujo, became a nationalist classic and was published under the title, *Inocencia de un patriota* (Buenos Aires, 1913).

35. The most clear-cut statement of Catalan regionalism from the viewpoint of economic interests was Guillermo Graell, *La cuestión catalana* (Barcelona, 1902).

36. After the restoration of universal male suffrage in 1890, the domination of the two major parties over Spanish affairs was based at least as much on apathy as on corruption. The shrewd Catalanist republican Claudi Ametlla has accurately observed, "If a district or a city had achieved political maturity, it voted as it wished, and sooner or later what it voted was counted in the ballot boxes. The *caciques* made and unmade elections only where there was no electorate sufficiently strong or civically conscious to make its wishes felt, where the voters neglected their duty. In that case, the election-makers substituted themselves for the electors; they made their opinion prevail because others had none. In a certain sense one can say that where that happened, the sole existing opinion was that of the

caciques. . . . What seems to me conclusive is that the so-called electoral farce did not prevent the Republic from being introduced by the ballot-box [in 1931] when a sufficient number of voters had achieved political maturity. For many years Spaniards either did not know how to vote or did not want to vote, lacking the necessary culture to realize its importance." *Memòries polítiques 1890–1917* (Barcelona, 1963, 53–54. Cf. the bitter remarks of the Conservative party cacique of Barcelona, Manuel Planas y Casals, as quoted by Amadeu Hurtado, *Quaranta anys d'advocat* (Barcelona, 1969), I, 69.

37. There is an excellent study by Isidre Molas, *Lliga Catalana* (Barcelona, 1972), 2 vols., which is the most thorough treatment ever made of a Spanish political party.

38. On the failure of Catalan industry to develop competitive leadership and full-scale modern organization, see E. Pinilla de las Heras, *L'Empresari català* (Barcelona, 1967).

39. The best contemporary account of Catalan industry at that time is Edouard Escarra, *El desarrollo industrial de Cataluña (1900–1908)* (Barcelona, 1970), first published in 1908.

40. For a later perspective, see José Félix de Lequerica's brief *La actividad económica de Vizcaya en la vida nacional* (Madrid, 1956) and also *El Banco de Vizcaya y su aportación a la economía española* (Bilbao, 1955).

41. Jaime Vicens Vives, *An Economic History of Spain* (Princeton, 1969), 691.

42. García Venero, *Nacionalismo vasco*, 304.

43. Ibid., 305. García Venero's transcription of the text seems to be garbled at one point.

44. This letter was first published by Ramiro de Maeztu in *ABC* (Madrid), Oct. 16, 1934, and reprinted in the Centro de Información Católica Internacional's *El Clero y los catolicos vasco-separatistas y el Movimiento Nacional* (Madrid, 1940), 36–37.

45. Quoted in the article by Areilza.

46. For example, Elías de Gallastegui, *Por la libertad vasca* (Bilbao, 1935), 88–89.

47. The best analysis is given in Aranzadi's *Ereintza*, 134–49, and the article by Areilza previously cited.

4

THE SLOW GESTATION OF THE NATIONALIST MOVEMENT, 1903 – 1930

facing a difficult uphill struggle, the nationalist movement paid increasing attention to practical organization in the early years of the century. Angel de Zabala, Arana's successor as president of the PNV, stressed the use of electoral democracy among the Basque people. Capable young leaders such as José Horn y Areilza, the son of an English immigrant who had married into a prominent Vizcayan family, worked to provide the party with the organizational infrastructure usually lacking among Spanish political groups of that period. In the 1903 provincial elections, the party placed two representatives in the Vizcayan provincial assembly and during the next decade regularly won between one-fourth and one-third of the seats on the municipal council in Bilbao, with individual seats in smaller towns.

The base of the movement remained in Vizcaya, and for years there was some resentment in other parts of the Basque region against the *bizkaitarra* nature of the PNV. The first Basque Center in San Sebastián was not opened until 1904 (the same year that the Basque Nationalist Youth of Vizcaya were formally organized), followed by other centers in Vitoria (1907) and Pamplona (1909). Growth remained slow and difficult.

In 1906 Basque nationalism obtained a brief doctrinal compendium similar to the one that Prat had earlier prepared for Catalanism. The booklet *Ami Vasco* was written by a Navarrese Capuchin, Padre "Evangelista de Ibero" (whose original name was Goicoechea Oroquieta) and was faithful to the Aranist conception. *Ami Vasco* emphasized the singularity and purity of the "Basque race" but grounded its racism more in culture and moraltiy than in biology.

> Eminent anthropologists have demonstrated that the Basque race differs physically from all the others that inhabit the globe. But that physical difference will never be as important, as intimate, as scientific, as that of language and moral character.[1]

Evangelista de Ibero was clear on the goal of the nationalist movement, which was absolute independence. Violence, however, was to be eschewed as a tactic.

> For the Basque nationalist party, war is the greatest calamity that could happen to Euzkadi, which has already suffered enough with the two that it waged during the past century in support of Carlism. . . . Weak and cowardly men have always called impossible that which is arduous and difficult in order to justify their sloth and vileness. When a united people fights with indefatigable determination for its liberty, it eventually obtains it. It may take 50, 100, or 200 years to shake off its chains, but it will break them in the end, if it never gives up. . . . For it is not so much independence itself that saves a people, but the love of independence. Let Euzkadi restore its language, purify its race—isolating it more and more from foreign character and customs—recover its ancient religious fervor and demonstrate on every occasion its determination to be free. That will suffice for the security of Euzkadi, which will endure with vigor and prosperity to the end of time.[2]

Aside from Navarra, which always voted resolutely Carlist or Integrist, the political life of the Basque provinces comprised heterogeneous personal and practical interests. Their only common denominator was their Catholicism and greater or lesser conservatism (even in the case of the dynastic Liberals), aside from the Socialists and the small republican groups around Bilbao and San Sebastián. Personal factions of "Catholic Independents" or "independent Catholic regionalists" regularly won seats on the provincial and occasionally on the national level, and official sections of the Spanish Conservative and Liberal parties were not organized in Vizcaya until 1909–10, though their nuclei had always held the majority of parliamentary seats. The Conservatives were the stronger of the two major parties and often were able to withstand electoral manipulation by Liberal governments in power in Madrid.

One of the reasons for the weakness of the nationalist movement was that nearly all these parties and factions defended at least a limited degree of Basque provincial particularism, though they differed considerably over its precise form and extent. The first issue to draw diverse interests together was the government's proposal for a slight revision in the *concierto económico* in 1905–06 to include a direct central excise on alcohol, a main source of local Basque tax revenue. Guipuzcoan representatives took the lead in organizing a *Liga Foral* that was joined by nearly all political elements in the three provinces save the Socialists and anarchists. As usual, the central government proved conciliatory. A satisfactory agreement, raising the quotas slightly but freezing them for twenty years, was negotiated in 1906.

The PNV stood aloof from this temporary *Liga Foral*, for the latter accepted the basic structure of the Spanish constitutional system to concentrate almost exclusively on fiscal privileges. Mere foral leagues were held to be the antithesis of true nationalism. A divergence of emphasis on economic issues was also beginning to develop between the nationalists and the dominant conservative interests of Vizcaya. Whereas the latter favored big business, the PNV strove to foster mesocratic and public concerns. PNV representatives in Bilbao took the lead in establishing a municipal savings deposit system for the benefit of the lower middle classes, which later (1920) was extended to the provincial level, in spite of the opposition of the major banks. Nonetheless, with political conflict increasing in the Basque provinces as throughout Spain, there was a growing tendency within the nationalist movement to engage in at least a limited degree of electoral cooperation with other Catholic groups.

As the role of the Basque Jesuits in La Coruña and that of Padre Evangelista de Ibero indicated, no sector of society was so sympathetic to nationalism as the clergy. This was due to the fact that nearly all the Basque clergy were local Basques who served in their native region, and to the fact that religion and local mores were probably more deeply interconnected than anywhere else in Spain.[3] Though the local church hierarchy was relatively unsympathetic to political nationalism, the parish clergy, save in Navarra, grew increasingly well disposed, and interest in nationalism among young priests at the only seminary in the Basque country (Vitoria) began to mount.

Nonetheless, there were at least two conflicts between the nationalist movement and the church during the early part of the century. One concerned the use of Euzkeran forms of Christian names from Arana y Goiri's *Ixendegi* (list of names) by nationalist parents for the baptismal registry of their children. Though the bishop of Vitoria at first forbade parish priests in the three western provinces to use Euzkeran names instead of the customary Castilian forms, this decision was later reversed by Rome in favor of the nationalists. The second concerned the defense of individualism as a philosophical doctrine mounted by Angel de Zabala in his *Historia de Bizkaia*. This was condemned by the bishop, and the nationalists withdrew the disputed material.[4]

Meanwhile, political attention continued to be focused on the Barcelona region because of anarchist outbursts, the growth of left Republicanism, and finally the military attack on a Catalan satirical publication[5] that led to a repressive new press censorship law by the Liberals in 1906. The consequence was a grand coalition of all three Catalan regional forces—the middle-class Catalanists, Catalan Carlists, and autonomist Catalan republicans—in the "Solidaritat Catalana" that swept the 1907 elections in the region, winning forty-one of forty-four regional seats in the Spanish Cortes.[6]

Antonio Maura's Conservative government, which came to power, made the most energetic effort yet seen under the 1876 constitution to grapple with the issue of local self-government. Its reform measures ultimately failed because of a combination of opposition from the extreme left—which opposed local corporate representation—and the centralists of the Liberal party. Even so, the relationship between Cambó and the *Lliga* and Maura's Conservatives remained friendly. At one point Prat even advised Cambó that the *Lliga* should unite with the pro-autonomist Spanish Conservatives, becoming the Catalan branch of the party.[7]

To hostile observers in other parts of Spain, it seemed that the real aim of the Catalanists, as of the very weak regionalist groups in Galicia and Valencia,[8] was to gain tax advantages similar to those of the Basque provinces.[9] This was a gross oversimplification; as events were to show, Catalanism was a matter of psychology and group identity, or "sentiment," as Cambó defined it a quarter-century later in the Spanish parliament.

When Maura introduced his local autonomy legislation in 1907, representatives of the Basque provincial *diputaciones* urged that it be broadened to include the restoration of the Basque foral systems prior to 1876. The prime minister considered this a gross abuse of the intent of the (abortive) new legislation and, since various sectors of Basque politics ranging from liberal to ultraconservative disagreed among themselves almost violently as to the exact terms a broadened autonomy should take, nothing was changed under the Maura government of 1907–09.[10]

The Conservatives were the leading political force in Vizcaya, and within a few years of Arana's death the PNV made a stronger bid for the number two position. This also raised the question of confrontation or cooperation with the Conservatives. In the 1907 election for Bilbao, a direct contest between Conservatives and nationalists created the danger of a victory for the growing leftist vote in the industrial region. Moderate nationalists urged support for the Conservative candidate, but the intransigent majority in the *Bizkai-Buru-Batzar* temporarily expelled several of them for this stance. As it turned out, the Conservative candidate bested the Socialist leader, Pablo Iglesias, by a two-to-one vote, and the nationalist candidate came in a poor third.[11]

The Maura government, though uninterested in reactionary foralism, hoped to attract Basque nationalists to its program of

Conservative decentralization, just as in the case of the Catalanists. Nationalist representatives were temporarily appointed mayors of Bilbao by decree in both 1907 and 1909. The crown had been generous in its attention to the Basque elite during the past generation, and had begun to reward industrialists with new titles of nobility. In a summer visit to the Vizcayan coast in 1908, Alfonso XIII made personal contact with Bilbao's leading shipping magnate, Ramón de la Sota,[12] who, though a native of Santander, was the only top industrialist who directly supported Basque nationalism.

The fall of the Maura government and the brief rise of the Liberals under José Canalejas in 1910–12 coincided with a surge of strength by the Socialist trade unions in the Vizcayan industrial centers and a major church-state confrontation over the regulation of Catholic orders. The Liberals temporarily broke the Conservative dominance over Vizcayan elections in 1910, and the clerical-anticlerical struggle that divided much of Spanish politics during the next two years also split the PNV. Basque nationalism had been firmly set in an ultra-Catholic mold by Arana, and this seemed in natural consonance with the strong religious traditionalism of the great majority of the inhabitants of the Basque region. However, a small minority of the urban middle-class following of the PNV became increasingly dissatisfied with the movement's clerical orientation. This splinter group split off in 1910 under the slogan *Aberri eta Askatasuna* (Fatherland and Liberty) to found a tiny *Centro Nacionalista Republicano Vasco*.

Anticlericalism was not as yet a major problem even in Vizcaya, but the steady growth of Socialist trade unionism was. There were already approximately fifty small Catholic syndical groups in the four provinces, mainly in Vizcaya and Guipúzcoa, but the nationalist movement was to this point almost exclusively a middle-class (and Vizcayan) enterprise, nourished by a sense of middle-class cultural and moral superiority in an environment of altered mores and apparent degradation. In Vizcaya and Guipúzcoa, however, class differentiation under the impact of industrialization was reaching significant proportions. A major Vizcayan miners' strike in 1910 was influential in winning national legislation for a nine-hour maximum workday in the mines. The nationalist movement could not hope for ultimate victory in an increasingly industrialized environment unless it could make an impact on the workers as well. To this end the first nuclei of the *Solidaridad de Trabajadores Vascos* (STV), a Basque nationalist trade union organization, were formed in Vizcaya in 1911. The new initiative was met with extreme hostility by the Socialist UGT, as well as by anarchist groups, and progress was at first very slow and again limited to Vizcaya. The initial support came mainly not from blue-collar industrial workers, but from white-collar clerical employees,[13] exactly as in the case of the only significant Catalanist syndical group, the white-collar CADCI in Barcelona.

Catalanism took a major step forward in 1913 when the Liberal government then in power in Madrid approved the formation of a *Mancomunidad*—a concentration of major aspects of the local administrations of the four Catalan provinces under a joint regional administration in Barcelona. The *Mancomunidad* arrangement did not devolve any major new powers of local autonomy or administration, but did make it possible for the entire region to coordinate such facilities as it already possessed. Under the leadership of the *Lliga*, the *Mancomunidad* administration carried out an energetic, if limited, program to improve local services and administration during the next decade.[14] Even so limited a gesture of decentralization split asunder the tenuously organized and essentially procentralist Liberal party, which was never effectively reunited again.

The outbreak of World War I soon gave an enormous incentive to manufacturers in Spain, which became the major neutral power in Europe. The regions that benefitted most were Catalonia, the Basque country, and Asturias. When the war began, Vizcaya was producing 80 percent of all the steel in Spain;[15] after that point Basque mining, metallurgy, and shipping continued to advance rapidly. There were already 58 joint-stock companies registered in Vizcaya by 1914; as wartime profits poured in, a total of 34 new ones were created in 1917, and in 1918 an all-time record of 219 new companies worth 417 million pesetas.[16] This was accompanied by new cultural investment as well: the first institution of higher learning in the Basque country was founded with the opening of the Commercial University of Duesto in 1916. The novelist Pío Baroja wrote a few years later that

> Bilbao is a town that daily grows more concentrated and more interesting. Its estuary is one of the most impressive things in Spain. I do not think there is anything else in the Iberian peninsula that gives such an impression of strength, labor and energy as those 14 or 15 kilometers of waterway.[17]

The wartime expansion reinforced the position of leadership, indeed virtually of hegemony, being acquired by Basque heavy industry and finance. To that extent it tended to accentuate the *españolismo* of most of the Basque bourgeoisie, interested in expanding its activities through other parts of northern Spain.[18] The Basque business elite enjoyed the best of both worlds, battening off the Spanish and international markets while enjoying the local Basque benefits of the *concierto económico*. Though they had little interest in Basque nationalism, they vigorously resisted any effort to change the existing tax structure. For example, the most active figure in the Liberal coalition government of 1916, Santiago Alba, minister of finance, proposed a modest excess profits tax on manufacturing and exports throughout Spain to help balance the budget and promote national development.[19] This roused a storm of protest among both Catalan and Basque businessmen, whom Cambó united in successful opposition to the proposed taxation.

The year 1917 was a time of political crisis in Spain. The radical changes imposed by the war, the example of the Russian revolution, spiraling wartime inflation, barracks revolts by much of the army officer corps against favoritism, corruption, and low pay, widespread middle-class political dissatisfaction, and the seeming inability of the political system to cope with these problems, all converged to create what seemed to many a prerevolutionary situation. The development of "military syndicalism" by the *junta* movement inside the army was followed by an ad hoc "Assembly of Parliamentarians" in Barcelona in July led by the *Lliga* to demand major constitutional reforms. This was followed in turn by the Socialist general strike of August 1917, which brought a week of crisis in industrial areas and constituted the gravest labor disturbance to that date in Spanish history.

Wartime pressures also had a strong impact in the Basque country and had already led to the second split within the nationalist movement. The PNV's leading ideologist and propagandist, Engracio de Aranzadi ("Kizkitza"), editor of the PNV's daily, *Euzkadi* (founded in Bilbao in 1913), was determined to open the movement to the broader currents of European politics. To this end he publicized the struggles of subjugated nationalities (Irish, Czech, Croat, Polish, etc.) and after the war began came out strongly for the Entente, which he saw as the natural liberator of oppressed peoples in central and eastcentral Europe. (Needless to say, Aranzadi found it convenient at that point to ignore the Irish and the great array of oppressed minorities within the Russian empire.) The increasing orientation of the movement's leadership toward the search for allies was symbolized by the change in its official title from "Basque Nationalist Party" to "Basque Nationalist Communion," (CNV), a more vague and less exclusive name.

By contrast, Luis de Arana y Goiri, president of the *Bizkai-Buru-Batzar*, was pro-German and strongly objected to the Aranzadist orientation in foreign affairs, while feeling that the movement was becoming too cooperative and compromising at home. In 1915 Arana was ousted from the presidency, but for some time he insisted that his small faction constitute the sole legitimate leadership of the movement. Though Arana was later elected a nationalist Cortes deputy from Vizcaya (1919), he remained hostile to official CNV policy.

By 1916 the CNV was beginning to function in terms of a minimal and maximal program. The minimal program was represented by a CNV proposal for a sort of "Little *Mancomunidad*" in the Basque region to coordinate the administration of judicial appeals, higher education, and other specific interests. The maximum program was presented by the Basque delegation that attended the "Conference of Nationalities" at Lausanne in the same year. It called for *Lagi-zarra*, the "old laws," and the restoration of the full degree of foral autonomy that existed prior to 1839.[20]

Under the impact of the multiple crises of 1917, the demand for autonomy grew on all sides. In new elections the CNV captured majorities in both the Vizcayan provincial assembly and the city

council of Bilbao. Provincial government leaders in Guipúzcoa
then took the initiative in calling a meeting of representatives of the
three provincial *diputaciones* in July 1917 that voted to petition the
government for restoration of the foral system. The assembly was
held in Vitoria to win over Alavese opinion, which tended to fear
the domination of wealthier, more populous Vizcaya and Guipúzcoa, and the Alavese Conservatives, at that point the major force
in the province, remained hostile.[21] Attitudes in Navarra were
uncertain, though the nationalists judged them to be favorable to an
all-Basque *Mancomunidad*.

The temporary solution to the political crisis of 1917 was
formation of a Liberal coalition government in Madrid in which
two seats went to the Catalanists. Parliamentary elections were
held in February 1918, and this campaign represented the highwater mark of the *Lliga Regionalista* in its effort to make creative
regionalism the cornerstone of Spanish modernization. Cambó,
minister of development in the new government,[22] had led the
Lliga in the last elections on the platform of *Per Catalunya i
l'Espanya gran*; in 1918 he traveled to the Basque country and
other regions to encourage a maximal effort by regionalists. A total
of more than one hundred regionalist candidates presented themselves in various parts of Spain, including provinces where regionalism had been unheard of a few years earlier.[23] The great
majority of these were defeated, but the new regionalist enthusiasm
lifted the PNV to its first national political breakthrough as it won
seven of the twenty seats in the four provinces: five of six in
Vizcaya, one of five in Guipúzcoa, and one of seven in Navarra.

These elections were among the most representative in
Spanish history to that point; consequently, given the extreme
division of opinion, they produced complete political fractionalization and an unworkable parliament. The Liberal coalition was
briefly replaced by a concentration "cabinet of notables" under
Antonio Maura, the "fireman of the monarchy," which remained
in office until the end of the World War. By that time the collapse of
the empires of central and eastern Europe and the apparent triumph
of Woodrow Wilson's program of national self-determination
raised the hopes and demands of regionalists—particularly among
the more radical anti-*Lliga* Catalanists—to their zenith.[24] Basque

nationalism was also stimulated by the outcome of the war; on October 25, 1918, the nine nationalist congressmen (seven deputies, two senators) sent a telegram to Woodrow Wilson on the seventy-ninth anniversary of the original abolition of the *fueros*, hailing the allied victory and expressing the hope that the rights of all nationalities would soon be recognized.[25]

Alfonso XIII then appointed a new Liberal minority government under the Conde de Romanones in November 1918 with the express charge of reaching an accommodation with Catalan and Basque regionalists—though not with the formulae of extremist nationalism. With this incentive, a large assembly of Navarrese autonomists met at Pamplona on December 30, 1918. CNV spokesmen pushed a resolution calling for immediate and total restitution of the pre-1839 *Lagi-zarra* of Navarra. In traditionalist and royalist Navarra, little affected by the pressures of modernization so keenly felt in Vizcaya and Guipúzcoa, the outright supporters of nationalism were few. Instead, a large majority at the assembly approved an essentially Carlist resolution calling on the Spanish government to restore "the integrity of foral powers," retaining "the special characteristics of this ancient kingdom adapted to the current needs of Navarra and harmonized with the proper faculties of the Spanish state."[26]

On January 2, 1919, a special interparliamentary commission on autonomy began its labors in Madrid under the leadership of Maura and other notables. While the main group prepared a draft project for Catalonia, a subcommission prepared new recommendations dealing with the Basque region. There was no Catalanist member of the main commission, but two of the three members of the subcommission were Basque nationalists and the third a Basque Integrist. Their proposal recommended the restoration of broad foral autonomy for each of the three western provinces, including administrative control of nearly all local affairs. It was suggested that taxes be made proportionate to those paid by all the rest of Spain and that the provinces would be subject to the military draft, but would enjoy complete freedom in their form of recruitment. Draftees would only be required to leave the home provinces in time of war. The final recommendation of the subcommission was that the exact proposal for the adjusted structure of autonomy for each of the four provinces (including Navarra) should be initially drafted by representatives of the municipal governments in each.[27]

This golden opportunity for a new system of Basque provincial autonomy was ruined by the veto of the Catalan draft statute by radical left-wing Catalanists, who repeated their earlier maneuver of 1908 against the Maura local government bill. Radical Catalanism was lower-middle-class, anticlerical, prorepublican, socially oriented, and extreme in its demands for autonomy. For a decade it had been laboring to turn the flank of the moderate, "bourgeois" *Lliga*. Though the proposed Catalan autonomy statute was a fairly broad and generous document, offering most though not all that the *Lliga* had been seeking, elements of the *esquerra* or Catalan "left" rejected a statute drawn up without Catalan participation, which also failed to meet their maximal demands. In an increasingly hopeless effort to maintain some sort of unity between radical and moderate Catalanists, the *Lliga* also rejected the draft statute. A separate autonomy proposal drawn up by Catalanists was approved by Catalan municipal councils, but the Spanish government then shelved the entire autonomy issue.

The question was quickly overshadowed in Catalonia by the outbreak of severe social strife. There the anarchosyndicalist CNT had reached mass proportions and completely dominated urban labor. The next four years were a period of constant strikes and spiraling terrorism. Middle-class Catalanists were completely diverted from regionalist/centralist controversy by the sanguinary employer/worker conflict at home. They tended more and more to fall back on the strong hand of central government to maintain order, as class struggle replaced regional struggle. Left Catalanism gained in strength, and the *Lliga's* support waned; in May 1923 Cambó announced his retirement from politics.[28]

The end of the war caused severe economic readjustment in Vizcaya and Guipúzcoa as in Catalonia, though at first social strife was less intense in the Basque country. The CNV promptly lost four of its seven newly acquired parliamentary seats in new elections held in 1919, retaining only three of the six seats for Vizcaya. By 1920 terrorism was spreading in the Bilbao district, as the extremist elements of Vizcayan socialism fell under the influence of the revolutionary maximalism of the Third International. The rate of political killings proportionate to population was lower than in Barcelona, Valencia, or Zaragoza,[29] and more emphasis was placed on pure incendiarism—whose most spectacular product was the burning of the new transatlantic liner *Alfonso XIII* as it neared completion in a Bilbao shipyard in November 1920—but the effect in polarizing society was much the same as in Catalonia. A main difference in the political consequences was that in the Basque region joint Conservative-Liberal monarchist tickets—the *Liga de Acción Monárquica*—swept the elections between 1920 and 1923.

As an electoral force the CNV was squeezed out much more than was the *Lliga* in Catalonia. In 1919 *Euzkadi* proclaimed that "whoever votes for a Conservative votes against the Basque people,"[30] but the nationalist delegation was reduced in both the national and Vizcayan provincial elections. CNV spokesmen put the best construction on things, claiming that the party had done well to retain four of the eight seats in the provincial assembly for Bilbao and to elect one provincial deputy in Guipúzcoa, since "money" was strongly arrayed against them and San Sebastián had become "an international cesspool."[31] The nationalists had reached the point where they had to fight on two fronts—on both right and left—and lacked the means to cope effectively. They suffered like most other sectors from the increase in violence, were occasionally fired upon by opponents, and sometimes engaged in brawls. They also suffered from the hesitant, intermittent waves of repression timidly essayed by the authorities and in one instance a young nationalist group was arrested for merely singing a nationalist anthem in public. In turn, CNV spokesmen became more sweeping in their condemnation of the unstable and apparently inept Spanish political system whose government was "pure vaseline."[32]

Militant young nationalists had become increasingly radical under the tensions of the war and the postwar domestic crisis. The Nationalist Youth of Vizcaya dominated the journal *Aberri* (Fatherland), formed their own "Action" group and called a special assembly of their own in the autumn of 1920 to sit in judgment on the course of the movement. They found the leadership of the CNV too stodgy, unenergetic, compromising, and conservative. The rebel bloc of nationalist youth wanted a more intransigent policy that was also more attuned to social issues. Their main leader was a radical young nationalist ideologue and activist, Elías de Gallastegui (who wrote under the pseudonym "Gudari"— Warrior) and they represented somewhat the same radicalization of regional nationalism as did the rising new left Catalanist parties in Barcelona. Unlike the latter, the *aberrianos*, as the young Basque radicals were called, were not anti-Catholic and only mildly anti-clerical. Though they talked of social reform and though Gallas-tegui later even had kind words for Vizcayan Communists, their socioeconomic program was vague and secondary, and was not much more advanced than the reformist program propounded by the CNV leadership.[33] What was at issue was a policy of radical intransigence and greater activism compared with the moderate, middle-class electoral tactics of the CNV. A complete split de-veloped after a national assembly of the movement in San Sebas-tián.

The *aberrianos* joined forces with the small faction led by Luis de Arana y Goiri—no one was more intransigent than he,[34] and this suited their mood—reconstituting themselves in July 1921 under the original title of Basque Nationalist party (PNV) with Angel de Zabala as president once more. They carried most of the party membership with them in Vizcaya and also enjoyed consid-erable support in Guipúzcoa.

The schism consummated the elimination of nationalism as an electoral force. In the last two parliamentary elections under the constitutional monarchy the nationalists were reduced to one un-contested seat in Navarra.

The last months of Spanish parliamentary government were a time of growing domestic terrorism, radicalization on the extreme left and severe internal cleavage over the colonial military problem in Morocco. *Aberri* reflected all these trends. It denounced Spanish activity in the Protectorate and came out for Moroccan indepen-dence,[35] as did its Catalanist counterparts. It avoided the use of the term "regionalist" altogether and classified the Basque, Catalanist, Galicianist, and Valencianist movements as "separatist," hailing the growth of left Catalanism as "the resurgence of revolutionary nationalism."[36] An attempt to reach an understanding with the CNV in June fell through,[37] and the latter was denounced as having "sold out to the *Liga*"[38] (that is, the Vizcayan Conservatives). By August the PNV had joined the new "Triple Alliance" that the left Catalanists had proposed for the radical sectors of the Catalanist, Basque, and Galicianist movements.[39]

On July 20, 1923, *Aberri* saw the breakdown of the Spanish system close at hand:

> Cultured people know how to make revolutions. Uncultured peoples can only make great butcheries. Spain is one of the most backward peoples on the globe, and the revolution that might occur in Spain would be a model of savagery and bloody reprisals.
>
> If we do not prepare outselves, if we remain indifferent, we shall not be able to draw aside when the moment comes but will sink with Spain into the precipice that opens at its feet.

The collapse of the Spanish polity would provide the opportunity for Basques, if fully prepared, to break away and establish their independence.

The breakdown of the Spanish constitutional system was much less dramatic than *Aberri* supposed. In fact, it was completely bloodless, casting some doubt on the absolute savagery of Spaniards in which the *aberrianos* so fanatically believed. The most immediate cause of General Miguel Primo de Rivera's *pronunciamiento* in September 1923 was the seemingly insoluble dilemma of national humiliation in Morocco (which the *aberrianos* had of course gloated over), but it was also directed against social disorder and political dissidence. Within three days the new head of government obtained the royal signature for a law banning separatist agitation, a move directed mainly against the radical Catalanists and the *aberrianos*. On the following day, September 19, the editor of *Aberri* was temporarily arrested, and informed that both the content and titles of the paper must change.[40] It reappeared on October 6 under the title of *Diario Vasco*, bereft of political agitation or nationalist propaganda, with the label "Organ of the Basque Nationalist party" removed from the front page. On October 28 the Civil Guard closed down a total of 34 *aberriano* PNV centers in the province of Vizcaya.[41] Though the repression was directed more against the PNV[42] than the more temperate CNV, all political activity by Basque nationalists was proscribed for the duration of the dictatorship.

The dictatorship was introduced not as a modern new system of authoritarianism but as a dictatorship of the classical sort, a temporary suspension of the constitutional system to resolve a national crisis. While lacking a concrete program, Primo de Rivera saw his government as the continuation of fin-de-siècle Spanish Regenerationism. Among other things, this was held to mean renewed attention to the problem of local self-government, whose importance had been impressed on him by his year of service as captain-general of Barcelona, where he enjoyed cordial relations with moderate elements of the *Lliga*. Under his Military Directory of 1923–25, Primo appointed the able young Maurist José Calvo Sotelo to the post of director general of local administration with the task of preparing a new statute of local self-government.

The presidents of the three western Basque *diputaciones* visited Primo de Rivera in Madrid on September 25, 1923, only twelve days after his seizure of power. The new dictator seemed fully receptive and authorized each of the three provincial governments to begin work on its draft project for a system of autonomy. Their confidence was soon afterward shaken by the dictatorship's ouster of all incumbent municipal governments throughout Spain, which were replaced with new central appointees led by *delegados militares*, but nonetheless the provincial governments persevered with their drafts. The greatest zeal was shown by that of Guipúzcoa, which completed a draft on December 29 that provided both for autonomous local government for each of the three provinces as well as a system of regional government for their common affairs.[43] Navarra was excluded from the project because its earlier foral system was both more complete and separate than that of the three "Castilian" provinces. The proposal was, however, rejected by the *diputación* of Vizcaya, dominated by the Conservatives. In a statement written by the talented young Conservative politician José Félix de Lequerica (thirty-two years later Spain's first ambassador to the United Nations), the Vizcayan government observed that "never in history have the Basque provinces formed a single region" and refused to participate in a separate entity intermediate between provincial and national government.[44]

By this time Primo de Rivera was losing his early concern for local autonomy, due in large measure to heavy pressure from his centralist colleagues in the military hierarchy. Early in 1924 the Catalan *Mancomunidad* was dissolved, and all other existing provincial government officials were ousted, save for those of the four Basque provinces—a presumed reward for their conservatism and reliability. The local government bill prepared by Calvo Sotelo was never actually promulgated, and there was no further discussion of autonomy while the dictatorship lasted.

The main concern of established Basque interests vis-à-vis the central government in 1925–26 was the renewal of the *concierto económico* at the close of its current twenty-year term. The minister of finance in Primo de Rivera's new "civilian" government, inaugurated at the close of 1925, was Calvo Sotelo. He made the most determined effort in all Spanish history to introduce a few modest but fundamental features of tax reform in the direction of graduated levies and in the process hoped to reduce the great tax advantages enjoyed by the wealthier Basque provinces. When all variables are taken into account—including gross population, nature of the economy, its ability to pay, and per capita income of the region—it is difficult to resist the conclusion that Basques paid little more than half of the proportionate tax burden of other Spaniards.[45] The system had been of great advantage in the development of modern Basque industry. In addition the Basque economy derived enormous benefits from the steep Spanish tariff and from government subsidies, especially to shipping. Whatever politically or ideologically motivated autonomists might say, Basque business interests were well aware of the advantages they enjoyed and were eminently satisfied with the system. After negotiations, the *concierto* was renewed with slight increases.[46] In general, after a downturn at the start of the decade, the 1920s were a period of further prosperity for the Basque economy. Steel production registered a spectacular increase of 235 percent between 1920 and 1930, and by that time the elite status of Basque industry within the general Spanish economy was higher than ever.

The dictatorship repressed all direct regionalist political activity but made almost no effort to censor regional cultural publications or hinder regional cultural growth. Somewhat paradoxically, the 1920s thus became the decade of the flowering of twentieth-century Basque culture, as both Catalan and Basque nationalism broadened their bases by greatly intensifying regional cultural awareness. In the case of the Basques, this once more underscored the anomalous development of nationalism. Nearly everywhere else in Europe, national cultural revival had preceded and prepared the way for political nationalism.[47] In the Basque territory, political nationalism preceded and stimulated the main cultural revival, though it is only fair to add that not all the Basques who participated in the cultural revival were willing to support political nationalism.

Wartime prosperity had made it possible for nationalists and other Basque cultural promoters to found a *Junta de Cultura Vasca*,[48] followed by the establishment of the *Sociedad de Estudios Vascos* in Bilbao (modeled to some extent on the *Institut d'Estudis Catalans* in Barcelona) and the *Academia de la Lengua Vasca*. Several small bilingual schools opened in Vizcaya, offering regular instruction in *Euskera* for the first time, and a few newspapers began to print regular columns in the language. Publication of books and magazines in *Euskera*, and even more in Castilian about Basque history, culture and institutions, expanded greatly. The Basque area in Spain had always published fewer books per capita in *Euskera* than had the French region,[49] but the new promotion of literacy in *Euskera* attempted to create a broader audience for the modest growth of Basque literature.[50] It was an uphill fight, for of the approximately 1,200,000 inhabitants of the Spanish Basque region at the end of the decade, no more than 400,000 were primarily *Euskera*-speaking.[51] Though a portion of the bilingual population could read *Euskera*, few of the *Euskera*-speaking peasants could do so. Thus the radius of publications in *Euskera* as compared with those in Castilian about Basque topics remained small. Castilian would always remain the overwhelmingly predominant medium of cultural development and political proselitization, but the cultural expansion of the 1920s created a greater sense of Basque consciousness both among *Euskera*-speakers and middle-class people in the larger towns who were ignorant of the ancestral tongue.

Though political activities had to be abandoned,[52] auxiliary groups of all kinds were expanded. The "scouts" or "mountaineers" organization of the *Mendigoitzales*, originally founded in 1908, was enlarged as a recreational association and surrogate nationalist youth movement. Basque music, dancing, and art organizations rapidly grew in number, adding color and liveliness to nearly every aspect of nationalist affairs in the years to come.

While the nationalist movement would never win majoritarian support in the Basque country as a whole, as distinct from Vizcaya, by 1930 it was finally on its way to becoming the largest single political force in the region. In one of the more oft-cited assessments of the appeal of nationalism, Gerald Brenan reached the somewhat superficial conclusion that its attraction in Vizcaya and Guipúzcoa was due to the fact that the two industrial provinces looked outward, away from Spain, whereas Alava and Navarra, where nationalism was much weaker, looked southward toward the rest of Spain, of which they were more of a geographic and spiritual continuation. This is rather misleading, since in economic terms Vizcaya and Guipúzcoa were more closely and profitably connected with the rest of Spain than were Alava and Navarra.

The tendency to "look away" was not due primarily to foreign association but to the challenges posed by the modernization process and the continued use of *Euskera* in rural districts. Modernization in terms of urbanization and industrialization had gone farther in Vizcaya and Guipúzcoa than anywhere else in Spain save Barcelona, creating major tensions and challenges to status, values, and identity. Even the medium and smaller towns in these two provinces were more genuinely urbanized than those elsewhere. In Andalusia towns of forty thousand people or more remained the centers of exclusively agricultural districts, much of their population made up of farm laborers who went out daily to the surrounding countryside. In Vizcaya and Guipúzcoa even small towns had been strongly affected by industrialization and changes in business and social organization. They had a high literacy rate, lived within the structure of modern communications, and were fully aware of the non-Basque immigration into the industrial areas and the pressures for secularization and rapid change radiating from those zones.

Conversely, the use of *Euskera* remained more common among the rural population of the inner Basque zone of the north—Vizcaya and Guipúzcoa—than in the south and east. The language had nearly disappeared even in the more remote rural districts of Alava, and this was true of much of Navarra as well.

By 1930 the societies of Vizcaya and Guipúzcoa had become extremely complex, in some ways more so than those of any other provinces of Spain. At that time, the socioeconomic categorization of the population of the three western provinces was approximately as follows:[53]

	Vizcaya	Guipúzoca	Alava	Totals
Industry	81,787	41,460	7,456	130,703
Smallholders	32,922	50,663	19,282	102,867
Commerce	23,380	4,661	1,220	29,261
Professionals	10,324	11,224	6,868	28,416
Housekeeping	115,757	81,049	25,132	221,938
Renters and pensioners	3,660	2,681	758	7,036
Miscellaneous	135,491	84,288	32,754	252,533
	403,321	275,963	93,470	772,754

The interaction of these complex sociocultural forces in the Basque territory led not to dichotomization but to triangulation. The main support for nationalism was drawn from the lower middle classes and the small town and rural population in the industrialized provinces. Nationalism did not rest on either of the two main sectors of the industrialization/modernization process—upper bourgeoisie or urban workers—but on the marginalized elements in between or along the side, whose identity and status were most questioned by current changes. By 1930 many of the industrial workers were non-Basque immigrants, and they were almost completely under the influence of the all-Spanish left, especially the Socialists, who largely rejected nationalism as clerical and reactionary.[54] By contrast, the wealthier upper middle classes—the most cosmopolitan elements who had the closest contacts with the outer world—thought largely in terms of all-Spanish politics and supported the Spanish right. So in a different way did the still largely agrarian and traditionalist provinces of Alava and Navarra, which continued to back traditionalist right-wing Carlist provincialism and other conservative forces flanking it. The lower middle classes and peasants in these two areas had not been marginalized or threatened by urbanization, industry, or secularization. They could not be attracted to new formulae that went much beyond traditionalist Catholic provincialism and were willing to ally for common goals with the all-Spanish right. Thus in an increasingly triangulated political society, the right would rest on the industrial rich and the traditionalist poor, the left on the industrial workers and radical, secularized elements of the lower middle classes, and nationalism on the main strata in between in the two advanced provinces.

When the Primo de Rivera dictatorship came to an end in January 1930, nationalism had ceased to appear as radical, romantic, and extravagant as in earlier years. To many in the lower-middle classes it began to appear the most effective means of defending their interests and way of life. As the foundations of the Spanish monarchy began to crumble and civic institutions were threatened with collapse, Basque nationalism provided a new means of identity and security, a firm defense of values both traditional and modern. To middle-class youth, it had a new allure as a creative and reforming (temporarily underground) force, radical with respect to the pre-existing political structure yet pious, middle-class and integrative.

In Vizcaya and Guipúzcoa nationalists considered Basques the economic elite of Spain, which, rather than providing new opportunities, was holding them back. In the years that followed, nationalists argued that, with only 5 percent of the total Spanish population, the four Basque provinces together produced the following percentages of total Spanish wealth:[55]

Banking capital of all Spain	24	Iron products	62
Bank deposits	42	Paper	71
Bank of Spain stock	34	Shipbuilding	71
Personal savings	33	Merchant marine	69
Fishery production	40	Electrical products	33
Iron	78	Chemical products	32
Steel	74	Gas and electricity	35
Coke	65		

After the experience of the dictatorship there emerged a greater willingness among nationalist leaders to cooperate in a new system of democratic reformism and also a greater stress on the norms of liberal democracy in political functioning. A new generation of leaders stepped forward to take charge, chief of whom was the twenty-seven-year-old José Antonio de Aguirre, former Catholic Action leader and one-time soccer star. On February 24, 1930, less than a month after the fall of Primo de Rivera, a pledge was made in San Sebastián to abstain from participation in any position or function of local government until popular sovereignty had been allowed to express itself on that level. It was signed by the several sectors of Basque nationalism, by a small coalition known as the United Republican party of the Basque country, the moderate Jaimist sector of Carlism, and the Socialist party in the Basque country, though ultimately only the Jaimists and nationalists fully honored it.[56]

Meanwhile efforts were made to unite the two sectors of the nationalist movement, and these produced an agreement on April 29, 1930, for the official reunification of the more intransigent PNV and the more moderate CNV under the regular title of Basque Nationalist Party (PNV). The accord was formally ratified by a meeting on November 1.

No sooner had it been accomplished, however, than a new schism developed, though this was less serious than that of the previous decade. A small minority of the more liberal activists split off to organize a separate party of *Acción Nacionalista Vasca* (ANV) on November 30. Their name and inspiration were in large measure derived from the liberal, anticlerical *Acció Catalana* party that had threatened to outflank the *Lliga* in Catalonia during the early 1920s and was strongly oriented toward cooperation with the rising tide of anticlerical Republicanism. Paradoxically, the chief leader of the ANV was the Catholic moderate liberal Anacleto de Ortueta,[57] who had remained with the CNV in the preceding split and had rejected the *aberrianos*. He and a number of other leaders were in fact practicing Catholics, the new cadres of the minuscule ANV being formed by an amalgam from both the old CNV and PNV. In its opening manifesto, *Al Pueblo Vasco*, the ANV emphasized the need to support a completely democratic program, representing all religious, philosophical, and social interests willing to back nationalism. It was not anti-Catholic or even particularly anticlerical, but stood on the principles of aconfessionality, republican democracy, and greater attention to social reform. As it turned out, the Basque country was considerably less secularized than Catalonia, and even in the latter region, *Acció Catalana* was in the process of being undercut by the more radical lower-middle-class *Esquerra Catalana* (Catalan Left). The ANV never at any time mobilized any significant following or electoral force.

One of the main reasons why an attempt at an aconfessional nationalist party was doomed to impotence lay in the fact that nationalism's main single mobilization force was the large pronationalist sector of the clergy. In small towns and rural areas the clergy still played their traditional role of civic intelligentsia as well as spiritual counsellors, whereas in Catalan society a modern anticlerical secular intelligentsia had largely established its dominance.

The year 1930 was the period of the most rapid organizational expansion in the history of the PNV. Nationalism mobilized a significant following in Guipúzcoa for the first time, and the chief organizer there was a progressive young priest, José de Ariztimuño.[58] Altogether, by the end of the year a total of more than two hundred local *batzokis* (centers) were operating,[59] and there was a great increase in the study of Basque language, culture, and music, as well as further expansion of athletic activities. The *Mendigoitzales* continued to grow in numbers, and the *Emakume Abertzale Batza* (Women's Patriotic Association)—earlier organized after the example of an Irish nationalist counterpart—reappeared and also expanded its membership and activities. The enthusiasm of the young people was the most notable feature of the Basque revival, but equally impressive was the choreography of nationalist meetings and festivals—the marches, national costumes, music, dancing, displays, and parades.

Basque nationalism had normally never looked upon the divided and heretofore impotent factions of Spanish Republicans as allies, for Republicanism was associated with anticlericalism and a degree of political and cultural—though not social or economic—radicalism that was repugnant to the mainstream of nationalism. When a self-selected committee of Republican or pro-Republican notables, representing diverse factions of the center and moderate left, met at San Sebastián in August 1930 to concert their strategy for overthrow of the monarchy and establishment of a new regime,

they invited representatives of the *Esquerra* and *Acció Catalana*.
There is no indication that they ever seriously considered inviting
Basque nationalists, even though they were meeting in the Basque
country. One of the main products of this conclave was the so-
called Pact of San Sebastián, whereby the Republican conspirators
won the support of the left Catalanists by promising to present a
project for Catalan autonomy to the first Republican parliament as
soon as possible.

Though all Spanish politics was in a general way informed of
the development of Republican plans, there is no indication that the
reunified PNV made any effort to associate itself with the Republican committee. In 1929 one sector of the nationalists had agreed
somewhat vaguely in principle to support an armed revolt against
the faltering dictatorship, but the only gesture during 1930 was a
public statement by a major leader at the Aberri-Eguna commemoration that Basque nationalism would support a Republic only on
condition that it pledge the full restoration of the pre-1839 *fueros*.
After the first abortive Republican revolt in mid-December, *Euzkadi*, the official organ of the PNV, reiterated that the movement's
overriding concern was Basque autonomy and that it had no interest
in a change of regime as such. When the monarchy finally collapsed in April 1931, Basque nationalism was stronger than at any
previous time, but it stood as an independent and virtually isolated
force.

NOTES

1. *Ami Vasco*, third edition (Buenos Aires, 1957), 18.
2. Ibid., 52–53.
3. The nature of religious sentiment among the rural population is
discussed by Caro Baroja, *Los vascos*, 351–83.
4. Isidro Muñatones, "El Partido Nacionalista Vasco: Su desarrollo,"
Alderdi, no. 262 (April 1971), 28–32.
5. See Lluís Solá, *¡Cu-cut! (1902–1912)* (Barcelona, 1967).
6. J. de Camps i Arboix has written a full-scale *Història de la Solidaritat Catalana* (Barcelona, 1970).
7. According to personal remarks quoted by Eduardo Aunós, *Discurso de la vida* (Madrid, 1951), 343.

Cambó and the politics of his time are the subject of Jesús Pabón's magisterial *Cambó* (Barcelona, 1952–68), 3 vols. See also Josep Pla's *Cambó* (Barcelona, 1930), 3 vols. In addition to the exhaustive study by Molas, cited earlier, there is a brief synopsis of the political history of the *Lliga* by Modest Sabaté, *Història de la 'Lliga'* (Barcelona, 1968).

8. The basic literature on the small Valencianist movement consists of M. Sanchis Guarner, *Renaixença al País Valencià* (Barcelona, 1968), Alfons Cucó, *Aspectes de la política valenciana en el segle XIX* (Barcelona, 1965), and above all Cucó's *El valencianisme polític 1874–1936* (Valencia, 1971). On Valencian radicalism, see also F. León Roca, *Blasco Ibáñez* (Barcelona, 1970).

9. Antonio Royo Villanova, *El problema catalán* (Madrid, 1908), 8. Royo added that "it always turns out that regionalism is something like growing pains that are hard to diagnose either as illness or as remedy." He insisted that his native Aragón was simply not wealthy enough to become regionalist, but noted the deplorable weakness of some aspects of government services that encouraged regionalism in the more advanced areas.

Royo became perhaps the most vocal anti-Catalanist in Spain and was adept at attacking Catalanists at one of their main weak points, the internal imbalance of Catalan society. He pointed out that despite their self-assurance concerning the superiority of Catalan culture, Catalonia had a mediocre record in the development of common educational facilities. In terms of schools per capita, the provinces of Old Castilla, the Basque country and Teruel led the list, while Barcelona ranked forty-third among fifty-one (p. 120). This part of Royo's argument was, however, somewhat misleading, for in some provinces the number of schools per capita merely reflected the dispersion of population, Teruel actually had one of the higher overall illiteracy rates in Spain.

Royo quoted (pp. 252–53) Luis Sánchez Fernández's "Avance a la antropología militar de España" from *Higiene Militar* to obtain statistics on the percentage of military recruits from various provinces who were fully literate in terms of being able to write as well as read. By this index, provinces were ranked in order of their degree of popular culture as follows:

1. Santander	7. León	13. Salamanca
2. Valladolid	8. Oviedo	14. Barcelona
3. Palencia	9. Madrid	22. Gerona
4. Alava	10. Segovia	23. Tarragona
5. Soria	11. Zamora	30. Lérida
6. Burgos	12. Vizcaya	

10. The two main books on the problem of local government and its reform in these years are Adolfo Posada, *La Evolución legislativa del régimen local* (Madrid, 1910) and H. Puget, *Le Gouvernement local en Espagne* (Paris, 1920).

11. The fullest account of these maneuvers is in Ybarra y Bergé, 276–89.

12. On Sota, see Rafael Ossa Echaburu, *Riqueza y poder de la ría 1900–1923* (Bilbao, 1969), 41–73.

13. The only study of the STV is an article by García Venero, mistitled "La Solidaridad de Obreros Vascos (1911–1937)," *Revista de Trabajo*, no. 8, 3–21.

14. There is a brief sketch of the work of the *Mancomunidad* by J. de Camps in Arboix, *La Mancomunitat de Catalunya* (Barcelona, 1968).

15. R. H. Chilcote, *Spain's Iron and Steel Industry* (Austin, 1968), 27.

16. Ossa Echaburu, 115–21.

17. *Horas solitarias* (1920), quoted in Ibid., 193.

18. An example of Vizcayan development ideas for the province of León was given by Julio de Lazúrtegui, *Una nueva Vizcaya a crear en el Bierzo* (Bilbao, 1918).

19. The leader of the *albista* liberals in Vizcaya was Gregorio de Balparda, sometime mayor of Bilbao. A staunch opponent of the extremes of foralism and nationalism, he stood for the creative integration of the Basque country in Spain. Such gestures as his invitation of a Protestant minister to a public function in 1906 earned him the undying hatred of Catholic ultra society in Vizcaya. His principal writings against Basque nationalism were *Errores del nacionalismo vasco* (Madrid, 1919); *¿Federalismo? ¡Feudalismo!* (Bilbao, 1931); and *La crisis de la nacionalidad y la tradición vascongada* (Bilbao, 1932). Balparda also prepared a three-volume *Historia crítica de Vizcaya y de sus Fueros* (Madrid, 1924–45).

20. Délégation Basque, *La Question Basque* (Lausanne, 1917).

21. According to a leaflet of the *Agrupación Nacionalista Vasca* of Vitoria, dated Feb. 25, 1918, in *Euzkadi* (Bilbao, March 5, 1918).

22. Cambó has written a brief memoir of his experiences, *Vuit mesos al Ministeri de Foment* (Barcelona, 1919).

23. See, for example, Juan Luis Corder's *Regionalismo (Problemas de la provincia de Cáceres)* (Barcelona, 1917). What Extremaduran "regionalists" meant by this term was merely greater attention to concrete local interests.

24. Josep M. Poblet, *El moviment autonomista a Catalunya dels anys 1918–1919* (Barcelona, 1917), and, on the Catalan reaction to World War

I, E. Cortada, *Catalunya i la gran guerra* (Barcelona, 1969).

25. The text is in Ybarra y Bergé, 498−99. Foes of Basque nationalism liked to point out that of the nine signatures on the telegram, the first four were of non-Basque origin: Horn (English), Campión (Italian), Chalbaud (French) and Sota (Castilian).

Tension between pro- and antinationalist Basques nearly reached the breaking point. On December 15, 1918, a nationalist mob in Bilbao sacked the offices of the Conservative antinationalist daily, *El Pueblo Vasco*, and as a consequence the nationalist mayor of Bilbao was removed from office by government decree. In the next electoral campaign (May 1919) an attempt was made on the life of the antinationalist Gregorio de Balparda. Disorders and irregularities during electoral campaigns were not uncommon in the Basque country, just as elsewhere, but attempted assassination was unusual there. Ultimately Balparda was murdered by the revolutionary left in Vizcaya after the civil war began in 1936.

26. García Venero, 400.

27. The full texts are in José de Orueta, *Fueros y autonomía* (San Sebastián, 1934), 24−64.

A full collection of all the laws and administrative orders of the Spanish government pertaining to the four provinces since 1836 was subsequently published by José Ma. Estecha y Martínez, *Régimen político y administrativo de las Provincias Vasco-navarras* (Bilbao, 1920).

28. For an interesting critique of Cambó together with key colleagues and rivals, see Antoni Rovira i Virgili's *Els polítics catalans* (Barcelona, 1929).

29. Between 1917 and 1922, casualties in political *attentats* in the six major cities were:

Barcelona:	255 dead, 733 injured	Zaragoza:	23 dead, 51 injured
Valencia:	57 dead, 120 injured	Sevilla:	12 dead, 42 injured
Bilbao:	24 dead, 145 injured	Madrid:	8 dead, 62 injured

The proportionate incidence was as follows:

Number of political crimes 1917−22		Population in 1920	Percentage per inhabitant
Bilbao	152	114,351	0.00132
Barcelona	809	710,335	0.00113
Zaragoza	129	141,350	0.00091
Valencia	151	239,800	0.00062
Sevilla	104	205,527	0.00050
Madrid	127	751,352	0.00016

SOURCE: José Ma. Farré Moregó, *Los atentados sociales en España* (Madrid, 1922).

30. *Euzkadi*, July 2, 1919.

31. "Kizkitza" in Ibid., July 17, 1919.

32. Ibid., Nov. 5, 1917.

33. Near the end of 1921 the CNV announced a long social program that included attention to lowering rents, raising wages, providing better housing, a system of social security, family assistance, strengthening of and freedom for trade unions, and measures to democratize industry. It proposed no drastic redistribution of property but advocated maintaining and perhaps expanding the modest forms of collective properties and cooperatives that existed in Spain. Ibid., Dec. 11, 1921. This was as advanced a social Catholic program as would have been found elsewhere in Europe with only one or two exceptions, and the *aberrianos* did not have much more to suggest.

At that point the STV was still struggling for members, having enrolled about 8,000. Ibid., April 25, 1936.

34. Luis de Arana stressed that the movement's goal had always been "absolute independence" in his pamphlet, *Formulario de los principios esenciales o básicos del primitivo Nacionalismo Vasco contenidos en el lema 'Jaungoikua-eta-lagizara'* (Bilbao, 1932—first published in 1922).

35. *Aberri*, May-Sept., 1923, passim, and Gallastegui's article reprinted in his *Por la libertad vasca* (Bilbao, 1935), 179-81.

36. *Aberri*, June 15, 1923.

37. Ibid., May 30-June 10, 1923.

38. Ibid., July 15, 1923.

39. Ibid., Aug. 4-Sept. 12, 1923.

40. Ibid., Sept. 19, 1923.

41. *Diario Vasco* (Bilbao) Oct. 30, 1923.

42. As early as mid-1922 fourteen members of the PNV were being held in jail on various charges. Memo of the president of the *Bizkai-Buru-Batzar* of the PNV to the PNV's *Junta Municipal* of Algorta, June 6, 1922. Serie B, Bilbao, Legajo 186, no. 64. Jefatura de Servicio Documental, Salamanca. (Hereafter cited as JSD).

43. The full text is given in Orueta, 76-95.

44. *Contestación de la Excelentísima Diputación de Vizcaya a la Memoria que la Excelentísima Diputación de Guipúzcoa proponía se elevase al Directorio Militar sobre el régimen de las provincias vascongadas* (Bilbao, 1924).

45. Interesting statistics are given by José Calvo Sotelo in his memoir *Mis servicios al Estado* (Madrid, 1931), 82-94.

46. Details may be found in Orueta, 105-64, 321-53. An overall exposition of the concierto at that time was published by Federico Zabala y Allende, *El Concierto Económico* (Bilbao, 1927).

47. By contrast, the movements in Catalonia, Valencia, and Galicia followed the normal sequence, as did the major regionalist movement in France, that of Brittany. On the latter, there is a thorough and informative study by J. E. Reece, "Anti-France: The Search for the Breton Nation (1898–1948)" (Ph.D. diss., Stanford, 1971). It might be noted that political Bretonism first began to take organized form at almost the same time (1898) as the Catalan and Basque movements started to generate political support, but it was much weaker than either.

48. The proceedings of the *Primer Congreso de Estudios Vascos* (Bilbao, 1919) were published soon after the first general congress on Basque studies was held in 1918. The most important of the new cultural journals were *La Revista Internacional de Estudios Vascos* (1907) and *Eusko-Folklore* (1921).

49. The following statistics have been given concerning the number of books published in Euskera prior to the twentieth century:

	16th cent.	17th cent.	18th cent.	19th cent.
Spanish Basque Country	2	5	34	301
French Basque Country	3	20	47	220
Total	5	25	81	521

"Ibar," *Genio y Lengua* (Tolosa, 1936), in Sierra Bustamante, 84.

50. The best general history of Basque literature is Luis de Michelena, *Historia de la literatura vasca* (Madrid, 1960).

51. According to Padre Estella's *Historia de los vascos*, in Sierra Bustamante, 83.

52. The only section of the nationalist movement to collaborate with official institutions under the dictatorship was the STV, which joined small Catholic syndicates in vying with the Socialist UGT for elections to labor arbitration boards after 1926.

53. I am following the results of the 1930 census as quoted in I. P. Trainin's subsequent Marxist analysis, *Baski v borbe za svoiu natsional-nuiu nezavisimost* (Moscow, 1937).

The social structure of Navarra was roughly similar to that of Alava. Population of the four provinces in 1930 was:

Vizcaya	500,453
Navarra	351,090
Guipúzcoa	311,146
Alava	105,278

54. This was succinctly expressed in a pamphlet by Felipe Carretero, *Crítica del nacionalismo vasco* (Bilbao, n. d., apparently about 1918).

55. Andoni de Soraluze, *Riqueza y economía del País Vasco* (Buenos

Aires, 1945), 185–86. The other side of this argument, of course, is the vital importance of the Spanish market for the Basque economy, a point effectively established in the writings of the non-nationalist Basque economist, Joaquín Adán, especially in his *Obra póstuma* (Bilabo, 1938).

Other indices of Basque economic well-being were (to some extent) the diffusion of property owning and the superior physiological measurements of the military-age population. By 1930 37 percent of Vizcayan farm operators owned their own land, and most of the rest enjoyed stable and reasonable rental conditions. Over a fifty-year period in the late nineteenth and early twentieth centuries, approximately half the farm renters in Guipúzcoa gained ownership of their properties, according to Sierra Bustamante, 260, though this was assisted in the 1930s by vigorous support from the PNV for easier purchase terms and rural credit. In Guipúzcoan industry, small shops still predominated. According to a 1933 industrial census, 22 percent of the industrial workers in Guipúzcoa owned their own shops.

The superior nutrition enjoyed by much of the population in the Basque country was reflected in the physiological measurements of army draftees. In 1913 only 14 percent of Spanish recruits were listed as comparatively "tall" in stature, compared with 27 percent of those from the three northwestern provinces. Applying approximately the same standards, the percentage of "tall" recruits from all Spain had risen to 27 by 1958, but that of the three Basque provinces increased to 44. J. M. Martín de Retana, "Antropometría vasca: La mayor talla, peso y caja torácica," *La Gran Enciclopedia Vasca*, III, 574–77.

56. José Antonio de Aguirre y Lecube, *Entre la libertad y la revolución 1930–1935* (Bilbao, 1935), 33.

57. Ortueta was himself a rather moderate man and a devotee of medieval Navarrese history. His principal works on the latter are *Nabarra y la unidad política vasca* (Barcelona, 1931) and *Sancho el Mayor, Rey de los Vascos* (Buenos Aires, 1963), 2 cols.

58. Ariztimuño's main published work was *La democracia en Euzkadi* (Zarauz, 1934). For a critique, see José Múgica's pamphlet, *La democracia vasca* (San Sebastián, 1935).

59. Aguirre, *Entre la libertad*, 164.

5

BASQUE NATIONALISM
AND THE SECOND REPUBLIC
1931–1936

The second Spanish Republic was inaugurated on April 14, 1931, without serious opposition from any quarter. For the Basque country, its coming raised the following issues and opportunities: the apparent introduction of complete and direct democratic constitutionalism, which could fundamentally alter the structure of Spain's government; the potential inauguration of a new era of social reformism, promoted especially by the Socialist constituency in the industrial districts of Vizcaya and Guipúzcoa; close identity with the goal of regional autonomy, at least for Catalonia, as had been postulated in the original Pact of San Sebastián in the previous year; and the threat of the inauguration of a radical anticlerical policy, long the rallying cry of most Republican factions.

The dominant force in the new Republican government was the anticlerical lower-middle-class Republican left, which found a leader several months later in Manuel Azaña. Regional government in Catalonia was immediately seized by the *Esquerra*, the lower-middle-class Catalanist "Left" federation led by the elderly Francesc Macià, which completely undercut the former power of Cambó and the middle-class *Lliga*. Other regionalist counterparts of the Republican left emerged as small groups in Valencia and in Galicia, where they formed an Autonomous Republican Galician Organization (ORGA).[1]

For Basque nationalism the new regime thus offered both a maximal opportunity and a worrisome threat. The PNV had nothing to do with the coming of the Republic, but certainly did not oppose it, as was made clear in an official statement on April 16, 1931, two days after the installation of the new regime. The new nationalist leadership in Vizcaya moved quickly to grasp the initiative by calling a meeting of pronationalist mayors in Guernica, ancient site of Vizcayan foral oaths, on April 17. Republican authorities were anxious about the direction that nationalist enthusiasm might take and dispatched military units to maintain close supervision. The occasion was, however, used by Aguirre and the young nationalist leaders to edge the movement into a more liberal and pro-Republican stance; the meeting's official manifesto hailed the constitutional Republic and called for an autonomous Basque regime within a system of Republican federalism that also recognized the "liberty and independence" of the Catholic church.[2]

Four days later, on April 21, the Republican government replaced the old monarchist provincial *diputaciones* in Spain with new *comisiones gestoras* (administrative commissions). In the Basque territory these were composed of representatives of the left Republicans, the Socialists, and in some cases of the ANV. The latter had joined the Republican-Socialist alliance that preceded the fall of the monarchy and placed a handful of representatives among the new leftist majorities that had been established on most Basque municipal councils in the elections of April 12. Thus the ANV, which lacked any future as an independent force, planned to further the cause of autonomy by close collaboration with the ruling leftist coalition.[3]

The PNV continued to pursue its independent course. An assembly of pronationalist mayors from Vizcaya, Guipúzcoa, and Alava was called in San Sebastián on May 8 to initiate plans for an autonomy project. This was a bold move, for the recent expansion of nationalism had not yet been tested in direct elections. In Vizcaya, where the movement was strongest, there were 175 nationalist *concejales* (municipal councilmen) and 235 non-nationalist *concejales*.[4] The governing coalition of the moderate left ruled most of Vizcaya and Guipúzcoa, while the support of Navarra for a nationalist autonomy project was uncertain. On the other hand, the inauguration of a new regime, and the resultant confusion and realignment, together with the broad, if diffuse support for the goal of decentralization, made the moment propitious.

To head off what it feared might be a conservative nationalist proposal, the *comisión gestora* of Guipúzcoa announced on May 7 the formation of a new foral commission charged with preparing a proposal of provincial autonomy for Guipúzcoa.[5] It was to be composed of members of the *comisión gestora*, further representatives of the three coalition parties, and representatives of the municipalities. Subsequently a joint autonomy commission from the *comisiones gestoras* of all four provinces was established to present a general autonomy proposal.

The pronationalist assembly of mayors moved more rapidly. Initiative was exercised on the municipal level because of the importance of local rights and representation in Basque legal history and because the preliminary autonomy proposal by the Spanish parliamentary subcommission in 1918 had recommended that details be formulated by municipal representatives. The prestigious *Sociedad de Estudios Vascos*, which since its founding thirteen years earlier had become the fulcrum of culture and erudition in the Basque region, was already sponsoring a study commission to draft an autonomy project, and the mayors' assembly formally requested it to present the full terms of a draft statute as soon as possible.

Working rapidly, the commission produced a General Statute of the Basque State on May 31. It declared that the "Basque state" would be "autonomous within the totality of the Spanish state." The Spanish government would have jurisdiction over foreign affairs, communications, the armed forces in a general sense, currency, commercial and criminal law, church-state relations, and the terms of suffrage for national elections. The Basque region would enjoy full authority over all other spheres of jurisdiction, as well as the administration of nearly all government functions within its borders, whether or not of its ultimate competence. This included control of the police and the armed forces, the latter to be known in the Basque region as the "Basque militia" and to serve outside the region only for indispensable technical training or in cases of national emergency. Municipal elections were to be held on the basis of universal direct suffrage, but indirect provincial elections were not excluded. A regional government of *Euzkadi* would be elected with its own parliament to administer the autonomous system, but at the same time each of the four provinces would enjoy the greatest latitude in their own local autonomy.

During the next few weeks there occurred the most intensive propaganda campaign in the history of the Basque region. It was led by the PNV, which accepted the draft statute at a national congress of June 7 even though its members objected to granting jurisdiction over church-state relations to the (now presumably anticlerical) Spanish government. The movement distributed more than four million posters, five thousand large mural announcements, and several million leaflets on behalf of the autonomy statute.[6] The Socialists and Republicans agreed to support the statute, though with reservations. The Carlists, who were being revived and reorganized as a political force, took the same position, though with different objections. They disliked the concept of a "Basque state," an innovation that sounded modern and radical, and like the PNV desired full freedom of action on the church-state issue. Relations between the nationalists and Carlists were already strained. The latter accused the former of being too ingratiating to radical Republicanism, while the PNV lamented the Carlists' apparent lack of overriding commitment to the autonomy issue. Indeed, when new municipal elections were held in Pamplona on May 31, the small nationalist minority there supported the left, giving the Republican-Socialist coalition a majority in the municipal government of the Navarrese capital.[7] Despite these triangular frictions, however, the councils of more than 480 of the 520 municipalities in the four provinces declared their initial support for the project.

A broad assembly of municipal delegates was scheduled to meet in Pamplona on June 14 to discuss the draft statute. However, the Carlists scheduled a unification rally for their newly reorganized *Comunión Tradicionalista* on the same date, infuriating the nationalists, who switched the autonomists' assembly to the historic Carlist capital of Estella (Navarra). Amid colorful mass parades, the assembly approved the statute article by article, adding a crucial amendment granting the Basque region complete autonomy in church-state relations and the right to negotiate a separate concordat with the Vatican.

This was only the first step, however. It would next be necessary to win government approval for an all-Basque plebiscite on the statute and then obtain its ratification by the Republican parliament. The first Cortes elections under the new regime were scheduled for June 28, only two weeks after the Estella assembly. They would select a constituent assembly to write the constitution and lay the groundwork of the new regime, and their outcome was crucial. Moreover, to overcome the fractionalization of the multiparty system, the new government authorized a voting system based on province lists and large urban districts rather than single-deputy units, with the victors to win between 67 and 80 percent of the seats so long as they gained at least a 40 percent plurality in the popular vote. According to this system—somewhat similar to that inaugurated by the Fascist government in Italy eight years earlier—the Basque territory was divided into four provincial districts, plus the separate urban "circumscription" of Bilbao, slightly gerrymandered to include surrounding industrial suburbs that would guarantee the left at least one safe electoral zone in the region. The arrangement made large coalitions indispensable.

Despite their increasingly liberal stance since the establishment of the republic, the leaders of the PNV had little option but to form an alliance with the right rather than the left. The movement's history, the sharp line drawn with the left over the religious issue and the latter's lukewarm—though not directly negative—attitude on the Basque autonomy issue resulted in the formation of a *vasconavarra* (nationalist/rightist) coalition in each province save Alava, emphasizing the twin goals of autonomy and defense of

Catholicism. Even amid the pro-Republican and progressivist euphoria of 1931, this could not fail to be a winning combination in the Basque territory. While the leftist coalition swept the elections in most other parts of Spain, the *vasconavarra* ticket won a clear victory, gaining fifteen of the twenty-four Cortes seats for the four provinces. Seven nationalists were elected, together with five Carlists and three Catholic Independents.[8] The coalition won 132,446 votes against 95,222 for the left.[9]

TABLE 1

Results of the 1931 Parliamentary Elections in Percentages

Province	Participation	Right	PNV	Left	ANV	Communists
Alava	81.3	30.6	17.7	32.7		
Guipúzcoa	85.5	49.0		35.4		
Navarra	83.5	53.1		30.7		
Bilbao	76.8		31.9	44.8	3.8	6.7
Vizcaya	80.0		61.3	18.6		

SOURCE: Javier Tusell Gómez and G. García Queipo de Llano, "Introducción a una Sociología Electoral del País Vasco durante la Segunda República" (1973), Table 1.

The nationalists had dominated the province of Vizcaya and, with the help of the right, made a strong minority showing in the Bilbao district. The traditionalist right dominated Navarra and, with strong nationalist support, won in Guipúzcoa. A mutually destructive contest between the two forces in Alava had thrown that province to the left. The left, however, could only approach a majority in the Bilbao district, though it also won all the other three provincial capitals (including Pamplona) and also the non-*Euskera* speaking rural districts of southern Alava and Navarra—regions partially controlled by landlords and the scene of more social conflict than other parts of the Basque countryside. The ANV, running alone in Bilbao, failed to gain a seat.

Altogether, the Basque region stood out in 1931 as the major conservative region in Spain. It was vehemently denounced by Socialists and Republicans as the "Vaticanist Gibraltar" of the north, and Catholic traditionalists were labeled *cavernícolas* (troglodytes). The latter was a particularly lame epithet since the literacy rates of the Basque provinces were among the highest in Spain. The other north Spanish provinces with high literacy rates also tended toward the center and right, and within the Basque region the only zones to vote left were those with the higher rates of illiteracy. The leftist detractors of the Basque coalition were usually most solidly based in the most illiterate, backward provinces. Not surprisingly, Basque representatives questioned who were in fact the real troglodytes,[10] but as the constitutional commission of the new Cortes got down to work it became clear that the conservative forces of the Basque territory stood no chance amid an overwhelmingly Republican and Socialist parliament.

Thus it was not surprising that a handful of monarchist conspirators looked toward militant Basque nationalism as a possible ally in overthrowing the Republican government. A leading conspirator, the retired General Luis Orgaz, was spending the summer in Deva (Guipúzcoa). He was placed in contact with PNV leaders and witnessed a parade of between ten thousand and fifteen thousand *mendigoixales* (Basque scouts; lit. "mountaineers") in Deva. Though Basque nationalism was not committed to sustaining a regime of the Republican left, an interview with Aguirre was at best inconclusive.[11] Meanwhile, the Carlists had already begun to reorganize their militia, the *Requetés*,[12] and conservative newspapers in the Basque country combatted the government vigorously. This led to a crackdown by authorities on August 20–21. All conservative newspapers in the Basque country were temporarily closed, the Eibar (Guipúzcoa) arms factory was occupied by troops, and public rallies momentarily prohibited.

Meanwhile representatives of the Navarrese municipal councils had met on August 10 to consider the autonomy issue. The nominal occasion was the submission of a Navarrese statute by the provincial *comisión gestora*, but instead representatives of 89.5 percent of the Navarrese population voted in favor of a common statute for all four provinces. This was a decided triumph for the nationalist idea, but when the question of the Estella statute was presented, it was approved by a smaller majority, representatives of 172,026 voting in favor and those of 147,977 against.[13] The only direct opposition to autonomy came from the leftist and liberal municipal councils of the Ebro valley (Ribera) in southern Navarra, but there were reservations about the new Estella statute on both left and right.

The nationalists redoubled efforts at political negotiation. On September 22 a delegation of 420 mayors appeared in Madrid to hand the prime minister, the liberal Catholic Alcalá Zamora, a copy of the statute with a request for assistance in achieving its legal recognition. Alcalá Zamora assured them that he wanted the constitution of the Republic to "incorporate" (lit., *recoja*)[14] the aspirations of all regions and transmitted the document to the government.

By that point, however, tension between the Catholic minority and anti-Catholic majority in the Cortes was nearing its high point. The debate of September 25–26 ended in a decision that the religious clauses in the Estella statute would be unconstitutional and so killed the entire measure. Within three weeks, the Cortes enacted the famous Article 26 of the Republican Constitution that not merely separated church and state and cancelled the subsidy to the church but also prescribed legislation that would outlaw much of the work of Catholic orders and eliminate Catholic education in Spain. The nationalist spokesmen, together with other Catholics, made the fundamental point that there could be no constitutional democracy in Spain if full and equal civil and social rights were not enjoyed by Catholics and the clergy. They accused the Republican-Socialist majority of stifling liberty instead of establishing democracy. When the major anti-Catholic legislation was passed on October 14, the nationalists answered Republican cries of *"¡Viva la República!"* with shouts of *"¡Viva la libertad!"* and Jesús María de Leizaola, their most prominent spokesman after Aguirre, was assaulted by a Republican deputy. With autonomy temporarily closed off and Catholic rights proscribed, Aguirre declared that further "reasoning in the Cortes was completely useless,"[15] and the entire *vasconavarra* delegation walked out, together with the other deputies of the conservative Catholic minority. The next five years would prove correct the contention that Republican democracy could only flourish on the basis of equal laws and rights for all individuals and groups.

For the Carlists and other ultraconservative Catholics in the

Basque region, passage of the anti-Catholic legislation created an unbreachable gulf with the Republic. The younger leadership of the PNV was much more flexible and ordered its priorities differently. Their main concern was *Euzkadi*, not the Republican constitution, and they noted that in and of themselves the people of the Basque region had never ratified directly any of the modern constitutions of Spain. For all its anti-Catholicism, the new Republican regime approved the issue of autonomy in principle, and a decision was soon made to distinguish between the form of a liberal democratic system per se and the content of specific legislation, in this case "unjust, antidemocratic and antiliberal."[16]

A policy of careful cooperation was also encouraged by some elements of the Basque clergy, who from beginning to end were perhaps the strongest single bastion of the nationalist cause. Aguirre's personal confessor, for example, took the position—then almost unheard of among Spanish Catholics but thirty years later increasingly accepted among Catholics as a whole—that the identity of church and state need not be made a touchstone of politics. On October 6, 1931, he wrote to Aguirre that

> Basque nationalist deputies ought not to cling solely to the religious issue. The defense of the church is first of all the duty of the clergy rather than of Catholic laymen.[17]

He suggested that nationalist leaders must use secular political opportunities primarily for secular political goals, chief of which was the conquest of Basque autonomy.

The issue of autonomy in church-state relations would clearly have to be given up, and that meant going back to the original approach of the commission from the *Sociedad de Estudios Vascos*, which now received the endorsement of the *comisiones gestoras* of the four provinces. On November 6 the government decided that the *comisiones* should be responsible for drawing up a new draft, and during the month that followed the PNV leadership apparently conducted negotiations about participating in the work. On December 8 a government decree announced that the new commission would be composed of a representative from each of the four *comisiones* and three representatives (presumably either nationalist or pronationalist) from Basque municipalities. This arrangement was apparently acceptable to the PNV,[18] though soon afterward the membership of the commission was increased to ten, incorporating three new Socialist members from the Basque region after the latter complained that all four of the *comisión* representatives were middle-class Republicans. The commission was charged with adjusting the preceding Basque autonomy statute to the new Spanish constitution, and this formula restored collaboration between the PNV and the Republican regime. The new constitution, finally approved on December 9, declared the Spanish Republic to be "an integral state," but "compatible with municipal and regional autonomy." Soon afterward the PNV deputies demonstrated their conditional reconciliation with the new regime by voting for the liberal Catholic Alcalá Zamora for the presidency of the republic, while the rest of the Catholic minority abstained.

By the end of 1931 the *vasconavarra* coalition was beginning to break up, as differences between the nationalists and Carlists widened. The latter had refused to cooperate with the regime in any way after October. On December 20 Basque Carlist leaders decided not to have anything to do with an autonomy statute prepared primarily by the Republican *comisiones gestoras*. Incidents between Carlists and Socialists reached a high point early in 1932 when three of the latter were killed after they came to protest a Carlist meeting in Bilbao.[19] Soon afterward the reunified Carlist Traditionalist Communion (CT) was organized on an all-Spanish level. The reorganization of Carlists tended to deepen the gulf between them and the Basque nationalists, for the regional Basque *jaimistas* who were rooted in local traditions and issues, and were often willing to collaborate with nationalists, were increasingly overshadowed by doctrinaire leaders of Integrist background. The latter figures, such as Juan Olazábal of the new CT provincial junta of Guipúzcoa, were much more hostile to the "temporizings" and doctrinal divergences of nationalism.[20] Moreover, conservative upper-class Catholic interests in Vizcaya and Guipúzcoa, which were *alfonsino* monarchist but not Carlist, were taking a more active political role and were increasingly hostile to the nationalists, whom they now began to see as selling out to the Republic.

Republican regulations required separate assemblies of municipal representatives from each of the four provinces to vote on the issue of an *Estatuto único*—a single autonomy statute for the entire region. These groups met on January 31, 1932, and approved the principle by a ratio of eleven to one, with representatives of eighty-five of the Navarrese town governments voting in favor.[21]

The PNV continued to expand its activities during 1932, building an extensive propaganda fund and carrying on widespread publicity. Youth organizations and cultural programs were still growing, and on Easter Sunday, March 25, 1932, the PNV held a massive commemoration of the *Aberri-Eguna*—"Day of the Fatherland"—with sixty-five thousand adherents parading in Bilbao.

The PNV leadership riveted its attention on the issue of autonomy irrespective of the question of regime and secondary implications. Though it was clear that an autonomy statute would need approval by the moderate left, the directors of the party did not think in terms of a genuine alliance with the latter—from whom they were still divided above all by the religious issue—and expected to be able to count on the Carlists at least as far as the issue of autonomy was concerned.[22]

The new autonomy draft was not officially presented for approval until June, but its outlines became known earlier in the spring. In general, the new statute would provide a somewhat more limited degree of autonomy than had the earlier document. It still preserved the basic features of local and regional self-government for internal Basque affairs in most aspects of law, social regulation, and economics, but it left greater authority in the hands of the Spanish state in matters of joint interest and of coordination with the rest of Spain. There was no mention of a "Basque state"; the new regional entity was termed "an autonomous politico-administrative unit within the Spanish state" that would be called *País Vasco-navarro* in Castilian and *Euzkadi* in *Euzkera*. Military service would still be conducted only in the Basque region, save for special training and emergencies, but there was no mention of a *Milicia Vasca*. All religious regulations had to conform to those of the Spanish state. The statute was based on the principle of the validity of the existing economic *concierto* and *convenio*, but the new system nevertheless required a redefinition and reallocation of taxes, about the justice of which there were conflicting opinions. Largely due to Socialist insistence, the proposed regional parliament would be composed half of deputies chosen by universal, equal, and proportionate suffrage from each of the four provinces equally and half from general slates elected by the entire region as a whole (giving somewhat greater voice to the leftist masses in the industrial areas). Each province would retain provincial autonomy, and broad self-government was provided for the municipalities.[23]

The opposition to the preceding draft had come from the left; the main danger to the new proposal came from the right. The Carlists were in fact divided. Though few were enthusiastic about the new statute, which was a project of the center and moderate left, regional autonomy—albeit in a different form—had always been a cornerstone of Carlist doctrine. On May 24, the leadership of the Traditionalist Communion declared that its members were free to vote their individual consciences on the issue. As the date for the general assembly of municipal representatives to approve the draft neared, Carlist opposition mounted. Only one of the top Navarrese leaders—the Conde de Rodezno—endorsed the concept of a Navarrese statute alone; even then he said that he was willing to support the Basque statute insofar as it retained the basic lines of the 1927 tax agreement and would establish regional control of education.[24] The most vehement Carlist opponent was Olazábal, the wealthy Guipuzcoan Integrist. In *La Constancia*, the Integrist organ of San Sebastián, he offered a prize of 5,000 pesetas to anyone who could find the word "God" in the draft, bitterly protesting the adjustment of Basque regulations to the anti-Catholic structure of the Republican state. Other Traditionalists complained that the whole statute was antifuerist, blurring over historic usages and creating a radically modern new entity.[25] To this PNV spokesmen replied that the true *fuero* would not conform merely to "the will of those who lived in the past, but of those alive today,"[26] faithfully echoing the position of Arana Goiri.

An assembly of municipal representatives was summoned to vote on the new document in Pamplona on June 19. Young Carlists waged a vociferous antistatute campaign. Though a narrow majority (127 to 115) of the municipal governments of Navarra voted to instruct their representatives to approve the statute, at the last minute the representatives of eight of those in favor changed their vote and eight abstained. The results of the voting were as follows:

		Vote by Number of Municipalities	Vote by Total Number of Inhabitants Represented
Vizcaya	In favor:	109	488,345
	Opposed:	1	1,066
	Abstained:	6	25,800
Guipúzcoa	In favor:	84	281,827
	Opposed:	2	5,708
	Abstained:	3	8,734
Alava	In favor:	52	89,956
	Opposed:	11	8,496
	Abstained:	14	7,647
Navarra	In favor:	109	135,582
	Opposed:	123	186,666
	Abstained:	35	28,859
Totals	In favor:	354	962,710
	Opposed:	137	201,936
	Abstained:	58	71,040[27]

Since the document had been prepared as an *Estatuto único* for the four provinces, its rejection by the Navarrese required the drafting of a somewhat different measure adjusted for the three provinces of the Basque country alone. Tension between nationalists and Carlists had reached a peak; on July 10, the Carlist *El Pensamiento Navarro* (Pamplona) complained of nationalist youths interrupting Carlist meetings in Guipúzcoa with shouts of "Long live the Republic!"[28] The *vasconavarra* parliamentary coalition, already in ruins, was officially dissolved by the PNV late in July.

Worse yet was in store for the nationalists, since the withdrawal of rural Navarra immediately began to increase doubts and reluctance in rural Alava. More important than the growth of reactive Carlist feeling in Alava was the concern that a lightly inhabited agrarian province would inevitably be dominated by populous and industrial Vizcaya and Guipúzcoa without the assisting counterweight of Navarra. The chief spokesman for this reluctance was the Carlist architect and top political leader in the province, José María Oriol,[29] who controlled one of the two main newspapers in Alava and began to prohibit publication of material expressing the nationalist viewpoint.[30]

The monarchist right in Vizcaya and Guipúzcoa also worked actively to undermine nationalism. At the beginning of August radical right elements published a pamphlet called *Nacionalismo, Comunismo, Judaismo* that sought to identify the Basque movement with the subversive goals of "Jewish Bolshevism." This effort to tar the regionalists with the charge of heresy was officially disavowed by the bishop of Vitoria in a letter of August 8, though it was not made public until two and a half months later.

At that point the top Spanish politician in the Basque region, Indalecio Prieto, saw an opportunity to utilize the widening gap between the nationalists and the ultraright in order to attract the former into closer cooperation with the moderate left. Prieto was the leader of Vizcayan socialism, an innovative Republican public works minister and the most practical and flexible politician in the Spanish cabinet. He was no regionalist and had long been apprehensive of the conservative tone of Basque nationalism, earlier helping to popularize the phrase about a "Vaticanist Gibraltar" in the north. For that matter, he had not even favored leftist Catalan regionalism, though out of deference to his allies had not combatted it in parliament. The Catalan autonomy statute was finally approved by the Cortes on September 9, 1932. Once this had become a fact, Prieto grapsed that the same means might be used to win Basque nationalism over to a center-left Republic.

At Prieto's suggestion the statute was officially signed into law on September 15 at San Sebastián, site of the original Republican-left Catalanist agreement. The ceremonies became the occasion for a vivid display of Catalan-Basque solidarity, as the differences between ardent Catholics and zealous anticlericals were momentarily submerged under the regionalist issue. Basque nationalist parades and flags were a highlight of the festivities, and the Republican president, Alcalá Zamora, went out of his way to assure the nationalists that the Republican system offered the same opportunity for them as for the Catalans.

The political climax occurred later in the day when Prieto met with the Basque Cortes deputies at the offices of the Guipuzcoan provincial government. He emphasized that the way was now clear for Basque autonomy. All that was needed was to follow the Catalan precedent and, if the Navarrese really did not want to participate, adjust the regional system to three provinces instead of four. In fact, he suggested, the Basques were perhaps more likely than the Catalans to make a success of autonomy,

> given Basque administrative experience and the general atmosphere of morality among the Basque people. On the other hand, I must loyally point out that one may doubt the effectiveness of its establishment in Catalonia. Everyone is aware that in times past the city government of Barcelona has had the most corrupt administration in Spain.[31]

Prieto had recently observed that "the political psychology of the Basque country is going to change rapidly."[32] In San Sebastián he went on to insist that autonomy could not be an end in itself. Separatism would be "asphyxiation"; once autonomy had been achieved, nationalists would learn to set new goals, "and I harbor the hope of seeing them join forces, even while maintaining their special norms, with those of us who seek greater social justice."[33] Prieto was categorical that the future lay in cooperation with the alliance of the moderate left. Soon afterward he wrote to a PNV leader that, should there occur a dissolution of the present Republican and Socialist parliament or the formation of a more conservative cabinet, the autonomy "project might perhaps encounter serious difficulties."[34]

On October 19 a meeting of provincial and municipal representatives in San Sebastián appointed a new commission to prepare a statute for three provinces only, excluding Navarra. The commission was composed of four Republicans, three Socialists, three PNV members, two representatives of ANV, and two Carlists. Lower-middle-class Republicanism was grossly overrepresented, due to their current dominance of executive power. Moreover, the Republicans were not quite so interested as Prieto in winning over Basque nationalism. For them the religious issue was still predominant, and though not opposed to autonomy per se, they did little to hasten the work of the commission. When the Republican government presented its crowning piece of anticlerical legislation in March 1933, outlawing teaching by Catholic orders in Spain, the Basque parliamentary delegation denounced it as "pure fascism," the arbitrary suppression of religion by the state.

The clearest sign of the continuing tension between Basque nationalism and the Republican regime throughout 1932 and well into 1933 were the numerous arrests of nationalist activitists. During 1932 more than two hundred were detained by the police, mainly on charges of "subversive propaganda" and "public disorder."[35] The frequency with which Republican authorities censored expression of ideas produced great resentment. More militants were arrested when the nationalists successfully led a major protest in Bilbao in February 1933 against plans of the Republican-Socialist municipal government to tear down a large monument dedicated to the Sacred Heart of Jesus. Still others were detained when the first municipal elections were held under the Republic on April 23, 1933. This contest was a great triumph for the nationalists; the PNV and ANV combined won more than two-thirds of all the municipal council seats in Vizcaya and Guipúzcoa, winning 285 of 409 in the former province.[36]

On May 2 the Republican president paid a formal visit to Bilbao. Seventy-one nationalists currently held in a nearby jail mainly for their activities in propaganda and demonstrations declared a hunger strike. On the morrow a demonstration in Bilbao was forcibly repressed by the police. The STV declared a general protest strike for May 4 and was seconded by the local sector of the CNT. This virtually closed down Bilbao for a day, even though the Socialist UGT refused its official support, maintaining somewhat perversely that the strike was in fact being backed by the "reactionary, nationalist, and clerical" business interests of Vizcaya.[37] The left was in general still unable to distinguish very clearly between the several non- and antileftist political forces in the Basque country.

Partly for this reason, work on the new autonomy statute proceeded with agonizing slowness.[38] By 1933 the Republican-Socialist coalition was beset with manifold problems and was steadily losing support. This had first been shown by the municipal elections; a second blow was struck by the selection of members of the new Republican Constitutional Court, who were chosen by municipal councils early in September. Opposition forces won an overwhelming victory, and in the Basque country the two members chosen were a nationalist and a Carlist, with no one for the left.[39]

In the meantime, a new three-province statute based on the document drawn up in the preceding year had finally been completed by the commission. On August 8 it was approved by representatives of municipal governments of the three proautonomist provinces (excluding Navarra) at an assembly in Vitoria. Within less than two months the Spanish parliament in Madrid reached a deadlock, and new national elections were scheduled for November 19. It was agreed, however, that the plebiscite on the new statute, which was required by Republican constitutional procedures, would be held in the three provinces two weeks before the national elections.

The position of the left was unenthusiastic but for the most part mildly favorable to autonomy. On the other hand, the Carlists and other forces of the right, who outnumbered the nationalists in Alava, were divided. Ultra-Catholic opinion held that it was not licit to vote for a Republican autonomy statute, for that would be equivalent to recognizing an impious regime. The bishop of Vitoria, Mateo Múgica, was appealed to and tried to lay this issue to rest by opining that there was no incompatibility in opposing Republican anticlericalism and yet voting for autonomy under the Republican system. Leaders of the monarchist right in Vizcaya indicated that they would discourage opposition to the plebiscite in Alava if the PNV would agree to forming a broad new *vasconavarra* coalition in the forthcoming national elections. The official leadership of the *Comunión Tradicionalista* decided to support the statute in a meeting of October 25, but the chief organ of Alavese Carlism, *El Pensamiento Alavés* (Vitoria), was vehemently opposed, saying that it would do away with the *concierto económico* and raise Alavese taxes. "If it is expensive and goes against both God and Spain, how can we who are Catholic, Spanish, and lovers of our regional economy vote for that?"[40]

In the plebiscite of November 5, 1933, the autonomy statute was approved by a vote of 411,756 to 14,196. The nominal participation of 87 percent of eligible voters was the highest for any contest in Spanish history. The balloting was, however, conducted rather loosely, and a few leftists complained of irregularities, even though the latter could scarcely have affected the general outcome. The slightly higher degree of support that was registered in Guipúzcoa compared with Vizcaya was apparently due to a stronger turnout by the left in the former province. The major weakness, as expected, was in Alava. Division among the ultraright and opposition by the left resulted in an abstention rate of nearly 42 percent, and only 46.4 percent of the registered voters actually voted in favor of the statute.

TABLE 2

Results of the Autonomy Plebiscite of November 5, 1933

	Registered Voters	Ballots in Favor	Ballots Against
Alava	56,066	26,015 (46.4%)	6,695 (11.9%)
Guipúzcoa	166,635	149,177 (89.5%)	2,436 (1.5%)
Vizcaya	267,466	236,564 (88.4%)	5,625 (2.1%)
Totals	490,167	411,756 (84.0%)	14,756 (3.0%)

SOURCE: *Euzkadi* and *La Voz de Guipúzcoa*, Nov. 10, 1933, in Tusell Gómez and García Queipo de Llano, Table 4. Cf. Aguirre, 403, and Sarrailh de Ihartza, 450.

The subsequent electoral contest for seats in the Spanish parliament was completely fractionalized in the Basque region as in most other parts of Spain. Carlists, nationalists, the moderate center (extremely exiguous in the Basque region), the middle-class Republican left, and the Socialists all entered separate candidacies. In the three western provinces, the Carlists attacked the nationalists as directly as they did the left. In Navarra, however, they concentrated their fire on the Republicans and Socialists, while the weak nationalist forces in that province attacked the Carlists more vigorously than they did the left, recognizing the former's greater strength there.

In the elections of November 1933 Basque nationalism won the greatest ballot-box triumph in its history, garnering twelve of the twenty-four parliamentary seats in the four provinces. Since all the non-Carlist forces failed to gain a single seat in Navarra and Alava, the nationalist representation was in fact confined to Vizcaya and Guipúzcoa, where it won twelve of the fifteen seats contested. Overall, however, the rightist alliance of the Carlists and their associates won a total of ten seats, while the left was almost completely eliminated, winning only the two minority seats for the Bilbao district.[41]

This electoral triumph for Basque nationalism coincided with the victory of the parties of the center and moderate right in Spain as a whole. It meant that the forces dominating the new parliament in Madrid were likely to be even less receptive to Basque autonomy than their predecessors, since the recent experience of the Catalan statute had identified regional autonomy with leftist politics. This tendency had been accentuated during the summer of 1933 when an informal regionalist alliance had been formed between the PNV, the left Catalanists of the *Esquerra* and the weak left Galicianists of the ORGA, who were defeated in the 1933 Cortes elections in Galicia,[42] though less severely than their left Republican allies in Spain as a whole. This alliance was given the name of *Galeuzca* (Galicia-Euzkadi-Catalonia), realizing a design conceived a decade earlier by the left Catalanist writer Antoni Rovira i Virgili. Despite the overwhelming leftist defeat in the national Spanish elections, the *Esquerra* still dominated the Catalan government (*Generalitat*), and the PNV leadership was interested in forming a strong alliance of all the autonomist forces to push the Basque statute through the new Cortes. However, the strongest regionalist party in the parliament was still not the PNV, but the moderate Catalanists of the *Lliga*, who had won fourteen seats. Their astute leader, Francesc Cambó, opposed a formal alliance of autonomist groups, believing that it would only harden antagonisms and elicit the organization of a much stronger antiautonomist bloc.

On December 22, after the new Cortes had opened, a Basque commission appeared in Madrid to present the draft autonomy statute to the leaders of the new government. The latter promised it swift parliamentary consideration. That same day, however, representatives of fifty-seven of the seventy-seven municipal governments in Alava informed the government that they rejected further Alavese participation in the autonomy project. These municipal councils had all been chosen by direct democratic suffrage, and their position was not greatly disproportionate to the minority vote actually given the statute by Alavese in the plebiscite. Moreover, in the parliamentary elections the antistatute Alavese Oriol had won a heavy majority. The decision of the Alavese municipalities was a grievous blow for the nationalists and retarded the constitutional gestation of the statute. During the next six months the parliamentary committee entrusted with its consideration moved rather slowly, held back particularly by disputes over the place of Alava in the proposed system. The concept of a loose confederal "Conference of Representatives" replaced that of a regular Basque regional parliament.

The spring and summer of 1934 was a time of mounting tension. Neither the Socialists nor the left Republicans accepted the victory of the center-right in the last elections, and the Socialists—despairing of full triumph by parliamentary means—were beginning to plan a revolutionary insurrection in conjunction with other forces of the extreme left. The middle-class elements of the Republican left encouraged this by making clear their refusal to cooperate with, or even tolerate, any conservative forces in government.

The first major conflict between Madrid and the new autonomous government of Catalonia erupted in June. The Catalan body had recently passed a new tenancy reform law enabling long-term renters to purchase titles to land. This was vigorously combatted by Catalan conservatives, and since the constitution reserved to the central government the right to alter contractual law, the Spanish supreme court declared the legislation unconstitutional.[43] The left Catalanist forces were thrown into an uproar, and on June 12 the Basque nationalist deputies walked out of the Cortes as a gesture of support for them. During the next three months, an adequate compromise solution for the Catalan agrarian reform legislation was negotiated between Madrid and Barcelona, but in the meantime radical left Catalanists prepared to use the issue to spark Catalan participation in a national leftist revolt that would topple the Madrid government and make Catalan autonomy absolute.

The persistent frustration of the Basque autonomy statutes, contrasted with the success of the Catalanist left, and the growing tension between Catalan autonomists and the moderate government in Madrid, all led to extended contacts between the PNV and proautonomy forces of the left. Just as the radical *Estat Català* faction was coming to the fore in Barcelona, an extremist section of the PNV youth led by Elías de Gallastegui, had virtually split off in 1932 and began to publish their own paper, *Jagi Jagi* (meaning "arise" or "upward").[44]

Even before the blowup over the Catalan issue, political passions in the Basque country had been vehemently aroused by a new proposal in the Madrid Cortes to reduce excise taxes on wine throughout the country to increase consumption and stimulate the economy.[45] So far, the tax rates established for the Basque country under the old monarchist *concierto* still applied, and Basque local government derived most of its income—superior to that of local governments elsewhere—from high excise taxes, particularly on wine, which was consumed in great quantities but produced nowhere in the Basque country save in the southern tip of Alava. Joined with this fiscal concern was mounting protest over the failure of the Republican government to hold provincial elections; there had been none for eleven years, and provincial administration was still conducted by *comisiones gestoras*. An ad hoc meeting of municipal representatives in Bilbao on June 5 led to plans to conduct elections in municipal councils throughout the Basque country on August 12 for members of a new Basque provincial government executive commission to safeguard the tax structure.[46]

Most political opinion opposed the continuation of the *comisiones gestoras*, and therefore the moderate centrist Republican cabinet promised to hold provincial elections within three months and safeguard the *concierto*. By the summer of 1934, however, nationalist opinion, especially in Vizcaya, had become wildly excited. Though the government declared the proposed municipal council elections illegal and threatened sanctions, the nationalists went ahead with plans to hold the special municipal council meetings and have them coincide with public homages to the late Francesc Macià, first president of the Catalan *Generalitat*. Anonymous pamphlets in Vizcaya called for the establishment of "national independence," concluding with slogans of "Long live the Basque revolution!" and *"¡Gora Euzkadi Azkatuta!"* (Up with Free Euzkadi).[47] The Socialists, left Republicans, and Catalan *Esquerra* strongly supported the Basque initiative, but government measures prevented the special elections from being carried out in the majority of municipal governments. A total of forty mayors and fifty-three municipal councilmen were then arrested for proceeding with the voting.[48]

The nationalists insisted that, despite the government pressure, most municipal councils had carried out the election of commission members, at least in Vizcaya and Guipúzcoa, and a special assembly was scheduled to meet in Zumárraga (Guipúzcoa) on September 2. Left Catalan representatives from the Spanish Cortes promised to attend along with the Basque nationalist parliamentary delegation and the two Socialist deputies from Bilbao. The assembly was held on schedule despite forceful government opposition that prevented many delegates from attending. Immediately afterward a number of Basque municipal officials were arrested, and on September 4 the intermunicipal Executive Commission urged that all municipal councillors in the Basque country resign in protest. Apparently a majority in Vizcaya and Guipúzcoa did so. In the aftermath, according to Aguirre, a total of approximately fifteen hundred municipal councillors and employees were either arrested, arraigned, or fined. The intermunicipal commission then urged the Basque parliamentary delegation to cease all bargaining with the government until this policy was reversed, and on September 11 Aguirre attended a meeting of the leftist parties of the Basque country in San Sebastián, where the PNV pledged to do all it could to resist a monarchist restoration or a rightist rebellion.

In the summer of 1934, however, the most immediate threat was a revolutionary insurrection by the left, led by the Socialists, whose plans were an open secret. The nationalist leadership in no way supported such plans, and at the September 11 meeting rejected a request that the PNV join an interparty council with the left. At the same time, in *Euzkadi* Aguirre ridiculed the fears of "revolution" currently shared by moderates and conservatives,[49] saying that in a modern state no revolution could triumph by force. All the Spanish government need do was to maintain constitutional law and order, without going to extremes of license or repression. He ridiculed conservative big business in Vizcaya and Guipúzcoa for having created the very conditions that currently threatened them:

Poor industrialists, who in years and years have never left the merest trace of a Catholic school in their mines; who abandoned their mines and factories to the socialists; who did nothing, nothing, absolutely nothing at all to indicate that the owners of these properties were in any way Catholic; who through their egotism, their ambition and their boundless lust for wealth, together with their absolute lack of concern for the bodies and souls of their workers, did everything, everything, absolutely everything needed to make the humble renounce their beliefs and abandon forever a religion that must seem false when those who proclaim it with their words deny it with their deeds! With what right do you now trumpet hypocritically against revolutionary extremism?[50]

Thus, on the eve of the revolutionary insurrection of 1934, the PNV leadership—and most of the party militants—had taken the position that the main danger and obstacles lay on the right. Without in any way directly supporting the anti-Catholicism and social revolution of the left, they blamed the country's current problems mainly on the right, for having blocked democracy and self-government and for having prostituted religion and pursued a policy of social exploitation. Like the revolutionary left and the protofascist right, Basque nationalism spoke of a need for "The New Man." Its cultural and psychological formula, however, was based on social Catholicism of an economically reformist and culturally liberal kind,[51] and this differentiated it from both extremes, including the variant of conservative Catholic authoritarianism represented by Spain's largest political party, the CEDA.

On September 24 a Basque nationalist delegation arrived in Barcelona to affirm its support of the Catalan *Generalitat*. At the same time, the Basque leaders had shown that they did not share the leftist ideological hysteria about anathematizing Catholic conservatives as "fascists" and limited their struggle to civil, not military, action. In Barcelona the Catalanist leaders apparently pledged that they were not committed to any subversive plot with the revolutionary left,[52] but events soon demonstrated that this was not exactly true.

The PNV decided to send its parliamentary delegation back to

Madrid for the new session of the Spanish Cortes, which opened on October 2. At that juncture, the Catholic CEDA, only organized in 1932 but already the strongest force in parliament, brought down the minority centrist cabinet. This necessitated a new center-right coalition—the only feasible way of achieving a workable majority in the current parliament and sustaining constitutional government—that included three CEDA members, one of them a Basque, Rafael Aizpun, who became minister of justice. This was the signal for the long-planned revolutionary insurrection, since the entire Spanish left held the doctrine that the CEDA was "fascist" and must never be allowed to enter the Republican government, despite its great strength in the democratically elected Cortes.

The left Catalanist revolt in Barcelona was pure farce and was quelled in less than twenty-four hours. The revolutionary insurrection of the Worker Alliance in the mining region of Asturias in northwest Spain was another matter. It lasted two weeks, caused much destruction and took over a thousand lives, requiring large-scale military intervention.[53]

The only other part of Spain where the revolt achieved any significance was in Vizcaya and Guipúzcoa, due to the action of the Socialists and also the small Communist group. Nearly four months earlier, in June, the civil governor of Vizcaya had talked both with Aguirre and with leaders of the STV concerning their position if and when a leftist revolutionary insurrection occurred. They assured him that they would "oppose" any "Marxist revolution."[54] When the insurrection began, the PNV sent instructions to all sections to "abstain absolutely" from joining any kind of movement.[55] After the Marxist organizations declared a general strike in the two industrial provinces on October 5, the STV directed its members to report for work wherever they could do so without risk. Since that condition could not be met in many of the mining or industrial areas, large sectors of the STV apparently respected the terms of the general strike so long as it lasted. There were indications that in some districts this reflected genuine support of the STV for the revolutionaries' goals. In at least one locality—Baracaldo (Vizcaya)—the Socialist-Communist alliance distributed leaflets declaring that the PNV and STV supported the strike, but this was officially denied by the latter organizations.

For several days the Vizcayan mining district was under paramilitary occupation by the UGT. The same was true of key industrial and coastal districts such as Eibar, Mondragón, and Portugalete. Though order was maintained in Bilbao, there were several days of skirmishing in that capital. The principal victims of assassination by the left in the Basque country were three local Carlist leaders in Eibar and Mondragón, one of them a former deputy in the *vasconavarra* delegation of 1931. The army had to be called out in both provinces to restore order and end the strike, with considerable loss of life.[56]

The official position of the PNV throughout was one of neutrality. However, the fact that several small nationalist extremist circles had supported the insurrectionists and that many STV workers had respected the strike made Basque nationalism a secondary target of government suspicion during the period of repression that followed. In its defense, the PNV made two main contentions. One was that in some towns the strikers so outnumbered other elements that they simply forced STV and Catholic workers to go along with them, as in Arboleda (Vizcaya) where fifteen hundred Socialist *ugetistas* completely dominated any possibility for resistance by the fifty-one local members of the STV.[57] The other contention was that in certain areas the PNV itself was a major target of the left, as in Hernani (Guipúzcoa), where eighteen of the twenty names on a captured Socialist *lista negra* of the left's principal enemies were those of PNV members.[58] Both the claims used by PNV spokesmen in the party's defense seem to be largely correct, though not valid for every local situation. Nevertheless many PNV centers were closed in Vizcaya—though not in Guipúzcoa, and on October 29 the whole leadership of the PNV in Vizcaya was arrested and its headquarters and records impounded. A few of the rank and file were subjected to severe beatings, though most were eventually released. In the immediate aftermath, a group of conservative nationalists in Alava broke away from the PNV to form a small *Derecha Autónoma Vasca*.

The revolutionary insurrection of 1934 thus clearly revealed the full dilemma of Basque nationalism. Despite the growth of the movement in 1930–33, it did not have a majority in the Basque country but was merely one of three forces—left, right, and nationalist center. Neither of the other two shared its deepest values and goals, but in an atmosphere increasingly polarized between right and left, nationalism could not triumph by itself. Given the semicentralist orientation of the Catholic right, Catholic Basque nationalism had a natural tendency to gravitate toward the anticentralist but also anti-Catholic left, though only partially and not with a clear conscience. Then, as the right triumphed over the left, nationalism also suffered the consequences.

The cultural work of the movement continued to expand, and by 1935 the Federation of Basque Schools had thirteen hundred children in Basque-language schools.[59] Yet this was a mere beginning, and in general propaganda work, as in overall support, nationalism accounted for only about one-third the activity in the four provinces.[60]

The year 1935 was a time of growing exasperation and radicalization for Basque nationalism. The Republican transition of 1931−33 had seemed to foster not merely a great growth in the strength and numbers of nationalism but also a modification in spirit and tactics that would encourage cooperation in the winning of a reasonable autonomy status. By 1935 this hope had been frustrated with respect both to the moderate left and moderate right. Failure had been due, among other things, to the inherent division of the Basque population and to the continuing maximalism of nationalist demands. The movement had to face severe contradictions. It could not resign itself to a nationalism based on Vizcaya and Guipúzcoa, the only two provinces in which it could hope to gain a workable majority. On the other hand, due to the nationalists' Catholicism, conservatism, and exclusiveness, the moderate left had long remained hostile and only changed its attitude when the Republican-Socialist coalition was losing its grasp on power. Conversely, moderate conservatives, who in some ways would have been more sympathetic, had become quite cool because of the growing identity between regional autonomy and leftism, because of the opposition to nationalism among traditionalist sectors of Basque Catholicism and because of the growing liberalization of tactics and political ideology of the movement. Nationalism was too conservative for the moderate left in 1931−32 and too liberal for the moderate right in 1934−35.

All hopes for further progress on the autonomy statute in 1935 were killed by the repression that followed the revolutionary insurrection. The Basque movement, in the eyes of moderate and conservative opinion, was at least partially identified with the rebels. Because of the suicidal policy of left Catalanism, regional autonomy was for the time being associated with subversion. On the other hand, Catalan autonomy was a legal fact and though aspects of the autonomous regime in Barcelona were temporarily taken under central control once more, Catalan autonomy was not abrogated. Moreover, political Catalanism was a broad popular movement represented by both a left and a moderate right of conservative liberals. The latter, the *Lliga Catalana*, acted as representative and defender of Catalan autonomy during the conservative reaction of 1935. The astute politicians of the *Lliga* even managed to establish themselves as official allies of the governing center-right coalition, gaining one cabinet seat in a government reorganization of mid-1935.

Basque nationalism altogether lacked such flexibility and diversity. The genuine Basque right was traditionalist and *españolista*. The PNV was in fact the Basque center and was no more liberal in its general orientation than the Catalan *Lliga*. But in its case there existed no fait accompli of Basque autonomy that it could take a conservative position in defending; rather, it was far outflanked to the right by its own Basque enemies, who stiffened government resistance against it.

This situation, plus the partially unjustified repression to which the movement was subject in 1934–35, pushed the movement farther to the left. Though the official position of the PNV was one of staunch opposition to what its leaders called the "Marxist revolution" of October, during 1935 local sections of the STV made common cause with the Socialist and Communist trade union groups in assisting workers incarcerated by the authorities.

Growing exasperation and radicalization led some Basque spokesmen to revive the extreme separatist and anti-Spanish tones of the early Sabino Arana. After a major meeting in San Sebastián on November 25, 1935, Basque Cortes deputies were quoted by the Spanish press as insisting that

It is not a question of regionalism or federalism; it is a question of the fatherland, and Euzkadi is the fatherland of the Basques. When they call you separatists, be even more separatist. . . . We want a Statute in order to follow the path of Cuba and the Philippines, the peoples who have become emancipated.[61]

This provoked an explosion by the extreme right in the Spanish Cortes. On December 5, José Calvo Sotelo, leader of the small protofascist Spanish nationalist *Bloque Nacional*, introduced a motion that the government actively repress Basque "separatist" agitation. He then read into the Cortes record some of Arana's most vicious statements,[62] while noting that Basque interests opposed construction of a new Bilbao-Santander rail line and that the *concierto económico* was much more valuable to the Basques than the economic provisions of the Catalan statute were to Catalonia.

The Basque deputies replied in white heat. Telesforo de Monzón declared that "The time will come when the mere autonomy that you will offer our people will not satisfy us. When all Basques demand more than mere autonomy, you will want to concede a small slice, but then it may be too late, as in the case of Cuba." Aguirre proclaimed that "Basque nationality" already held "sovereignty over its own destiny," and warned that "If you impede the solution of our aspirations, the responsibility will be yours," to which a centrist Radical deputy later replied, "For regionalism, understanding; for separatism, executions in the public square."[63] This livid session occurred less than ten days before the final breakdown of the regular Spanish Republican parliamentary system. After an extraparliamentary government was appointed on December 15, the country headed for new elections in February 1936.

The Spanish elections of 1936 became a sort of plebiscite between the left and right. The Popular Front stood for the legitimization of the 1934 insurrection and the establishment of a radical new leftist system. Its rightist enemies stood for the inauguration of a more conservative and at least semiauthoritarian regime. Neither of these goals was at first a viable alternative for Basque nationalism. The Popular Front was viewed as "Marxist," and was radically anti-Catholic, though it supported Basque and Galician autonomy. The right was officially Catholic, but also Spanish nationalist and willing to accept only extremely limited autonomy at best for Catalonia and the Basque country. Hence Basque nationalists decided that they had no alternative but to stand alone in the elections.

All the right-wing forces, CEDA, Carlist and monarchist, formed a counterrevolutionary electoral alliance in the Basque country, and through the church hierarchy strong pressure was placed on the nationalists to unite with these forces. The Vatican attempted direct suasion. The occasion for this was provided by negotiations begun between the Vatican and the PNV during 1935 with regard to church organization in the Basque region, currently divided among two different archdioceses (Burgos and Zaragoza). In mid-January 1936, the Vatican requested that a nationalist delegation come to Rome as soon as possible. Ten of the outstanding figures in the movement, led by Aguirre, arrived in Rome on January 18. Due to news of the death of George V, there was a delay of two more days in receiving the Basque delegation. During the interval, wealthy Catholic monarchists in Vizcaya learned of the visit and brought Catholic influence to bear urging the Vatican to force the nationalists to support the rightist list in the new elections. The delegation was received on January 20 by Monsignor Pizzardo, secretary general of the Vatican Secretary of State, who insisted that the forthcoming Spanish elections would be a struggle between "Christ and Satan." Unless the nationalists would sign a document agreeing to support the Catholic right, it would be impossible for the secretary of state to discuss the issue of ecclesiastical structure with them. The nationalists, determined to hold to their independent liberal position, insisted that such an interpretation was an oversimplification and that they could not accept church tutelage in party politics.[64] The visit was a complete failure. At approximately the same time, in response to a query from the Vatican, the vicar-general of the bishopric of Vitoria declared in an official note "that the nationalists were just as Catholic as the so-called right and that one could lawfully vote for either of them.[65]

The PNV's official slogans in the official campaign were "For Christian civilization! For Basque liberty! For social justice!"[66]

The first slogan differentiated the nationalists from the Popular Front,[67] the second reaffirmed their basic goal of autonomy, and the third slogan differentiated them from the rightist bloc. Care was taken to delineate the nationalist social program. It included major expansion of education, realization of the social Catholic goal of a family (rather than merely individual) salary, worker participation in industrial councils, fostering of new savings plans, broad extension of health and medical facilities, a basic system of relief for the poor, protection of family-enterprise fishing boats, and new measures to enable modest family farmers to remain on the land.[68] The PNV's social program was not directed toward general Spanish problems so much as specific grievances in the Basque country.

The STV received more publicity than before. According to official statistics, since its founding in 1920 it had grown to an organization of thirty-six thousand workers,[69] second only to the Socialist UGT in the two industrial provinces. In addition, the family-farmer organization of *nekazaris* included five thousand families in Guipúzcoa alone.

The independent stance of the nationalists meant that the electoral struggle in the Basque region was not polarized, as in most of Spain, but triangulated between left, right, and center. The nationalists and rightists both argued that the other had betrayed the main priorities of what should have been a common cause. For the right the chief issues were preservation of social order and defense of Catholicism; for the nationalists the chief issues were winning autonomy and the defense of Catholicism. They deemed the establishment of autonomy as perfectly compatible with—indeed a prerequisite for—preserving a more just and meliorized social order. The right, however, vehemently insisted that social order and Catholicism could not be preserved without all-Spanish unity. By 1936 regionalism was seen as the entering wedge of "communism" and the collapse of Spanish civilization. José María de Areilza, one of the most active and intelligent young leaders of the Vizcayan monarchist right, declared that

> At present no problem is of such importance as this issue [of Spanish national unity]. Not even the religious persecutions or the crisis of authority which the state currently suffers are comparable to nationalism. . . . The problem of unity precedes all others.[70]

The nationalists agreed that it would be disastrous if the Popular Front made it possible for a Communist deputy to be elected from Bilbao, but insisted that the only alternative lay in nationalism, since the monarchist right could not hope to mobilize enough votes in the urban industrial areas to win.[71] Moreover, while staunchly opposing the anti-Catholicism and revolutionism of the left, the PNV stressed the need for basic social reforms. Its spokesmen also partially supported the Popular Front's demands for amnesty for those arrested in the aftermath of the 1934 insurrection, for that would free several hundred nationalists. Nonetheless, there were basic differences between the nationalist and the leftist position, since the PNV specifically excluded those guilty of common criminal acts (assault, murder, destruction of property) and rejected the Popular Front's reverse morality whereby amnesty should be merely the prelude to a series of reprisals against the center and right for not having capitulated to the insurrection.[72]

As it turned out, the triangulation of candidacies reflected a surprisingly proportionate triangulation of political opinion in the Basque region as a whole. In Spain the Popular Front went on to a narrow plurality in the popular vote—about 1 percent—that through the disproportionate bloc voting system of the Republic was eventually translated into a crushing two-thirds majority in the Cortes. In the Basque region, however, the results were divided almost evenly: nine nationalists, eight rightists (all but one of them Carlists), and seven seats for the Popular Front. The rightist list swept to a total victory in Navarra, shutting out all other forces, and won a majority in Alava. Compared with the preceding elections of 1933, the nationalists lost votes in every province save Navarra, and there they had no chance anyway. Overall, the right increased its popular vote in the Basque country by well over 30,000 and the left also made significant gains, but the nationalist total declined by more than 28,000. Half of this loss occurred in Bilbao, where the triangulation of candidacies gave victory to the Popular Front, though it had less than half the vote.[73] During the first round of the voting, none of the three lists won a quorum in the provincial voting for Vizcaya and Guipúzcoa. Since the right had run second to the nationalists in both provinces, it withdrew during the second round of voting on March 1, enabling the PNV to pick up seven seats, with minority representation in both districts going to the left.

Though the nationalists ended up with a parliamentary majority of one for the three western provinces,[74] they had gained only 35 percent of the popular vote, an enormous decline from the 45 percent that they had mobilized in a smaller electorate three years earlier. When Navarra was included, the nationalist share of the all-Basque popular vote dwindled to a dismal 28 percent. The bulk of this loss went to the right, which since 1934 had been gaining the support of the extreme conservative and ultra-Catholic sectors of the nationalist vote. The proportionate leftist vote increased only slightly, but was much more effectively concentrated than in the previous contest. On the morrow of the first round of voting, the elections were recognized by the PNV leadership as a "defeat," attributable to the effects of the left-right polarization that had tended to squeeze out the nationalist center, abetted by the appeal of the leftist social and amnesty program in the industrial areas.[75]

Despite this great disappointment, all was not by any means lost. The PNV remained the strongest single party in the Basque region, and despite nationalism's independent stance, the new leftist parliament was pledged to give sympathetic attention to the problems of autonomy and further decentralization.

NOTES

1. The ORGA had been organized in 1929 as a loose amalgam of Galician Republicans and pro-Republican Galicianists. The tiny *Partido Nacionalista Gallego* (PNG), formed in 1918, was more conservative and stood apart from it. A broader *Federación Republicana Gallega* (FRG) was set up in 1930 after civil liberties were partially restored, but the ORGA retained its separate identity. During 1931 it tended more and more to become the personal organ of Santiago Casares Quiroga, the new Republican minister of the navy (later of the interior) and a chief lieutenant of the key Spanish left Republican leader, Azaña. It won two seats in the 1931 Cortes elections. In May 1931 an ORGA assembly approved an outline of a proposed regional autonomy statute for Galicia, but Casares Quiroga showed little interest in promoting Galicianism. The autonomist banner was then borne most prominently by a reorganized *Partido Galleguista*, which superseded the old PNG in December 1931. The ORGA, FRG and PG were each represented by two Cortes deputies (the PG leaders being Alfonso Rodríguez Castelao and Ramón Otero Pedrayo), but all six

Sabino de Arana y Goiri, founder of the modern-day Basque nationalist movement; he died at age 38 in 1903.

Some of the ninety-three founding members of the first *Euzkel-dun-Batzokija* (Basque Nationalist Center), meeting in Arrigor-riaga, Vizcaya, on July 8, 1895.

Celebration of *Aberri Eguna* (Day of the Fatherland) in Bilbao, Spring 1932.

José Antonio de Aguirre y Lekube, elected president of Euzkadi in October of 1936. Formerly a representative of the Basque Nationalist Party (PNV) to the Spanish parliament; he served as president of the Basque Government-in-Exile until his death in Paris in 1960.

Passport issued by the Basque government. This document was widely used by Basque refugees and accepted by many governments throughout the world.

Identification card for soldiers serving in the battalions provided by the Basque Nationalist Party to the army of Euzkadi.

Gudaris, or Basque soldiers, manning the Vizcayan front. Since the Basque army had little artillery, the machine gun was its most effective weapon.

Basque troops relaxing during a lull in the battle for Vizcaya.

Basque soldiers attending mass at the front lines. Chaplains were assigned to all battalions which were supplied to the army by the Basque Nationalist Party.

The town of Guernica after being bombed by German aviators on Monday, the town's market day, April 26, 1937.

The funeral, in Bilbao, of Captain Cándido Saseta, killed while serving as commander of the Basque troops in Asturias in 1937.

Evacuation of Basque children from Bilbao to France, on board the steamer *Habana* during the Spring of 1937.

Ramón Aldasoro, Republican minister and delegate of the Basque Government-in-Exile to Argentina, presiding at the naming of Plaza Guernica, a square in Buenos Aires.

Delegation of the Basque Government-in-Exile presents its case to the United Nations ca. 1947. Delegates Antón Irala (left) and Jesús Galíndez flank the president of the assembly.

Jesús María de Leizaola, president of the Basque Government-in-Exile since 1960. During the Spanish Civil War he served as minister of justice under President Aguirre.

Basque Nationalist coat of arms, which includes the coats of arms
of the individual Basque provinces of Alava, Vizcaya, Guipúzcoa,
Labourd, Navarra, and Soule. The caption *Jaun-Goikua eta
Lagi-Zaŕa* means "God and the old laws."

united behind the ORGA in parliament, due to the influence of Casares Quiroga in the government. However, after the ORGA leaders refused to support the principle of Basque autonomy, Castelao and Otero withdrew from the coalition. There is an interesting unpublished article by the former Galicianist deputy—and top votegetter on the 1936 Popular Front electoral list in Galicia—Prof. Emilio González López, "El movimiento autonomista gallego entre 1931 y 1936."

2. José Antonio de Aguirre y Lekube, *Entre la libertad y la revolución 1930-1935* (Bilbao, 1935), 17–18. Aguirre's memoir constitutes the principal chronicle of Basque nationalist politics from 1931 to 1935.

3. The ANV saw the initial pro-Catalanist stance of the Republican leaders as having profound implications for the Basque cause. Cf. "Una referencia detallada del Pacto de San Sebastián," *La Libertad* (Bilbao), May 17, 1931. Its first statement after the change of government, a pamphlet called "A los ciudadanos de Euzkadi" (Apr. 17, 1931), stressed the opportunities offered by a thorough-going new democratic regime.

At the same time, however, the ANV lost its financial interests in the publishing company that had begun to bring out its new Bilbao daily, *Acción Vasca*, and was temporarily forced to cease publication. A private memorandum of June 11, 1931, by an ANV leader, José Domingo de Arana, complained bitterly that "the PNV, which has become a mortal enemy of everything that we propose, has taken command of the entire nationalist press." Bilbao Legajo 195, JSD. The PNV members were particularly incensed that the ANV had accepted participation in the new *comisiones gestoras* that were imposed on the Basque provinces by the central government without holding new elections.

4. According to a subsequent PNV tabulation. Bilbao Legajo 199, JSD.

5. Meanwhile a separate provincial autonomy project for Guipúzcoa was drawn up by a small federalist group there, but this drew no support.

6. Aguirre, 49.

7. R. M. Blinkhorn, "The Carlist Movement in Spain 1931–1937" (Ph.D. diss., Oxford University, 1970), 76–77.

8. The coalition system sometimes made it difficult to categorize individual candidates. Thus García Venero, in his *Nacionalismo vasco*, 495, gives a total of six nationalists, four Carlists, and five Catholics, and is technically correct in listing as Catholic Independents two deputies, one of whom was closely associated with the nationalists and the other with the Carlists.

9. According to Aguirre, 96.

10. One reply was a defensive pamphlet by Xavier Azcoitia, *Defensa de la obra de los vascos. ¡Cavernícolas, cavernícolas!* (Bilbao, 1931).

11. There are two versions of this. Aguirre, 152–53, insists that the initiative came entirely from the monarchists and that the PNV had little or no interest in such a venture. Orgaz's version emphasized that the conspirators were unwilling to meet the maximalist regional demands of the PNV, according to Sierra Bustamante, 124–30. Blinkhorn, 115, suggests that the discrepancies may be less than they appear, since the main contacts on both sides were arranged by secondary figures.

12. Jaime del Burgo, *Requetés en Navarra antes del Alzamiento* (Pamplona, 1954).

13. The different stands taken by municipal representatives nominally represented the following population totals:

In favor of a Basque-Navarrese statute	304,351
In favor of a Navarrese statute alone	2,808
In favor simply of "regional autonomy"	2,561
Against any statute	30,290

El Pensamiento Navarro, Aug. 11, 1931, in Blinkhorn, 113.

14. Aguirre, 139.

15. *Euzkadi*, Oct. 16, 1931. Further references are given in Domingo de Arrese, *El País Vasco y las Constituyentes de la Segunda República* (Madrid, 1931).

16. Aguirre, 160.

17. As quoted in *La Gaceta Regional* (Salamanca), Aug. 4, 1937.

18. Aguirre, 189.

19. *El Pensamiento Navarro*, Jan. 19–22, 1932, in Blinkhorn, 147.

20. Blinkhorn, 159.

21. Aguirre, 194.

22. Aguirre wrote to the moderate Catalanist leader Cambó on Jan. 27, 1932, "There will be no difficulty from the right in the Basque country. The uncertainty lies with the left, which is now compromised with the statute because they conceive the new draft to be their own project. That is not because of its content or the zeal that they feel for it but rather because the left considers it a triumph over the right, which according to them failed in the presentation of the Estella Statute. To us all this matters little; what is really important is the statute itself. . . ." Aguirre went on to condemn the Republican government's anti-Catholic policy as "sectarian" and "immoral," and declared that arbitrary actions by the present cabinet were "repeating the maneuvers of the dictatorship, which we still cannot say has completely ended."

During that same month of January Aguirre received numerous requests to make personal appearances on behalf of the reorganization of the Catholic right in Spain. Letters came from José Ma. Gil Robles, from the Catholic right of Valencia (DRV) and from such Catalan areas as Gerona. Bilbao Legajo 10, JSD.

23. There is a discussion in Aguirre, 196−217.

24. *El Pensamiento Navarro*, June 17, 1932, in Blinkhorn, 165.

25. Blinkhorn, 166.

26. Aguirre, 235−36.

27. *Euzkadi*, June 21, 1932; Aguirre, 285−86; Sarrailh de Ihartza, 449. It is interesting to note that a somewhat similar problem of integrating a region obtained in the Levant, where a three-province *anteproyecto* for regional autonomy was but feebly supported in Alicante and Castellón. Cucó, *El valencianisme polític*, 202−04.

28. *El Pensamiento Navarro*, July 10, 1932, in Blinkhorn, 171.

29. Oriol's clearest statement of Alavese opposition was made in *El Heraldo Alavés* (Vitoria), July 27, 1932.

30. Domingo de Arrese, the ultraconservative Catholic editor of *El Heraldo Alavés*, was sympathetic to nationalism. Early in 1932, in his *Bajo la ley de Defensa de la República* (Madrid, 1933), 28, he had written that the PNV and Carlists were brothers. However, by mid−1932 Oriol had imposed a policy of hostility toward nationalism. On July 9, 1932, Arrese wrote to the Vizcayan nationalist leader, Manuel de Eguileor, "Pardon me for not inserting the article 'Pro Nabara y Araba' that I received. You already know Oriol's opinion and that he would not forgive me for its appearance. . . . Some day I will tell you how much I have suffered from the intransigence of certain elements who do not allow me to develop in the newspaper the policy of profound cordiality that ought to reign between the two political parties of the Basque country. Both the Bishop of Vitoria and José Antonio de Aguirre are well acquainted with the difficulties of my position." Bilbao Legajo 186, JSD.

31. Joaquín Arrarás, *Historia de la segunda República española* (Madrid 1964), II, 17.

32. Ibid., II, 15.

33. Ibid., II, 18.

34. Published in *Euzkadi*, Sept. 23, 1932.

35. According to Aguirre, 245.

36. According to a tabulation by the PNV. Bilbao Legajo 199, JSD.

37. *ABC* (Madrid), May 5, 1933.

38. The most detached attitude, though one not shared by most Spaniards, was expressed in Ramón de la Mar's *El separatismo vasco-catalán favorece a España* (Bilbao, 1933). La Mar, who seems to have been a sort of bourgeois libertarian, argued that there was little reason to

oppose Catalan or Basque separatism, since the Catalans and Basques benefitted more from Spain and its market and tariffs than vice versa. Basques never paid their fair share of Spanish taxes, while Basque and Catalan industrial products could be replaced either by cheaper foreign imports or by industrializing interior Spain.

39. The percentage of municipal council votes for court representatives from the various parties in the Basque region was as follows:

	Carlist	PNV	Republican-Socialist	Radicals
Alava	52.	37.	11.	.0
Guipúzcoa	30.5	57.	12.5	.0
Vizcaya	21.	57.	22.	.0
All three provinces	32.3	51.3	16.3	.0
Navarra	77.5	.0	15.5	7.

SOURCE: *El Pensamiento Navarro*, Sept. 5, 1933; *El Siglo Futuro*, Sept. 4, 5, 7 1933, in Blinkhorn, 244.

40. *El Pensamiento Alavés*, Oct. 30, 1933, in Aguirre, 395. The nationalist position was that recent changes in the Spanish tax structure, with more direct and individual taxes, had outflanked the usefulness of the *concierto*. PNV spokesmen later presented figures to show that by 1934 the taxes paid through the *concierto* amounted to only 16.67 percent of all taxes paid by Basques with only 12.77 percent being raised for local use. They also claimed that in the limited categories covered by the *concierto*, Basques paid a per capita average of 99.78 pesetas compared with the general Spanish average of 66.78 pesetas. *Euzkadi*, Nov. 23, 1934.

Such figures, of course, would require objective verification. Many in the Basque provinces were still convinced that the *concierto* provided major advantages. Cf. Martín de Jústiz, *En defensa del Concierto Económico del País Vasco* (San Sebastián, 1936).

41. The results in the popular voting were:

ALAVA	VOTES	%		VOTES	%
Carlists	20,718	52	Left Coalition	4,856	12
Nationalists	11,525	29	Radical/Socialists	98	0.2
Radicals	2,382	06	Communists	109	0.2

Percentage of voter participation: 71.68

GUIPÚZCOA	VOTES	%		VOTES	%
Nationalists	60,860	36	Socialists	60,860	36
Rightist Union	31,925	19	Left Republicans	10,374	06
Radicals	3,458	02			

Percentage of voter participation: 78.08

NAVARRA	VOTES	%		VOTES	%
Carlists	107,529	71	Socialists	20,584	14
Nationalists	13,937	09	Left Republicans	2,851	02
Radicals	5,918	04	Communists	1,334	01

Percentage of voter participation: 80.59

VIZCAYA (Capital)	VOTES	%		VOTES	%
Nationalists	57,239	41	Socialists and		
Rightists	20,049	15	Republicans	50,467	37
			Communists	9,139	07
			Radical-Socialists	1,093	01

Percentage of voter participation: 77.95

VIZCAYA (Province)	VOTES	%		VOTES	%
Nationalists	39,629	57	Left Coalition	9,484	14
Rightists	19,679	28	Communists	503	01

Percentage of voter participation: 78.18

SOURCE: Javier Tusell et al., *Las elecciones del Frente Popular* (Madrid, 1971), II, 308–40.

42. An assembly of Galician municipal government representatives had met in Santiago de Compostela in December 1932 to consider procedures for drawing up a Galician autonomy statute. Galicia was the only region where the autonomy movement was strongly supported by the Socialists; this was due in part to the latter's weakness there but perhaps more to the fact that Galicianism was almost exclusively a movement of the middle-class left, lacking the conservative tinge of the Basque movement or of major sectors of Catalan and Valencian regionalism. The ORGA's leader, Santiago Casares Quiroga, was one of the chief lieutenants of Azaña and Republican minister of the interior in 1932–33. However, he identified primarily with all-Spanish Republicanism and had little personal interest in Galicianism per se. Since the movement was quite weak, the Republicans gave scant attention to the Galician autonomy issue in 1933, and in the elections the right carried three of the four provinces of that region. In La Coruña the rightist José Calvo Sotelo, former finance minister of the Primo de Rivera regime and an ardent foe of Galicianism, topped the winning majority list while Casares came out at the bottom of the minority ticket. Subsequently the ORGA was fused with the new Republican Left party of Manuel Azaña, though it did not lose its regional identity in Galicia. González López, "El movimiento autonomista gallego."

43. On the Catalan agrarian problem, see the excellent study by Albert Balcells, *El problema agrari a Catalunya 1890-1936* (Barcelona, 1968),

and J. de Camps i Arboix, *Història de l'agricultura catalana* (Barcelona, 1969), 207–70.

44. The ideology of the "Jagi" group and its leader are expounded in F. Sarraill, *La cuestión vasca* (np., n.d.).

45. For a comparison of a similar proposal under the dictatorship, cf. Primo de Rivera's National Assembly remarks of Jan. 30, 1929, on the need for a *desgravación de vinos* in the Basque country, in *Intervenciones en la Asamblea Nacional del General Primo de Rivera* (Madrid, 1930), 180–82.

46. *Euzkadi*, July 6, 1934, announced that approximately 200 municipal councils, representing 823,216 of the 881,000 inhabitants of the three provinces, had agreed to choose representatives for a joint commission to defend the fiscal structure.

47. Arrarás, III, 390–91.

48. According to the statistics in Ibid., 392–93.

49. *Euzkadi*, Sept. 21, 1934.

50. *Euzkadi*, Sept. 22, 1934.

51. Ibid., Sept. 23, 1934.

52. Aguirre, 529–33.

53. The revolutionary insurrection in Catalonia and its background are treated in Manuel Cruells, *El 6 d'octubre a Catalunya* (Barcelona, 1970), and Pabón, *Cambó*, III, 291–408. On Asturias, see Ricardo de la Cierva, *Historia de la Guerra civil española* (Madrid, 1969), I, 387–430.

54. Aguirre, 544.

55. Ibid., 545.

56. There are descriptions in Arrarás, II, 519–24, and in Francisco Aguado Sánchez, *La revolución de octubre de 1934* (Madrid, 1972), 407–25.

57. *Euzkadi*, Nov. 17, 1934.

58. Ibid., Oct. 13, 1934.

59. Aguirre, 573.

60. In partial data for the years 1933–35, Sierra Bustamante, 218, indicated that the five principal nationalist newspapers published 1,016,479 kilograms of paper per year while the eleven leading nonnationalist papers published 2,226, 916 kilograms per year.

61. Arrarás, III, 256–57.

62. Such as: "To love that which is Basque you must hate Spain." The Spanish are "the most vile and contemptible race of Europe." "The closer is our triumph the nearer Spain comes to prostration and ruin," and so on. Ibid. Cf. Aurelio Joaniquet, *Calvo Sotelo* (Madrid, 1939), 113–15, 228.

63. Ibid., III, 258.

64. There are several harmonious accounts of this visit by members of the delegation and their associates. The most explicit are those by Aguirre and by F. J. de Landaburu in the documentary collection, *El Pueblo vasco frente a la Cruzada franquista* (Toulouse, 1966), 106–22, followed by an anonymous diary of the visit by "L.", 123–47. There is also a brief statement by Manuel de Irujo at the beginning of his "La Guerra Civil en Euzkadi antes del Estatuto," Bayonne, Jan. 6, 1938. (Unpublished MSs, Bolloten Collection, Hoover Institution.) There is a doctoral thesis on the Basque ecclesiastical problem by J. Gutiérrez Alvarez, "La cuestión eclesiástica vasca entre 1931 y 1936" (Ph.D. diss., University of Madrid, 1970) that I have been unable to consult.

65. Arrarás, IV, 81.

66. *Euzkadi*, Feb. 4, 1936.

67. The ANV had moved steadily to the left during the past five years without notably expanding its meager following. In 1936 it formed part of the Popular Front in the Basque country, though by that time its original leaders had begun to feel themselves somewhat *desbordados* by the climate of radicalism in their minuscule party.

68. *Euzkadi*, Feb. 11, 1936, and the pamphlet *La labor del Partido Nacionalista Vasco en materia religiosa y social* (Bilbao, Feb., 1936).

69. This was broken down as follows:

Vizcaya	18,000
Guipúzcoa	15,000
Alava	3,000
Navarra	1,000

70. Quoted in *Euzkadi*, Jan. 31, 1936.

71. The PNV announced that it had a total of 93 different political and social centers in the Bilbao district alone, with a total of 12,550 registered members, including 5,650 in the women's auxiliary EAB. Ibid., Feb. 1 and 8, 1936. These figures do not include the STV membership.

72. Ibid., Feb. 7, 1936.

73. Official results of the popular vote totals for the Spanish elections of 1936 are not available. There is, however, an excellent study of the electoral campaign and general results for all of Spain by Javier Tusell et al., cited in fn. 41.

Various slightly conflicting statistics have been cited for the Basque provinces. Despite certain discrepancies, the figures given by Sierra Bustamante, 216, appear to be the most nearly accurate:

	Right 1933 Votes	%	Nationalists 1933 Votes	%	Left 1933 Votes	%
Alava	20,718	52	11,524	29	7,445	19
Guipúzcoa	31,925	25	59,044	46	37,094	29
Navarra	106,555	71	13,937	09	29,269	20
Vizcaya (province)	19,679	29	39,630	58	9,499	14
Vizcaya (capital)	20,037	16	57,314	45	50,475	39
Totals	198,914	39	181,449	35	133,782	26

	Right 1936 Votes	%	Nationalists 1936 Votes	%	Left 1936 Votes	%
Alava	24,701	57	8,958	21	9,521	22
Guipúzcoa	45,153	33	50,108	37	41,193	30
Navarra	111,442	69	14,799	09	34,987	22
Vizcaya (province)	24,726	35	36,013	51	10,424	15
Vizcaya (Capital)	30,274	21	43,548	30	69,684	49
Totals	236,296	43	153,426	28	165,809	30

This tabulation largely coincides with the results gleaned from newspapers by José Miguel de Azaola, *Vasconia y su destino* (Madrid, 1972), I, 543–46.

74. The results by party and district were:

Popular Front		Right		PNV	
Bilbao:	2 Socialists 1 Communist 1 Republican	Navarra:	4 Carlists 2 CEDA 1 Independent	Guipúzoca:	4
				Vizcaya:	3
Guipúzcoa:	1 Socialist 1 Republican	Alava:	1 Carlist 8	Bilbao:	2 9
Alava:	1 Republican 7				

75. *Euzkadi*, Feb. 18, 1936. The abstentionist behavior of the *Jagi* group may also have been a minor factor. Radical young nationalists rejected participation in the civic processes of the Spanish system and protested the PNV's failure to take an extreme stand in favor of outright independence.

6

CIVIL WAR: THE
AUTONOMIST BREAKTHROUGH

The Popular Front victory in February 1936 led to formation of a minority middle-class left Republican cabinet under Azaña. This government rested on the votes of the Popular Front parties but did not and could not lead them. Rather, it followed the spiralling trend of strikes, street fights, labor violence, and land occupations that stretched into the spring and early summer, creating what some historians have called a "pre-revolutionary situation" and leading to the absolute polarization of Spanish politics. After February 1936 the Republican constitutional system entered a process of dissolution.

In the early stages of this process the extent to which it would go was not foreseen by most of those active in politics. Basque nationalists continued to remain as apprehensive as ever about anti-Catholicism, but they grasped that the broad new leftist orientation of Spanish government involved the fundamental alteration of power relations and constitutional structure that could finally make autonomy a reality. On April 15 deputies of all parties from the three western Basque provinces submitted to the Cortes the autonomy statute that had been approved in the plebiscite of October 1933, and on the following day a new parliamentary commission was appointed to deliberate on the project. Indalecio Prieto was named chairman and Aguirre secretary.

The nationalist press claimed a new growth of support for the movement, citing an increase of four thousand members for the STV and in Guipúzcoa one thousand more families in the *nekazari* organization.[1] Work on the statute by the new commission proceeded about as rapidly as the disturbed state of affairs permitted. On May 12 the commission approved the validity of the 1933 plebiscite, with only the CEDA representative, Serrano Súñer, abstaining and also approved the validity of the three-province statute (including Alava), with only Serrano Súñer and the Alavese Carlist Oriol voting no.[2] Eight days later it agreed on a formula for simplifying the text in order to win speedier approval[3] and on May 29 approved the arrangements for each of the three provinces to enjoy provincial autonomy within the statute.[4]

The PNV leadership cautioned that the "statute is not nationalist" because of the limitations that it placed on full autonomy[5] but hailed the commission's progress and by the beginning of June believed that the completion of the work was at hand. By June 6 only three articles of the text of the statute remained to be approved.[6] Twelve days later the small Popular Front forces of Navarra—which included the tiny Navarrese ANV group—petitioned the government to include Navarra in the proposed legislation.[7] On July 7 the Republican council of ministers approved in principle the continuation of the basic features of the *concierto económico* under the new system,[8] and there was an expectation that the legislation might be completed before the summer parliamentary vacation.

In its parliamentary weakness the right did all it could to slow the commission's labors, insisting that if this measure were approved all other regions would have equal claims to autonomy. On July 10 the remaining questions were scheduled to be taken up in cabinet, hopefully with a date to be set for submission to parliamentary ratification, but other matters pushed them off the agenda.[9] On the following day, the rightist parliamentary delegation demanded full details concerning taxes and the distribution of state income, both under the present arrangement and the proposed autonomy legislation. This information was not at that point available. Two days later occurred the assassination of the rightist leader Calvo Sotelo and the breakup of the Spanish polity.

Deliberations on the Basque statute were accompanied by autonomist agitation in half a dozen other regions.

On May 2 representatives of the three Aragonese provinces met in Caspe; on April 20 the Cedista-Agrarians began to talk of a statute for Castilla (and another regionalist offshoot could be seen in León); on May 9 the mayor of Burgos endorsed a statute for Old Castilla; on May 29 another for Asturias was requested in Gijón; and on June 6, amid a new flowering of Andalusian autonomist dreams, the municipal government of Huelva proposed regional annexation of Murcia and Badajoz, and even threatened to withdraw its own province from Andalusia and unite it with an autonomous Extremadura.[10]

The small Valencianist movement had, however, split into several weak fragments; the Galicianist movement, on the other hand, gained force from the support of Manuel Portela Valladares, interim centrist prime minister in the winter of 1935–36, and the Popular Front victory in three of the four Galician provinces. The Republican Left party became the strongest force in that region, and cooperated with the four Galician autonomist deputies that were elected, though the most moderate of these, Otero Pedrayo, refused to be associated with the Popular Front.[11] The Galician left Republican Casares Quiroga succeeded Azaña as Republican prime minister early in May and in the meantime a Galician statute was being readied. It was submitted to a regional plebiscite on June 28. The right advocated abstention and most of the population there had never been mobilized by the autonomy movement, but an overwhelming majority was achieved. The right charged that tens of thousands of votes had merely been counted as yes without having been cast; Galicia had enjoyed in previous times one of the most deeply rooted systems of *caciquismo* in the peninsula. At any rate, the newly approved statute was presented to the minister by a delegation of elected Galician officials on July 17, the day that the civil war broke out.

The revolutionary extreme left went far beyond the middle-

class autonomist movements in seeking to dissolve the state structure of Spain. The official position of the mass anarcho-syndicalist
federation (CNT) was that the Spanish state must be replaced by a
series of locally and regionally federated Spanish communes. The
Socialist party remained semicentralist, admitting only limited
autonomy, but the small Spanish Communist party, which was
growing by leaps and bounds in the spring of 1936, stood for the
total disintegration of Spain as a nation or civic entity. As a tactical
ploy it advocated total independence for any region that wanted to
break away. The nominal Communist Party of Catalonia was
organized completely apart from the regular Spanish Communist
party, though the Communist Party of *Euzkadi* simply formed an
"autonomous" branch of the Communist party of Spain. The
Basque Communist chiefs, led by Jesús Larrañaga, were genuine
Basques and even given to speaking Basque among themselves in
private.

Archenemy of Stalinist Communism on the left was the small
Leninist but anti-Stalinist POUM of Catalonia, which stood for
regionalist and national Communism. One of the few things on
which they agreed with the Stalinists was that "Spain is a fiction. It
is not a federal state that should be built, but a federation of states
with complete sovereignty. . . ."[12]

Despite frenzied endorsement of regional independence by
the extreme left, the PNV endeavored to keep its distance from
both left and right throughout the ominous spring of 1936. On the
national level it drew increasing fire from the latter because of the
acceleration of the autonomist legislation. Church leaders found it
hard to overcome their displeasure with the recent nationalist
electoral tactics. In April the primate of the church in Spain, Isidro
Cardinal Gomá, sent a long report to the Vatican secretary of state,
Pacelli, in which he declared that he would not categorically
condemn Basque nationalism but noted what he termed its "dem-
agogic excesses" and its failure to support the common Catholic
cause.[13] Gomá also condemned Bishop Múgica of Vitoria for
having stated that Basque Catholics might vote either for
nationalism or the Catholic right with equally good conscience.
Múgica privately defended himself in a letter to Pacelli stressing
the Catholic fidelity and orthodoxy of the nationalists, saying that

allegations against them were either incorrect, exaggerated, or unproven and adding that in the three western provinces the majority of practicing Catholics were nationalist.[14]

Though some of the young militant radicals in the nationalist movement were willing to make common cause with the revolutionary left, ordinary lower-middle-class Basque nationalists continued to regard the latter with extreme aversion and even fear. The party leadership had even vetoed participation in the special national balloting for presidential electors (*compromisarios*) that elected Azaña to the Republican presidency, saying that such maneuvers had nothing to do with the Basque cause.[15] Hostility of revolutionary syndicates to the STV flared into the open again early in June when CNT and UGT workers declared a boycott against ships in the port of Vigo carrying STV crewmen. Though leftist leaders quickly intervened to recognize the principle of free syndicalization,[16] this was another indication of the constant tendency of the left to view Basque nationalists as, to quote one of their favorite epithets, "reactionary."

Since the spring of 1936 was full of constant alarms about leftist outbursts and violent strikes, rightist leaders in the Basque provinces were eager to assure the cooperation of nationalists in their plans to resist a revolutionary takeover. Nationalist leaders by no means discounted the danger of leftist revolution. It is alleged by hostile commentators that the former PNV deputy and Guipúzcoan leader Telesforo Monzón met with rightist representatives in San Sebastián at the beginning of April and dickered for arms for a Basque militia.[17] Though this particular meeting cannot be confirmed with the evidence currently available, there is ample testimony about subsequent arms negotiations with the right in Guipúzcoa.

One nationalist leader has testified anonymously:

> Two months before the revolution [apparently about mid-May] José de Ariztimuno, José M. de Lasarte, Iñaki de Lizaso, José M. de Benegas and myself met [in Guipúzcoa] to draw up plans for a secret organization apart from the PNV "in order to form an armed Basque militia that could go into action as soon as the Communist revolution that we thought imminent broke out." . . . Our organization was of a strictly

defensive type, . . . with the sole aim of saving the Basque country from "Communist chaos." . . .[18]

Another has declared that

This public fear of revolution was exploited by the right to raise money to organize resistance. In Guipúzcoa representatives of the Gipuzko BB [PNV provincial committee], the Carlists, the Falangists, the monarchists, and the CEDA met. Their joint action was to be directed solely to the defense of religious interests in the event of an attempted Communist coup. . . . The Gipuzko BB bought arms (pistols) in Eibar and in France that were distributed among these associated groups. These purchases were made with funds provided the GBB by the right. I myself delivered 50 pistols to rightist groups, but the nationalists did not receive their fair share in the distribution of arms. . . . Moreover, Fausto Gaiztarro, on behalf of the parties of the Rightist bloc, proposed the formation of a broader group led by army officers. Since this was contrary to the original agreement, the nationalists refused and went their own way.[19]

The nationalist leaders, like their counterparts in other parties, heard increasing rumors about a pre-emptive coup by the military, but since most of the public aggression came from the left, they were not fully prepared when the army revolt began on July 17. On the evening of that fateful day, one of the top nationalist leaders in Guipúzcoa, Manuel Irujo, emphasized to the civil governor of that province the PNV's opposition to authoritarian interference by the military in constitutional government. This declaration was then repeated by the Guipuzcoan governor in a radio broadcast at San Sebastián on the 18th. It caught other Basque leaders by surprise, and a special meeting of the *Euzkadi-Buru-Batzar*, the party's national council, was called in San Sebastián on the afternoon of the same day. The entire country was at that point prey to the most diverse rumors and no one knew exactly what was going on. Aguirre opined that the whole affair might be a stratagem of the weak left Republican government to discredit the right and consolidate the present cabinet. Therefore the PNV leadership agreed to publish a notice on the following day disauthorizing Irujo's declaration in so far as it might be taken to indicate support for the

Popular Front regime in a contest with the right. The desire of the party's leadership was as always to maintain neutrality in the left-right power struggle in Spain.[20]

From the following day, July 19, 1936, that opportunity would be permanently denied the nationalists. In Navarra and Alava the rightist Spanish rebels seized control; depending on individual cases, they either carried or forced the nationalists with them. In nearly all the urban and industrial centers of Vizcaya and Guipúzcoa, revolutionary worker groups began to take over the streets in force that same day and proceeded to arm themselves as speedily as possible. In most cases the middle-class left Republican authorities made common cause with them. Though few guessed its dimensions, civil war had begun throughout Spain and no middle ground was permitted. If the nationalists tried to completely dissociate themselves from the Popular Front forces in Vizcaya and Guipúzcoa, they would be suppressed along with the rightist groups. Thus the neutrality notice in San Sebastián was never published and, after the main group of leaders returned to Bilbao on the evening of July 18, they began to realize that the PNV would have to follow Irujo's position in order to preserve its freedom of action and also its hope for autonomy. As further news came in, it was clearer that a major military revolt was erupting, and that more was at stake than a mere strategem of the Azaña-Casares Quiroga regime. The PNV came down on the side of Republican constitutionality. On July 19, the PNV leadership declared in *Euzkadi* that the burgeoning struggle was one between "civil rights [ciudadanía] and fascism, Republic and monarchy," and consequently that "its principles lead it to come down on the side of civil rights and the Republic in consonance with the democratic and republican regime of our people during its centuries of liberty."

The problem that had made nationalist leaders hesitate was that by July 1936 civil rights existed only for leftists, and the Republican constitution was being progressively abandoned by the Republican government. Catholics were being openly persecuted in other parts of Republican Spain. Moreover, the civil war marked the beginning of violent social revolution in nearly all sectors of the Republican zone, including wholesale executions of nonleftists, especially of priests.

The civil war was not merely an internecine conflict between Spaniards as a whole, but also a civil war between the Basques of the four provinces. Navarra immediately became the strongest bulwark of the insurgent Spanish nationalist cause. It was taken over by army rebels under General Mola, supported unanimously by the Carlists, who even before the war had organized eighty-four hundred men in Navarra, sixteen hundred of them in militia groups,[21] albeit largely unarmed and untrained. In his official declaration of martial law on July 19, Mola declared that what remained of foral privileges in Navarra would be completely upheld. The leadership of the PNV in Navarra hesitated no more than twenty-four hours before repudiating the position taken by the top party spokesmen in Bilbao. On July 20 they issued a statement saying that the PNV of Navarra "does not support the Republican government in the present conflict."[22]

In Alava, where the military insurgents had also seized control, Basque leaders were placed under heavy pressure to support the rebels. On July 18 they had attempted to establish contact with the small middle-class Republican group in Vitoria to discuss resistance to a military takeover but failed to organize anything. As soon as the local army garrison in Vitoria seized power on July 19, its commander dispatched troops to close the nationalist offices in the city. The new rightist civil governor appointed by the garrison commander assured Alavese nationalist leaders that the military revolt in that region was Basque and regionalist, but the nationalist provincial leaders would go no further than to announce their neutrality. The former PNV Cortes deputy Javier de Landáburu and two other representatives were arrested on July 20 and forced to write a notice urging Basque nationalists in Alava to respect the new military authorities. Though this note was published on July 22,[23] Landáburu was arrested once more four days later and on July 30 was forced to write another note asking Basque nationalists in Alava to "support the [military] movement."[24]

Landáburu may have been on the verge of throwing in the sponge to the insurgents. On August 3 he and another Alavese nationalist who had joined the rebels wrote to Aguirre and the Vizcayan leaders that

. . . At the request of very respectable friends . . . (including the bishop of Vitoria), we have had several interviews with the local military commanders [of Alava], who are very worried about Vizcaya and Guipúzcoa and surprised to find the nationalists there on the side of the Reds, when so many sacred and fundamental things separate us from them. When the time comes, they will have to conquer those provinces by force and regret having Basque nationalists for enemies.

. . . If the nationalists limit themselves to protecting people and property so long as the Reds are in control there and do not take up arms against the army, they will be respected when the army takes over that zone.

. . . We are concerned to have your rapid reply so that we can justify you before the military authorities. Today we can intercede on your behalf; after the army takes over there it would be too late.[25]

These messages were followed by a series of declarations from local groups and councils of Basque nationalists in Navarra and Alava proclaiming their support for the insurgents and also declaring the dissolution of their local organizations. For several weeks the insurgents hoped for a change in policy by the main body of nationalists in Vizcaya and Guipúzcoa. However, after learning that the latter had firmly decided to continue to resist, Landáburu went into hiding on August 13 and later escaped from the insurgent zone. It was not until September 18 that Mola finally declared the forcible dissolution of Basque nationalist organizations. In the meantime a not inconsiderable number of nationalist youth in Navarra and Alava had volunteered for the Carlist and Spanish Falangist militia.

Complete order prevailed in Vizcaya, where no army revolt occurred. There the local garrison battalion remained loyal to the nominal authorities and was incorporated as a unit into the anti-insurgent struggle. In Guipúzcoa, however, which bordered on Navarra, the situation was more uncertain. In the capital, San Sebastián, an abortive revolt by garrison troops was eventually crushed by militia from the revolutionary groups (mostly Socialist and anarchosyndicalists), assisted by loyal Civil Guards. There the local PNV leaders played a moderating role, finally convincing the rebel commanders to surrender instead of fighting to the death.

Since regularly constituted Republican authority immediately collapsed almost everywhere in the so-called Republican zone, a series of ad hoc multiparty leftist *juntas* sprang up to assume the functions of local government. Only in Vizcaya and Guipúzcoa did a nonleftist party, the PNV, participate. In those two provinces a series of four *juntas* were formed: one in Vizcaya, one in eastern Guipúzcoa based on San Sebastián, one in the Eibar district of western Guipúzcoa that was dominated by the Socialists, and a fourth in the Azpeitia district of central Guipúzcoa to cover the gap in between the other two. The San Sebastián *junta*, which called itself the *Junta de Defensa de Guipúzcoa*, was composeed of two Socialists, two nationalists, one anarcho-syndicalist (CNT), one Communist, and one middle-class left Republican. The streets of San Sebastián and Irún were, however, dominated by uncontrolled militia squads or gangs of Socialists and anarcho-syndicalists,[26] who seized and shot scores of Catholics and non-nationalist conservatives. The key post of Interior Affairs in the San Sebastián *junta* was given to Telesforo Monzón, a top nationalist leader in the province, in an effort to provide some guarantee of public order. He found that impossible, however, and three successive PNV representatives resigned that position in the San Sebastián *junta* within forty-five days. Even rightist prisoners incarcerated in official prisons were not safe from lynch mobs, since revolutionaries carried out massacres in the jails at Ondarreta (San Sebastián). Guadalupe (Fuenterrabía), and Tolosa. Since the revolutionary militia had seized nearly all available arms, the nationalists were helpless to prevent these atrocities.[27]

The ad hoc alliance with the revolutionary left in Vizcaya and Guipúzcoa was in some respects a leap in the dark. On certain issues, the PNV probably had more in common with the insurgent Spanish Nationalists of Mola and Franco, sharing with them strong Catholicism and an emphasis on social order and discipline. The main point that the PNV had in common with the revolutionary left—since the middle-class Republican left no longer counted— was a determination to break up the existing structure of the Spanish state, but the rebels in their own way had a similar goal. Even the aim of a federalized and democratic state was not a true common value with the revolutionary left, for the most dynamic and effective force among the latter, the Communists, were determined to impose a more centralized, if only partially revolutionary, dictatorship as soon as possible.

It was not surprising that the nationalists were slower to mobilize paramilitary forces than were the parties of the extreme left. The latter began to form in both Vizcaya and Guipúzcoa on July 19. In Vizcaya PNV volunteers were serving as guards on July 23, but the first call for volunteers did not go out until the next day. It is not clear how quick was the response, since the first PNV militia parade in Bilbao was not held until August 5.[28] In San Sebastián the first formal call for PNV militia volunteers was not issued until July 29.[29]

The insurgents revealed much greater offensive capacity. During the first week of the revolt no less than eight small columns, were organized in Navarra—composed of several small regular army units and a few Falangists but above all of Carlist *Requetés*— that moved into southern and eastern Guipúzcoa. At first the leftist militia leaders in northern Guipúzcoa were self-confident, for they had at least twice the manpower as well as "superiority in artillery"[30] and better defensive position. However, the superior leadership, skill, and cohesion of the Spanish Nationalists— though most of the latter were also militia volunteers—brought a rapid penetration. On August 5 the three easternmost columns moved into northeastern Guipúzcoa to cut the border with France. Three days later, in view of the gravity of the situation, the PNV leadership in Guipúzcoa called for the formation of a *Euzko-Gudarostea*, or Basque army, that would be composed of all able-bodied male party members and united with similar formations in Vizcaya. However, this appeal was not rapidly implemented and had little effect on the immediate course of military operations. The insurgent columns continued to advance deeper into eastern Guipúzcoa. The fortress of San Marcial, defending Irún on the border, resisted eight days (August 26–September 2) and did not fall until after a battalion of the elite Spanish Legion was moved up from Morocco and several of the Spanish Nationalists' small stock of airplanes were committed to the assault. Three days later, on September 5, the insurgents occupied Irún, cutting the border with France. This was a grave blow to the defenders of the entire Republican northern zone (Guipúzcoa-Vizcaya-Santander-Palencia-Asturias), who were already isolated from the main Republican territory. Manuel de Irujo, the most influential Basque nationalist leader in Guipúzcoa, later wrote that "the loss of Irún demoralized all the troops [i.e., militia] of the San Sebastián district."[31]

The other columns from Navarra advanced into south-central Guipúzcoa, threatening to cut off San Sebastián. The Guipuzcoan capital was evacuated on September 12 and occupied by the Spanish Nationalists on the following day.[32] Though parts of Irún had been put to the torch by retreating revolutionaries, San Sebastián suffered little destruction thanks in large part to the efforts of the Basque nationalists. The insurgents stopped only two days to regroup, resuming the advance into western Guipúzcoa on September 15 and reaching the line of the Deva river on September 22. By that time Vizcaya, the home province of the Basque move- was in danger.

The political situation in Vizcaya remained relatively calm but nonetheless uncertain. Though the Republican civil governor, Echeverría Novoa, retained nominal authority, at first a confused set of "Delegations" and "Commissariats" had been created to exercise many of the functions of administration. On August 12 a new *Junta de Defensa de Vizcaya* was organized under the governor, and was composed of three left Republicans, two Socialists, two representatives of the PNV, and one each from the ANV, CNT, and the Communists.

Since the PNV had mobilized half the total nonrightist vote in Vizcaya only five months earlier, it was grossly underrepresented with only 20 percent of the *Junta* delegation. The nationalists were clearly at a disadvantage due to their lack of an armed militia but even so had much more influence in the province than their government representation would have indicated. For years they had denounced the authority of Madrid appointees in Basque administration, yet once the civil war started they did all they could to uphold the legal authority of the Republican civil governor against the revolutionaries,[33] while showing scant enthusiasm for having their young militants mobilized for the fighting front.[34] Nearly all the fighting in Guipúzcoa had been done by the revolutionaries, and a subsequent Republican army report on the loss of that province noted the lack of combativeness "among the greater part of the Basque population, perhaps more concerned about their regional interests than the common cause of the Republic."[35]

Indeed, throughout the month of August the nationalist leadership in Vizcaya remained profoundly perplexed and often doubtful that they had any reason being on the leftist side. The scores of murders by the revolutionaries had a "disastrous effect"[36] on nationalist morale. The PNV headquarters maintained intermittent contacts with Spanish rebel agents[37] and also talked from time to time with British representatives, hoping to use the long-standing financial and commercial connections between Vizcaya and England to gain British support for separate autonomous regime.[38]

As the military situation grew critical for the Popular Front, relations with the Basque nationalists of Vizcaya achieved great importance. This was made clear by the first all–Popular Front government established in Madrid on September 4 under the revolutionary Socialist Largo Caballero. Its goal was to create unity among the discordant left groups and develop an organized military force while there was still time. Since the beginning of the Civil War most of Republican Spain had separated into de facto autonomous regional units; hence there was no reason not to recognize formally such a situation in what remained of the Basque country so long as the nationalists would resolutely dedicate themselves to the Popular Front cause. Largo Caballero originally tried to include Aguirre in his cabinet as minister of public works, but the latter refused to be associated with a Popular Front government that included Communists[39] while the crucial issue of autonomy remained unresolved. Formation of the Largo Caballero ministry coincided, however, with a meeting of the Vizcayan *junta* and members of the Guipuzcoan *juntas* in Bilbao, where they agreed to set up an all-Basque regional *junta*.[40] This could be the first step toward an autonomous Basque government. On the "following day" (September 5), the new Republican foreign minister, the Socialist (and proto-Communist) Alvarez del Vayo established contact with the most cooperative of the top Basque leaders, Manuel de Irujo (then in imperiled San Sebastián), offering him a ministerial position. Irujo has written that he replied no Basque nationalist could participate in the Republican government until the autonomy question had been settled. When Vayo declared that the concession of the previously prepared autonomy statute could be completed almost immediately, Irujo telephoned the Vizcayan regional council of the PNV, which decided to send a commission to Madrid headed by Aguirre.[41] At the same time, the new Republican government moved swiftly to create, at least on paper, organized military districts and commands, forming a consolidated military district of Vizcaya, Santander to the west, and what remained of Guipúzcoa to the east. All these developments encouraged the Basque nationalists to accelerate the formation of a unified Basque provinces government, to which the leftist parties in most of Guipúzcoa agreed by approximately September 7.

The Basque commission evidently arrived in Madrid in mid-September, and talked first with Indalecio Prieto, the new Republican minister of the navy and air force. Francisco Basterrechea, one of the commission leaders, made it clear to Prieto that

> If you want the Basque country to resist the fascist assault, do all you can to have the statute granted to us, for only thus can we guarantee that it will resist. Otherwise, God only knows what might happen.[42]

This last phrase may have referred to the continuing contacts with the Spanish insurgents, apparently through the mediation of Basque Carlists. The secretary of General Mola has written that after the insurgent forces reached the Deva river line in western Guipúzcoa on September 22,

> Vizcaya was on the verge of surrender. Mola received reports that the Basque government [to what this refers is not clear] would agree to surrender if the general guaranteed the lives and property of both soldiers and civilians and if the entry of the [insurgent] troops was controlled by the League of Nations.[43]

The Basque nationalists were apparently guaranteed impunity for their rank-and-file, with the opportunity for the leaders to escape abroad, and only those guilty of common crimes were to suffer prosecution.[44]

However, the Basque hesitations ended when the Republican government promised to approve the autonomy statute as soon as the rump Republican parliament met in Valencia on October 1 and to send military assistance to the Basque front without delay. In a major gesture whose value was almost as much propagandistic as military, the main Republican fleet, which up to that point had been maintaining a blockade on the elite insurgent forces in Morocco, was ordered to abandon the southern coast and to proceed to Bilbao on September 24. The expedition was composed of one battleship, three cruisers, and five destroyers. Its supply vessels brought badly needed ammunition and equipment, and the flotilla remained in Bilbao for twenty days. This, together with arms imports that the nationalists had themselves arranged directly in western Europe and Mexico, helped stiffen Vizcayan resistance and raise morale,[45] but it also lifted the Republican blockade of the Moroccan straits, allowing Franco to complete the transfer of his elite units in preparation for the drive on Madrid. Meanwhile, Irujo entered the Largo Caballero government as minister without portfolio on September 26. The Republican defense line in western Guipúzcoa resisted an insurgent assault on September 29[46] and two weeks later, on October 12, General Mola canceled further efforts by the small insurgent units to advance. For the time being, Vizcaya was safe.

The Basque autonomy statute was formally voted by a rump session of the Spanish Republican parliament in Valencia on October 1, 1936, attended by only about 100 of its 470 nominal members. The goal had finally been achieved, but it had been made possible only by a total civil war. To nationalists the new autonomy statute was known as the *Estatuto de Elgueta*, for it had only been voted after the Spanish Nationalists neared Elgueta, the last remaining town east of the Vizcayan border. The outcome of the conflict hung in the balance; whether an autonomous Basque regime could long survive was by no means certain.

NOTES

1. *Euzkadi*, Apr. 25, 1936.
2. Ibid., May 13, 1936.

3. Ibid., May 21, 1936.

4. Ibid., May 30, 1936.

5. Ibid.

6. Ibid., June 6, 1936.

7. Ibid., June 19, 1936.

8. Ibid., July 8, 1936.

9. Ibid., July 11, 1936.

10. Ricardo de la Cierva, *Historia de la Guerra civil española* (Madrid 1969), I, 685.

11. González Lopez, "El movimiento autonomista gallego."

12. Jordi Arquer, *Los comunistas ante el problema de las nacionalidades ibéricas* (Barcelona, 1936).

13. Quoted in Juan de Iturralde (pseud. of P. Usabiaga), *El Catolicismo y la Cruzada de Franco* (Vienne, 1955), 411 − 16.

14. Ibid., 418 − 23.

15. *Euzkadi*, Apr. 17, 1936.

16. Ibid., June 10 and 12, 1936.

17. José Ma. Gil Robles, *No fue posible la paz* (Barcelona, 1969), 729; Sierra Bustamante, 155 − 56.

18. Quoted in *El pueblo vasco*, 90 − 91. It should be noted that in the lexicon of Spanish antileftists the term "Communist" was used however vaguely to denote the entire revolutionary left, just as the latter used the terms "fascist" and "reactionary" to refer to all their opponents.

19. Ibid., 91 − 92.

20. Irujo's account is given in Ibid., 207 − 08.

21. Gen. Luis Redondo and Maj. Juan de Zavala, *El Requeté* (Barcelona, 1957), 326 − 27.

22. *Diario de Navarra* (Pamplona), July 23, 1936.

23. Jaime del Burgo, *Conspiración y guerra civil* (Madrid, 1970), 67.

24. *El Pensamiento Navarro* (Pamplona), August 4, 1936. Landáburu explains the pressure to which he was subject in *El pueblo vasco frente a la cruzada franquista* (Toulouse, 1966), 162 − 71.

25. F. J. de Landáburu and Manuel Ibarrondo to J. A. de Aguirre, Aug. 3, 1936, in Joaquín Arrarás, ed., *Historia de la Cruzada Española* (Madrid, 1941), XIII, 560.

26. Cf. Irujo, 24 − 27, and A. de Lizarra (pseud.), *Los vascos y la República española* (Buenos Aires, 1944), 92.

27. José Antonio de Aguirre, "Informe" to the Spanish Republican government-in-exile, Oct. 15, 1950 (Hoover Institution), 7 − 8.

28. *Euzkadi* (Bilbao), Aug. 6, 1936, in Col. J. M. Martínez Bande, *La Guerra en el norte* (Madrid, 1969), 37. According to a memoir by Enrique

Iza, a battalion commander in the subsequent Basque army, these first paramilitary organizations were organized by the Bizkai-Buru-Batzar primarily to counterbalance the left and impress the Republican civil governor in Bilbao. Iza's remarks are quoted in M. Fernández Etxeberría, *Euzkadi, patria de los vascos* (Caracas, 1969), 135.

29. Irujo, 25.

30. Ministerio de Defensa Nacional (Madrid), "Informe sobre la zona cantábrica," Aug. 11, 1936, in Martínez Bande, 70.

31. Irujo, 74.

32. It may be noted that the latter made use of some of the first Italian military equipment to arrive in Spain: 5 light machinegun-carrying Ansaldo tanks (or, more precisely, tankettes). Emilio Faldella, *Venti mesi di guerra in Spagna* (Florence, 1939), 80.

33. Sir Henry Chilton, the British ambassador to Spain, wrote his government from Irún on August 17 that in Bilbao "the Civil Governor appears still to hold the reins of administration, notwithstanding the efforts of the political Junta to wrest control from him. His strength lies undoubtedly in the fact that the Junta is divided against itself on a number of points, the most important of which is the policy of moderation steadily pursued by the Basque Nationalists." Public Record Office of Great Britain (hereafter cited as PRO) 1936 W9528/62/41.

34. The British consul in Bilbao, R. C. Henderson, reported on August 28, "A recrudescence of rumours of differences between the Basque Nationalists and the Left Extremists is also reported. From what I hear the Basques feel more than unhappy over their political bargain of last month. . . . I have been told, too, that the Junta finds it more than difficult to persuade them to send detachments to the defense of San Sebastián." PRO 1936 W10370/62/41.

At that point the Vizcaya front (to the south) was almost completely inactive. The big military news in *Euzkadi* on August 27 concerned a militiaman who had fallen down a farmer's well and badly hurt himself.

35. Report of Gen. Martínez Cabrera, Republican Inspector General of the Army of the North, July 15, 1937, in Martínez Bande, 92.

36. Aguirre, "Informe," 8.

37. On August 1 the H.M.S. *Crusader* telegraphed the Foreign Office from the Bay of Biscay that the British consul in Bilbao was "informed by reliable source that rebel representative hiding at known address in Bilbao [was endeavoring to make?] contact with Basque nationalists [and?] allied Governments in order to agree terms concerning Basque self-government in return for Basque alliance with rebels." PRO 1936 W7519/62/41.

It added on the following day: "Basque representative is reported to be leaving Bilbao today Saturday proceeding Vitoria via sea route and France to discuss with rebel leaders terms for joining them." PRO 1936 W7516/62/41.

Chilton opined from Hendaye on August 15: "If the insurgents give the Basque leaders an acceptable assurance that their desire for autonomy will be satisfied, I doubt whether the Basques would have much interest in continuing the struggle." PRO 1936 W8874/62/41.

Iturralde, II, 288−92, gives the text of three letters by the Basque nationalist priest José de Ariztimuño from France in mid-September that refer to contacts with the Carlists and also with British representatives.

38. Most Basque iron ore exports went to Britain, where they played a minor role in the British rearmament program.

There were reports that even prior to the elections of February 1936 PNV leaders had made contact with British diplomats seeking protection for the Basque region in case of a revolutionary takeover of the Spanish state, according to the testimony of a former Spanish "Director General of the Department of Justice and Inspector General of the Ministry of the Interior," cited in the staff report of Lt. Col. Buzón Llanes to the Republican Ministry of War, June 2, 1937, in Martínez Bande, 153. If such conversations took place, I found no references to them in the diplomatic dispatches from Spain for 1936 in the Public Record Office.

The British ambassador to Spain, Sir Henry Chilton, telegraphed from Hendaye on August 3: "Just as I was leaving Zarauz on August 1st Basque Nationalist leader sought an interview with me and informed me that whereas Basques had joined 'Frente Popular' at the beginning of the conflict as that party had promised them autonomy, they were now disgusted with the horrors perpetrated by Communists, Anarchists, etc., in Basque territory, when rebel prisoners had been shot wholesale in cold blood and many persons inimical to Government parties assassinated. Basques were tired of Soviet regime in Guipúzcoa and would like to get rid of it. Unfortunately they had allowed themselves to be disarmed and were now powerless. With 800 rifles he was convinced they could deal with the Soviet forces in the province. Though he did not actually suggest that Great Britian should provide the arms the hint was obvious.

"I told Nationalist leader that Great Britain was neutral and could assist neither side in supplying arms." PRO 1936 W7908/62/41.

39. According to Francisco Largo Caballero, *Mis recuerdos* (Mexico City, 1954), 225.

40. Irujo, 69.

41. Ibid., 70.

42. Francisco Basterrechea, *Euzko-Deya de Buenos Aires*, May 10, 1945, in Iturralde, II, 228.

43. José María Iribarren, *Mola* (Zaragoza, 1938), 215.

44. According to the investigations of Vicente Talón in his *Arde Guernica* (Madrid, 1970), 204–5.

45. The British military attaché, Col. F. Beaumont-Nesbitt, was not however impressed by the state of morale in Bilbao when he visited the city late in September. He reported on October 5: "At Irún, recently liberated from the Reds, such people as one saw appeared to be comparatively cheerful. . . . In both Bilbao and Gijón it was entirely the opposite: everyone looked sullen, apathetic and depressed." PRO 1936 W13516/62/41.

46. On September 30 *Euzkadi* headlined "Three Gudaris Killed" in a skirmish, the first publicity drawn by any nationalist military casualties thus far.

7

THE LIFE AND DEATH

OF VIZCAYAN EUZKADI

In his official speech at the Valencian Cortes session that ratified Basque autonomy, José Antonio de Aguirre defined the Spanish Civil War as a struggle between "democracy" and "fascism." He reemphasized the absolute identity of Basque nationalism with the former and pledged that "Basque nationalism will remain firmly in its place until fascism is conquered."[1]

Aguirre also invoked the movement's Catholicism and its battle for "social justice." Replying to critics in the Catholic hierarchy such as the bishop of Pamplona who had condemned Catholics for resisting the Spanish Nationalist insurgents, Aguirre intoned,

> Why did Christ come to this earth? Did Christ come to the earth to aid the powerful or to raise and console the weak? We, between the powerful and the weak, are with the weak, with the people, for we are born of the people and are fighting for them.[2]

The argument was attractive, but somewhat casuistic. The

PNV had sided with the dominant force in Vizcaya—the "strong," not the "weak"—and it supported the Republican regime because the latter provided the strength and authority for autonomy. Similarly, in Navarra and Alava most members of the PNV had sided with the dominant local forces. It is probably correct that the unified antirightist coalition represented a majority of "the people" in Vizcaya, but it did not necessarily represent the Basque people as a whole. As Aguirre frankly admitted to the author twenty years later, in the Basque country as a whole, one-third of the people supported the antirightist coalition, one-third opposed it, and the remaining third were neutral.[3]

The autonomy statute voted for the Basque country was basically that prepared in 1933−36.[4] It provided an autonomous regional government for the three provinces of Alava, Guipúzcoa, and Vizcaya, though all that remained free of Franco's forces were Vizcaya and the western strip of Guipúzcoa around Eibar. For the time being, the president of a Basque provisional government was to be elected by the municipal councils of the territory remaining. The unanimous choice of *lendakari* (president) was Aguirre, who also held the chancellory of defense. Of the ten cabinet posts in his government, three were held by the PNV, three by the Socialists, two by the middle-class Republican left, and one each by the ANV and the Communists. The anarcho-syndicalist CNT, which had just decided for the first time to participate in regular government in Catalonia, was completely excluded. Basque nationalists detested the anarcho-syndicalists, as did, at the other end of the political spectrum, the Communists. By October effective working relations had been established between the nationalists and the small Vizcayan Communist party, since the latter supported the autonomy statute and a policy of "order." A delegate of the STV attended the Moscow ceremonies in October 1936 in honor of the Revolution of 1917,[5] whereas only a year earlier the PNV leadership—though admittedly not that of the STV—had thoroughly dissociated itself in almost every way from the Communists.

Though PNV representatives had negotiated and voted for the autonomy arrangement, the party itself never officially endorsed the new relationship as having met the full objectives of Basque nationalism. That degree of ambiguity was altogether unsatisfactory for the old-guard Aranist ultranationalists and the young radicals—the same conjunction of extremists that had first emerged fifteen years earlier—for both these elements regarded any kind of compromise within the Spanish state (or what remained of it) as a sellout. On October 7, when Aguirre officially swore his oath of office under the traditional Tree of Guernica, he was hooted at by young *gudaris* (Basque soldiers) who shouted "*¡Estatuto, no! ¡Independencia, sí!*"[6] That same day the veteran Luis de Arana y Goiri officially resigned from the PNV in protest against the compromising of nationalist principles and objectives, while nonetheless recommending that "all good nationalists remain within the party to restrain its deviations and eventually rectify its course."[7]

The nascent Basque government moved fairly rapidly to establish a new juridical order in the small district under its jurisdiction and, according to Aguirre, completed the task within fifteen days. He reported that "all those who held official positions"[8] in the legal structure were at first deposed and many new functionaries appointed, but in fact it seems that most aspects of the pre-established judicial system were maintained and the majority of the legal officers were reappointed. The major difference was that a series of new People's Tribunals were created to deal with political and military subversion in accordance with the system developed in the main Republican zone, though the nationalists had earlier opposed the development of such political courts. All the pre-existing security forces were dissolved and replaced by a new Basque police, the *Ertzaña*, under the councillor of the interior, Telesforo Monzón.

One achievement of the Basque government was to improve public order and, with a few major exceptions, bring political executions under control.[9] Even before October there had been fewer acts of violence and anarchy than elsewhere; under the autonomous regime the only major atrocity that occurred was the slaughter of 224 prisoners in the Larrínaga jail on January 4, 1937, by a battalion of mutinous Socialist militia.[10] After this outburst the government took stringent measures to strengthen military and police security in the Bilbao area.[11] In general the functioning of the People's Tribunals in Bilbao was comparatively moderate.[12]

Most political killings occurred either in leftist mob raids on jails or in Guipúzcoa during the first two months of the war. The most extensive account of the antirightist repression in Vizcaya and Guipúzcoa has compiled the names of 844 people killed between July 1936 and June 1937,[13] though another informed estimate reduced this to 766.[14] Though Aguirre's frequent contention that the Basque government prevented political executions is not entirely correct, it moved earlier and somewhat more vigorously to stop them than did any other institution on either side of the Spanish Civil War.[15]

During the first three months of the Civil War, numerous acts of vandalism and destruction were wreaked on Catholic churches in Vizcaya and Guipúzcoa by the revolutionary left[16] and approximately fifty clergy were murdered.[17] Minor harassment and one or two murders continued to occur after formation of the autonomous government, but the latter in general brought anti-Catholic excesses under control.

Basque nationalists of Vizcaya were fully aware of their propaganda value to the Popular Front regime as the latter's "only argument"[18] that there was any tolerance in the Republican zone toward Catholics. During the following year, this theme was widely used by Republican (and Communist) propaganda throughout the western world. Not the least of the ironies of the role played by Basque nationalism in the Civil War was that it used propaganda placards defining its struggle as a battle "for Christian civilization," employing one of the most common slogans of the Spanish Nationalists on the other side.

Social mores were less affected by the Civil War in Vizcaya than in any other part of the Republican zone. Even in Bilbao, the revolutionary style that was common in Barcelona, Madrid, and Valencia was largely lacking. Major Angel Lamas Arroyo, last chief of staff of the Basque army, noted with surprise when he arrived in Bilbao from the central zone in June 1937 that "above all, ordinary people had not lost their courtesy and good manners as in the rest of the country." He noted also that the public addresses of the Basque leaders were simple and direct, in contrast to the "speeches that were loud, truculent and explosive—both in tone and content—that were heard daily in any meeting or mere official visit in the Madrid region."[19]

Vizcaya was practically the only sector of the Republican zone where there were virtually no revolutionary changes in the basic structure of the economic system. State control (*intervención*) was established over industrial and commercial assets of those known to support Franco's Spanish Nationalists, and all aspects of military production were also placed under state supervision. There was, however, no official state socialization or nationalization (*incautación*) as in Asturias and some other provinces, nor any direct collectivization, as in Catalonia and Aragón. Wartime regulations were imposed on the general economy by the end of October, including strict rationing and price controls, but in general there was no change in the legal basis of property. The relative social conservatism of Basque nationalism combined with the diplomatic cautiousness of the Communists and Socialists (who were eager not to offend British interests and foreign opinion) to prevent genuine revolutionary changes in Vizcaya.

The new Basque government did, however, rapidly generate a sizable bureaucracy to staff all its new supervisory organs. This soon began to reach top-heavy proportions, termed by Indalecio Prieto, then Republican minister of the navy and air force, in a letter to Aguirre as a "scandalous development" of bureaucracy.[20] At the same time, the Basque government extended its own direct commercial representation to England, and Prieto had to reject Aguirre's proposal that Basque "counsellors" be placed in Spanish Republican embassies abroad.[21]

Under the autonomous government every effort was made to safeguard the economic resources of Vizcaya. Basque nationalists had been zealous in preserving the financial resources of Guipúzcoa as that province fell to the enemy, and some reserves were transferred to Vizcaya. Emphasis was placed on direct financial and commercial contact with England, and Aguirre tried to get the Republican government in Valencia to pay in foreign currency for Basque metallurgical goods shipped to other provinces.[22] On the other hand, Aguirre has written that approximately 70 million pesetas trade credit was made available by Vizcaya to the two neighboring Republican provinces of Santander and Asturias. Be that as it may, the revolutionaries who dominated the latter never lost their political and social resentment of Basque nationalists, whom they frequently termed "reactionaries." The Basques resisted any kind of genuine economic integration with the other two sectors of the northern zone. Thus a Republican staff report later lamented, "Asturian coal never entered Vizcayan factories, which imported it directly from England. A central, rational direction of war industries was impossible."[22a] This report calculated that in the northern zone as a whole, industry operated at scarcely 30 percent of its full potential, though it is doubtful that production ever declined anywhere near that much in Vizcaya.

Conversely, Ramón Salas, the exhaustive historian of the Republican People's Army, has judged that "due to the organizational capacity and political maturity of the Basques and Asturians industrial mobilization was much more effective than in the main Republican zone."[23] These contrasting analyses are not entirely antithetical, for in Barcelona, the industrial center of the chief Republican zone, industrial mobilization during the first year of the war was altogether feeble. There is little doubt that Basque and Asturian industry produced proportionately many more rifles and pieces of light artillery than did Catalonia, even though Asturian industry was in great disarray and Vizcaya did not achieve anything approaching a truly efficient mobilization. Distrust of conservative military personnel meant that little of the available talent was employed in Vizcaya, and retooling for major production of planes, tanks, and heavy artillery was in the short term beyond the limited resources of Vizcayan industry.

The great weakness of the northern Republican zone in the Spanish Civil War lay in the almost absolute disunity that prevailed between its three main sectors, Vizcaya, Santander, and Asturias, each of which cooperated only minimally with the others. In an official decree of October 26, Aguirre declared that all Basque armed forces were "under the superior authority of the Councillor of Defense for *Euzkadi*" (an office that he combined with the presidency), and hence virtually independent of central Republican military authority. Organization of the new Basque army was a major problem, not so much for want of material (though that was inadequate), as for lack of internal unity and trained leaders. There were proportionately many fewer reliable professional army officers in Vizcaya than in the central Republican zone—less than a dozen, according to Aguirre,[24] though this is perhaps an underestimate. A Communist general staff captain, Francisco Ciutat, was named by the Republican government on September 12 as director of operations for the entire northern zone with headquarters in Bilbao, but his advice was accepted only on occasion.

Aside from one infantry battalion in the Bilbao garrison, at the beginning of the civil war the only paramilitary forces in Vizcaya were the small, poorly trained, and largely unequipped *Miqueletes* of the provincial militia and the very small, clandestine units of the Communist *Milicias Armadas Obreras y Campesinas* (MAOC).[25] On October 16 the Basque government called up four yearly quotas of draftees (though the Republican government in Valencia had already gone farther than that). Basque agents were already busy purchasing arms abroad and even managed to buy Czech military equipment through German purchasing agents in Hamburg.[26] More spectacular, however, was the arrival in Bilbao in mid-October of a Russian military supply vessel, carrying fifteen Russian fighter planes (with their respective Russian pilots), six cannon, fifteen self-propelled guns, and other material.[27] A nominal general staff system was instituted for the new Basque army on November 7, and by November 20 a total of twenty-seven untrained infantry battalions of 750 men each had been organized into a 25,000-man "army of maneuver," which did not count between 12,000 and 15,000 volunteers in multiparty militia units that were holding the largely inactive front line. Moreover, the new Basque army set up three officer training schools, for infantry, artillery, and engineers, open theoretically to all "Spanish citizens," which eventually enrolled approximately four hundred candidates, including a few from Santander and Asturias.[28]

The chief defensive bulwark of Vizcaya's heartland—the industrial district around Bilbao—was to consist of an elaborate system of static fortifications termed the *cinturón de hierro*. Work on this system, conceived as a sort of Vizcayan Maginot Line, was begun on October 5, 1936. A month later it was discovered that the assistant director of the project, an army captain of engineers, was trying to establish contact with the Spanish Nationalists: he was quickly tried and shot. When the main enemy offensive was unleashed against Vizcaya in the early spring of 1937, the system was only 40 percent complete, and its director deserted on the eve of the attack, delivering much of the fortification plans to General Mola.

Defense was not an immediate problem for the autonomous government, however, for Franco's principal effort during the autumn and winter of 1936 was exerted on the central front, against Madrid. The insurgent positions east and south of Vizcaya were at that point thinly manned by only a scattering of Spanish Nationalist troops, and the Basques were urged to use the resources of thickly populated, industrial Vizcaya to mount an offensive from the north that would break Franco's rear and relieve the pressure on Madrid. This resulted in the only Basque offensive of the war, an attack due south into Alava.

It became known as the Villarreal offensive, since the entire operation converged on the small town of Villarreal, the principal insurgent defensive position in northern Alava. It was apparently planned by Ciutat but actually directed by Captain Arambarri of the new Basque general staff. A total of twenty-nine battalions participated, supported by five companies of engineers, twenty-five cannon, and eight Russian armored cars.[29] The total force of nearly thirty thousand outnumbered the Spanish Nationalist defenders by eight to one, but they lacked training, leadership, or military cohesion. Their officers were unprepared, and strategy was totally wanting.[30] The operation, which began on November 30, soon degenerated into a series of uncoordinated direct assaults on Villarreal. Franco hurried small units of reinforcements north, Basque losses were extremely high, and the attack was suspended on December 12. The subsequent Republican military inspector general in the north ascribed the defeat above all to the "lack of good commanders and of organization."[31] Due in part to lack of adequate sanitary facilities, more than 20 percent of the Basque casualties resulted in deaths, amounting to approximately one thousand fatalities.[32] It was a discouraging blow after the high hopes and loud talk of recent weeks, and helped earn for the stocky Aguirre the derisive epithet of "Napoleontxu" (little Napoleon) among the not inconsiderable number of people in the Basque country who sympathized with Franco's insurgents.

Yet the defeat did not have the effect of redoubling military preparations or prompting greater coordination with the new Republican People's Army in the central zone. The Basque leadership apparently believed that Franco would continue to exert his main energy in the south, and that Basque interests would be better protected by independent management. The Basque nationalists distrusted all military appointments made for the northern zone by the central Republican government and refused to accept the new Russian-derived system of political commissars that was being installed in the main sections of the People's Army. Instead of commissars, PNV battalions were accompanied by Basque priests as chaplains, to the shock and disgust of their leftist allies. The Basque leadership enjoyed cooperative relations with the local Vizcayan section of Communists (which claimed a nominal twenty-two thousand members by June 1937)[33] but much resented the growing influence of the central Spanish Communist party in military affairs. Aguirre later complained that the new general staff for the Republican Army of the North that was created in the autumn of 1936 "was composed from the beginning of people of civilian background who lacked the necessary technical preparation but who showed a marked inclination toward the Communist party," so that "elements belonging to Communist organizations or their allies could take over the channels of command . . . in order later to dominate the Basque [military] organization."[34] Thus Basque fears of central Spanish domination were compounded by concern over the growing Communist hegemony, especially in the People's Army.

On November 14 all forces in the northern zone were theoretically incorporated into a Republican Army of the North under General Francisco Llano de la Encomienda, but this unification remained on paper only. On December 18, Llano, from his new nominal headquarters in Bilbao, ordered the creation of a unified infantry officer's school in the Vizcayan capital to serve all the northern zone. The Basque government opposed this directive, which was never put into effect. Relations between the erstwhile commanding general and the Basque president grew worse and worse. Aguirre praised to the skies the Basques' own separate chief of staff, Major Alberto Montaud, on whom he greatly relied, while denouncing Llano for "absolute ineptitude."[35] On January 38,

1937, he wrote to Llano that "until the new organization of all forces, institutions, and material situated in Basque territory is approved [by the Basque government]; they will remain within the exclusive jurisdiction of the Basque government."[36] In February 1937, Llano de la Encomienda finally moved his headquarters to Santander and gave up any direct effort to command the Basque forces. Aguirre was fully aware that the Basque army needed topflight professional direction, but insisted on an apolitical commander who could be trusted. For several months he tried unsuccessfully to have the able, non-Communist General José Asensio sent to Bilbao as commander of the Vizcayan front. In an attempted compromise, the Republican ministry of war on March 12 named a new delegate inspector for the Army of the North (which as a coordinated unit still existed only on paper) in the person of General Toribio Martínez Cabrera, but it is not clear that he exercised much effective authority.

In an official report, Lieutenant Colonel Buzón Llanes, head of the second section of the general staff of the Army of the North, complained with scant exaggeration that the boundaries between the three main provinces in the northern zone were "much harder to cross than international frontiers."[37] Of Vizcaya he wrote,

In Vizcaya one had the feeling of not being at war. . . . Perfect order reigned, there was complete mutual tolerance in ideas, but nonetheless the civilian population began to suffer such shortages of food and other goods that it wished an end to the situation no matter what the means.

The defects of improvisation were felt in all services, together with the lack of preparation on the part of the leaders. The opportunism of appointing untrained young people to all positions of responsibility was one of many causes that eventually contributed to the loss of Bilbao.

The army suffered serious basic defects and lacked the necessary political commissars to inspire confidence in the troops. There were no units larger than a battalion and two different sets of command for each battalion, one military and other administrative, which resulted in troops being poorly fed and cared for. Arms and clothing were provided according to the influence of whichever political groups had

organized each battalion. Some were luxuriously cared for
and others went barefoot.

Until March 1937 morale was never tested. . . . Most
fortifications were mere slit trenches. . . . Discipline had
been relaxed (if indeed it had ever existed) and the commanders, who did not live in daily contact with their troops, spent
their days and especially their nights amusing themselves in
Bilbao. To sum up, people lived as if the war were already
won, and with this suicidal idea wasted a precious
year. . . .[38]

This portrait, while containing much truth, is nevertheless
somewhat overdrawn. However much the Basques distrusted the
revolutionaries in Santander and Asturias, they did provide them
with financial assistance. Perhaps more important, a total of seven
battalions were transferred to Asturias, where they gave a good
account of themselves in the final bloody Republican attempt to
conquer Oviedo in February 1937. These units were sent back to
Vizcaya when the Spanish Nationalist offensive commenced there
and were eventually joined by several Asturian battalions sent to
the aid of the Basques. Inept military preparations in Vizcaya were
primarily due to the lack of adequate military leadership, which
neither the young Basque political elite nor the worker revolutionaries could provide. Nor were the Basque leaders far
wrong in their complaints that the military officials sent by the
Republican government were of uncertain professional quality.

The most notable event of the early winter of 1936–37 was a
public exchange of letters between Aguirre and Cardinal Archbishop Gomá, primate of the church in Spain. Ever since the split
between the nationalists and the right in 1932, the latter had used
the defense of Catholicism as their main tool to try to dissociate
nationalists from the left. As early as August 6, 1936, the two
bishops of the Basque area, Múgica of Vitoria and Olaechea of
Pamplona, had issued a joint public letter (though not an official
pastoral) condemning strife among Catholics and calling for
Catholic unity.[39] Though no direct endorsement was given to the
insurgent Spanish nationalists, the clear intention was to condemn
the alliance of Basque nationalism with the left. Múgica was

himself an independent prelate devoted to spiritual leadership and at first refused directly to bless or endorse the insurgent cause, however Catholic its identity. Under suasion such an endorsement was finally issued in his name on September 8, but soon afterward he was forced into exile in Rome.[40]

Tension was increased by the murder of priests by both the revolutionary left and the right. The number of killings by the former eventually amounted to 6,832 throughout the entire leftist zone,[41] including the fifty-odd that were killed in Vizcaya and Guipúzcoa, but an equal scandal for Basque nationalists was the summary execution of fourteen nationalist priests by Franquist authorities during the autumn of 1936, all on the charge of inciting to rebellion. The most notable of those executed was José de Ariztimuño ("Aitzol"), who actually opposed alliance with the left and hoped to end the war by compromise. He was captured at sea when attempting to reach Vizcaya and was executed for subversion because of his previous role in the PNV. In reference to these executions, Aguirre delivered a speech in Bilbao on December 22 in which he defined the Civil War as a kind of socioeconomic class struggle in which the Basques supported the "poor" and demanded to know why the hierarchy had not protested the deaths of the fourteen nationalist priests.

Archbishop Gomá replied in a public letter on January 10, 1937, denying that the Spanish conflict was a social war pure and simple. He defined it as basically an ideological struggle, since it was the wealthiest provinces and best-paid sectors of workers who most vigorously supported the Popular Front. While not denying the gravity of the executions by the Spanish Nationalists, Gomá noted that the priests had been involved in politics and had suffered penalties resulting therefrom. As a counteraccusation he asked why Aguirre had not protested the murder of thousands of priests by the Basques' revolutionary allies and urged him as the leader of a Catholic province to seek means of achieving peace as soon as possible.[42] Aguirre replied that peace could easily be achieved as soon as Franco's forces surrendered to the Popular Front (defined somewhat ingenuously as the "legal government"). He denounced the hierarchy for supporting conservative interests and said that he "asked God . . . for a persecuted church rather than a protected church," for that was the way to true sanctity.[43]

This propaganda duel was a drawn battle, for the issue was too complex to be easily resolved by polarized positions. The alliance of Basque nationalism with the left remained a major source of perturbation for the church hierarchy and was a principle factor in restraining the hierarchy from clear-cut endorsement of Franco during the winter and spring of 1937. It was no mere coincidence that the collective letter of the Spanish bishops condemning the wartime Republic and blessing Franco's struggle as a crusade was not issued until July 1, 1937, a fortnight after the fall of Bilbao. The letter was not signed by Mateo Múgica, bishop of the western Basque provinces, in exile from Nationalist Spain.[44]

As the winter wore on, the suffering of the civilian population increased. To the inevitable shortages imposed by the naval blockade was added the burden of caring for nearly one hundred thousand refugees who had flocked in from surrounding provinces.[45] A certain amount of genuine hunger was unavoidable, and this merely increased the resentment of the approximately one-third of the native population that desired the victory of Franco.

One great advantage for the government was that interparty relations were relatively more harmonious in Vizcaya than in other sectors of the Republican zone. The secretary of the Basque Communist party, Manuel Astigarrabia, had a strong sense of Basque identity and might be considered as a Basque "Titoist" *avant la lettre*.

> He was a man who basically did not accept the domination of the Communist party of Spain. He placed *Euzkadi* before everything else and felt *Euzkadi* within himself. His relations with the Communist party of Spain had always been strained but he lacked the strength to declare his independence. He feared to do so because he knew that he would never be supported by the Comintern, which was already aware of his "independentist" ideas.[46]

Astigarrabia's leadership was nonetheless acceptable to the Comintern during the first part of the war as the most effective Communist policy for rallying a united anti-Franquist front in Vizcaya. The

Communists, Socialists, and middle-class left Republicans all cooperated in relative harmony with the Aguirre government for the first six months of its existence, until the Spanish Nationalist offensive opened against Vizcaya.

A major exception was relations with the CNT, which always remained poor. The Basques, supported by the other parties, refused to grant the anarcho-syndicalists a place in the government, stressing among other factors the CNT's own apoliticism and the fact that it was not a regular political party. Latent conflict and press polemics first reached a climax in mid-March, 1937, when the anarcho-syndicalist newspaper in Bilbao, *C. N. T. del Norte*, was seized by the government and its presses handed over to the Basque Communists. At the height of this brief confrontation the entire regional committee of the CNT was temporarily arrested.

Thus if the Basque government achieved a not inconsiderable degree of tolerance and harmonious relations, genuine unity was never in sight. This was clearer yet in the army, where integrated organization was never achieved. All battalions in the Basque army retained individual and discrete political identities. The approximately fifty battalions in existence early in 1937 were composed approximately as follows:

PNV	22
Socialist	14
Communist	7
CNT	6
ANV	2
Left Republican	1[47]

This is also perhaps as good an indication as any of the relative proportion of popular support for the various forces behind the Basque government, and underlines the extent to which the middle-class left Republican forces, with 30 percent of the cabinet positions and 6 percent of the battalions, were overrepresented.

Though the Basque government continued firmly to reject any form of unified command for the northern Republican zone, an attempt was made to increase mutual rapport by dispatching a half-dozen battalions to Asturias for the final attack on Oviedo in February 1937. This was reciprocated by the dispatch of several Asturian battalions for the defense of Vizcaya in April, but the appearance of "foreign" anticlerical revolutionaries drew renewed protests from old guard ultranationalists, who bitterly denounced the Asturians' exercise of military territorial jurisdiction, with temporary police rights, in one local district.[48]

The passive phase of the war in Vizcaya came to an abrupt end in the early spring of 1937. For eight months the province had been completely free of pressure from Franco's Spanish Nationalist forces. The latter, however, had failed in their major effort to take Madrid during the climactic battles of the late autumn and winter of 1936−37 in central Spain, ended by the dramatic check of the Italian corps (*Corpo di Truppe Volontarie*) at Guadalajara in March 1937. The main strength of the new Republican People's Army was concentrated around Madrid. By contrast, the northern zone was isolated; it constituted a valuable prize because of its dense population and because it contained the major concentration of heavy industry in Republican Spain. Occupation of the northern zone with its resources could decisively tilt the balance of power in the Civil War. Moreover, the northern zone was disunited and uncoordinated. Though more than one hundred thousand men were under arms—two-fifths of them in Vizcaya—they were poorly trained, organized, and led. Franco and his staff calculated that they would be able to destroy the three separate sections of the northern zone piecemeal, and that the new Republican People's Army in central Spain lacked the capacity for sustained offensive operations that could deter the main Spanish Nationalist units from concentrating on the north. In both calculations they were absolutely correct.

The offensive was scheduled to begin in Vizcaya, because of the province's great value and because it was judged that the Basque forces would not be able to put up serious resistance. Spanish Nationalist Intelligence calculated the number of regularly organized Basque troops at no more than thirty-nine thousand, with few aircraft and no more than one hundred forty pieces of artillery. General Mola planned to spearhead the assault with the four newly formed Navarrese Brigades, totaling 28,000 troops. These forces consisted in large part of right-wing Basque volunteers from Navarra, who during the preceding eight months had been carefully trained and organized by professional officers into first-class regular army units. In addition to troops from other parts of northern Spain, they included approximately ten battalions of Basques from Alava and Guipúzcoa,[49] and during the course of the northern campaign they were expanded to six brigades, ultimately of division strength. The assault on Vizcaya thus took the form of direct civil war between opposing sectors of the Basque population as a whole. However, the Carlist Navarrese suffered none of the moral and political uncertainties of the Basque nationalists of Guipúzcoa and Vizcaya. Their courage, determination, and offensive spirit made them perhaps the most effective single sector of Franco's army.[50]

By contrast, a staff report of the Spanish Nationalist Army of the North concluded that Republican forces in Vizcaya and the neighboring province of Santander (whose social composition was equally conservative)

> were weak and in most instances wanted the war to end. Their feeling for Basque nationalism was not so strong as to make them want to lose their lives for it. . . . A great mass of people eagerly awaited the arrival of our forces. . . .
>
> Shortages were already felt, and the arrival of large numbers of wounded from Asturias and the failure of the leftist offensive on that front [in the late winter of 1937] lowered morale, so that a sizable proportion of those mobilized were opposed to the Reds.[51]

Thus it was felt that the Basques would offer little resistance and that the entire province could be occupied "within a few weeks."[52]

The offensive opened against the eastern front of Vizcaya on March 31. Its greatest advantage was derived from the vigorous support offered by the main sector of Spanish Nationalist aircraft—some 140 planes including at least 65 of the 90 to 100 aircraft of the German Condor Legion. The bulk of the Spanish Nationalist artillery was also employed, by early April reaching a total of 200 pieces, including the seven batteries of the Italian "Legionary" artillery.[53] The effect of this firepower on the Basque defenders came as a shock. Though the Basque forces had enough material to arm all their regular troops,[54] their firepower was both uneven and dispersed, and they had at most approximately 35 planes, perhaps less. The reduced size of Vizcaya made an aerial warning system impossible and there was very little antiaircraft artillery. Thus General Mola's Navarrese brigades quickly pierced Vizcayan defenses, while the government in Bilbao ordered a general speedup in mobilization. Resistance by no means collapsed, despite the psychological impact of bombing and strafing. The mountainous topography of southern and eastern Vizcaya made offensive operations very difficult, whereas the small number of effectives used in the Nationalist assault were inadequate to cover their targets. Heavy rainfall completely grounded the aircraft and the offensive had temporarily to be suspended on April 7. A determined Basque counterattack momentarily regained one hill on April 13−14, and the rapid victory expected by Franco's headquarters was not in sight. A report by the chief of the operations section of Franco's headquarters on April 21 was not overly optimistic.[55]

However, General Mola, directing the offensive, enjoyed an ultimately decisive advantage in the technical skill and firepower of his aircraft and artillery, skillfully combined to disorient the defense. After several weeks the exiguous Basque air units were almost entirely destroyed. Though the Republican ministry of war in Valencia sent a certain amount of supplies, it was hard to pierce the naval blockade. Small quantities were dispatched periodically which weakened reserves in central Spain without actually meeting the needs of the Basques. The greatest lack was airpower, and in general at that point the Republican zone contained as many warplanes as did that of the insurgents. However, the Republican air force was completely controlled by its Russian advisors, who deceitfully alleged that it was logistically impossible to transfer planes to Vizcaya.[56] Direct shipments of aircraft from central-eastern Spain only began on May 8, after the situation had become critical. During the next five weeks approximately forty-five new planes reached Vizcaya, but they came in dribs and drabs and had to be committed piecemeal.[57] In addition to this crippling limitation, Vizcayan airfields were highly exposed and weakly defended, while the aerial forces also suffered from a certain technical inferiority of crews and combat formations. Thus all reinforcements were successively destroyed by the much more numerous, efficient, and concentrated squadrons of the enemy. Whenever weather conditions permitted, the Spanish nationalists were able to employ an overwhelming preponderance of tactical air support, the most important single factor in cracking the tough Vizcayan defense.

Thus when Mola resumed the offensive on April 20 his reinforced units began to gain ground more rapidly, moving deep into eastern Vizcaya. On April 26 there occurred the most famous incident of the Vizcayan campaign: the incendiary saturation bombing and partial razing of the historic "foral center" of Guernica by German planes of the Condor Legion, operating without the express consent of Franco, who normally tried to avoid the destruction of civilians and of economic resources.[58] Durango, the hub of eastern Vizcaya, was occupied on April 28, and in the week that followed the advance moved nearer the center of the province.

The crisis was compounded by a reawakening of latent problems of disunity and defection. On April 28 Aguirre sent out special orders to unit commanders to try to cut down on desertions.[59] Renewed efforts were being made by Basque rightists and by church leaders on Franco's side to negotiate the surrender of Basque forces. At the other extreme of the political spectrum, Vizcayan anarcho-syndicalists came close to open revolt as a result of the events of May 3–6 in Barcelona, which amounted to a miniature civil war between the CNT and extreme left on one side and the forces of the reorganized Republican state, led in considerable measure by the Communists, on the other in the Catalan capital.[60] Fearing that an all-out attempt was being made to suppress the CNT, several anarcho-syndicalist battalions momentarily abandoned their positions on the Vizcayan front before unity could be restored.[61]

By that time the main internal political pressure was coming from the Communists, who were demanding tight coordination and total mobilization for resistance. At the beginning of the offensive the central Spanish Communist command overthrew Astigarrabia as leader of the Basque Communist group, though he remained in the Aguirre government as Communist front-man to maintain appearances.[62] Communist propaganda demanded a struggle to the death and brushed aside complaints over the lack of aircraft by insisting that the proper use of shovels might be as effective as fighter planes in defense against enemy bombers.[63] After Juan Negrín formed a new Republican government under Communist tutelage in mid-May to foster all-out resistance, the Communists considered trying to overthrow the Aguirre regime in favor of a new policy of last-ditch revolutionary warfare, but Basque Socialists refused to assist them and the project had to be abandoned.[64] Tension between Basque nationalists and the Communists mounted steadily, and Aguirre later complained to the Republican President Azaña that "Communist propaganda in the Basque country produced a very bad effect because people there are Christians and democrats, and 'Mongolian' ideas are repulsive to them."[65]

On May 5 Aguirre assumed direct command of Basque military operations in an effort to shore up morale and mobilize for stiffer resistance. Soon afterwards all able-bodied men were summoned for military or fortifications duty, and at one point the Basque forces may have numbered a nominal seventy thousand men, though arms were lacking for many of them. Several battalions from Santander and Asturias helped to compose this total, but their violence and revolutionary hooliganism apparently alienated part of the native Vizcayan population.[66]

The climax of military operations was producing a politico-psychological crisis as well as a military crisis for Basque nationalists. Aguirre admitted soon afterward to Prieto, the Republican naval minister, that the moment when he took personal command was one of "maximum danger, above all for the Basque nationalist sector [of politics]."[67] Montaud, the earlier Vizcayan chief of staff, had acknowledged to other Republican commanders that "If you want to know the truth, our Basque peasants are at heart more with the enemy than with us."[68] A Republican military intelligence (SIM) report from Bilbao on May 9 was optimistic, but a week later, after the long expected aerial reinforcements failed to materialize, another report stated,

> The attitude of the troops and civilian population in Bilbao is that all is lost, especially since they are receiving no aircraft, in spite of promises. Many people think about surrendering, but this is always accompanied by great fear, since they are convinced that even if they surrender there will be many executions afterward [by Franco's forces].[69]

On May 18, Spanish Nationalist intelligence in Burgos received a report that declared,

> Those who arrive in Bayonne from Bilbao bring very gloomy impressions of the situation, which is considered ever more serious; of the arrival of wounded for whom there are no facilities; of hunger that is felt in all its crudeness; many people spend much of the day in shelters; Basque nationalist troops talk of surrender, but only in isolated groups.[70]

Barring a drastic change in the whole balance of the war or a major realignment of Republican priorities, Vizcaya's capacity to resist much longer was doubtful. Without a military miracle, the end of the autonomist regime was at hand.

NOTES

1. García Venero, *Nacionalismo vasco*, 593–94.

2. The translation is by G. L. Steer, *The Tree of Gernika* (London, 1938), 78.

3. Interview with José Antonio de Aguirre, Paris, Sept. 26, 1958.

4. The text is printed in full in Sarrailh de Ihartza, 466–73.

5. Jesús Hernández, *Yo, ministro de Stalin en España* (Madrid, 1954), 85.

6. Iturralde, II, 197–98.

7. Arana to Doroteo de Ciáurriz (president of the EBB), March 7, 1937, quoted in Sarrailh, *Vasconia*, 386–89, and Fernández Etxeberria, 111–14.

8. Aguirre, "Informe," 13.

9. Writing on December 8, 1936, the British consul declared that he had observed a great improvement after formation of the Basque government. He charged that prior to October 1, "One may well ask what the Basque nationalists were doing during these weeks to preserve themselves and their city from material and moral destruction. . . . They showed a complete lack of leadership and made no effort to assert themselves. In defence they plead extenuating circumstances." He went on to say that though "there have been isolated cases of murder by anarchists since they [the nationalists] came to power," the situation was in fact much more secure. PRO 1936 W 18036/62/41.

10. An eyewitness account is given by Steer, 113–21. He notes that six of the Socialist militia involved were later sentenced to death by Basque courts.

This slaughter was the most sanguinary of several assaults on prisons and prison boats in Guipúzcoa and Vizcaya. Such reprisals usually occurred after crowds became enraged by Spanish Nationalist air raids, forgetting that the policy of bombing civilian targets had been begun by the Republican government in the first days of the war. The British military attaché, who observed one of those mob rages in Bilbao on September 25, reported that the Spanish Nationalist attack "as the governor himself admitted, . . . was merely retaliation for similar action by Government aircraft against Vitoria earlier in the week." PRO 1936 W 13516/62/41.

Unlike the Republican central front, Vizcaya was virtually helpless against aerial assault. In the spring of 1937 these mounted in crescendo until they culminated in the Guernica disaster.

11. On January 31 Consul Henderson reported that "eight battalions of Gudaris—about 7,000—were pulled out of the front line for garrison duty in Bilbao after massacres earlier this month." PRO 1937 W 2828/1/41.

12. Records of the Tribunal Popular de Vizcaya have been preserved in the JSD, Salamanca. They indicate that the majority of death sentences were passed *in absentia*. Only a few score people were actually sentenced and executed. In one special instance, on January 20, 1937, fifty-one anonymous (nombre: "se ignora") executions were entered into the records, apparently to legitimize one of the prison massacres.

13. Dr. José Echeandía, *La persecución roja en el País vasco* (Barcelona, 1945).

14. Centro de Información Católica Internacional, *El Clero y los Católicos vasco-separatistas y el Movimiento Nacional* (Madrid, 1940), 161.

15. It should be noted that Basque nationalists also managed to play a moderating role during the main phase of the Red Terror in Madrid, where they won the release of several hundred people from the local *checas*. See Jesús de Galíndez, *Los vascos en el Madrid sitiado* (Buenos Aires, 1945).

16. According to *El Clero y los Católicos vasco-separatistas*, 124, a total of 286 churches were totally or partially destroyed in Vizcaya, a figure exceeded only by that of the anarchist-dominated provinces of eastern and southeastern Spain. However, it is not clear how many of these were damaged by bombing or other military action. The same may be said for the record of destruction compiled by a committee from the University of Valladolid, *Informe sobre la situación de las Provincias vascongadas bajo el dominio rojo-separatista* (Valladolid, 1938).

17. *El Clero y los Católicos vasco-separatistas*, 148−50, gives the names of all but one of fifty-one clergy reported to have been killed by the left in Vizcaya alone. Del Burgo, 95, lowers this total to forty-seven, the same figure given earlier by Pedro P. Altabella, *El catolicismo de los nacionalistas vascos* (Madrid, 1939), 158−64.

18. Aguirre, "Informe," 22−23.

19. Quoted in Lt. Col. J. M. Martínez Bande, *Vizcaya* (Madrid, 1971), 59, 244.

20. Prieto to Aguirre, n. d., reproduced facing p. 153 in Martínez Bande, *Guerra en el norte*.

21. Ibid.

22. According to the Vizcayan anarcho-syndicalist leader Horacio Prieto (Director general of foreign commerce in the Largo Caballero government), in his "Gobierno Vasco. Algunos antecedentes para el Libro Blanco de Euzkadi-Norte C. N. T.," in César M. Lorenzo, *Les Anarchistes espagnols et le pouvoir* (Paris, 1969), 167−69; Prieto's *Anarquismo relativo* (Mexico City, 1948), 244, in Ibid.; and Juan Peiro, *Problemas y cintarazos* (Rennes, 1946), 125.

22a. Quoted in Martínez Bande, *Guerra en el norte*, 154.

23. Ramón Salas, *Historia del Ejército Popular de la República* (Madrid, 1974), II, 1427.

24. Aguirre, "Informe," 29.

25. The latter was stressed particularly by José Rezola, Basque assistant councillor for defense in 1936−37. Interview in St.-Jean-de-Luz, Oct. 11, 1962.

26. José Antonio de Aguirre, *De Guernica a Nueva York pasando por Berlín* (Buenos Aires, 1944), 21. It might be noted that since the German government refused to commit itself so fully to the Spanish Nationalist cause as did that of Italy, at first it did not prevent private German firms from selling arms to Spanish Republican agents, even though the German government was shipping supplies on credit to the other side.

27. These and most other military statistics used in this study should be recognized as mere approximations. Concerning the Russian shipments in October, Aguirre gave slightly different figures in his later "Informe" compared with his earlier book, *De Guernica*. There are further minor differences in the account of an eyewitness, Steer, 96−97.

28. Aguirre, "Informe," 38−39.

29. Martínez Bande, *Guerra en el norte*, 170.

30. Aguirre, "Informe," 32−36, blames this—apparently correctly—on Ciutat's rigid staff work, which rejected a Basque plan for a three-pronged maneuver that could have turned the insurgents' flank.

31. Ibid., 202. Cf. M. Fernández Etxeberria, *Euzkadi, patria de los vascos* (Caracas, 1969), 135–40, and Gen. José Martínez Esparza, "El sitio de Villarreal de Alava," *Ejercito* (Madrid), no. 111 (April 1949).

32. Casualty report of the Army Corps "Euzkadi," in Martínez Bande, *Guerra en el norte*, 204–5. Total Basque casualties were at least 4,500, whereas those of the Spanish Nationalist defenders were only 255.

33. According to the secretary of the Spanish Communist party, José Díaz, in his *Por la unidad, hacia la victoria* (Valencia, 1937). The figure is probably too high. Just three months earlier, the Basque Communist leaders had only claimed a membership of 12,000, in Jesús Larrañaga, *¡Por la libertad de Euzkadi, dentro de las libertades de España!* (Barcelona, 1937). In the statements published by the latter pamphlet, the Vizcayan Communist leader Aurelio Aranaga claimed that 10,000 Communists were then serving at the front, which was undoubtedly an exaggeration, unless members of the Vizcayan Unified Socialist Youth were included. More nearly correct was the statement that the Communist organ in Bilbao, *Euzkadi Roja*, which began with a circulation of 17,000 in January 1937, had increased to 44,000 and achieved the largest circulation of any journal in Vizcaya, with the possible exception of *Euzkadi*.

34. Aguirre, "Informe," 37. The Vizcayan Communist leader Jesús Larrañaga was named chief commissar for the People's Army in Vizcaya by the Republican ministry of defense.

35. Ibid.

36. Quoted in Dolores Ibarruri, *They Shall Not Pass* (New York, 1966), 276.

37. Consul Henderson observed on Feb. 13, 1937: "The Basques, I have the impression, fear more 'Red' aggression from Santander and Asturias than the danger from the [Franquist] Military. To prevent the infiltration of undesirable elements from the West they have instituted a rigorous control of their Santander frontier." PRO 1937 W 4274/1/41.

38. Report of Lt. Col. Buzón Llanes, chief of the Second Section of the General Staff of the Army of the North, to the Republican Government, Nov. 21, 1937, in Martínez Bande, *Guerra en el norte*, 247–50.

39. The full text is given in Sierra Bustamante, 313–21.

40. In July 1937 Múgica publicly denied charges that the initial letter of August 6 had been issued under duress, and in a technical sense he was correct. Nonetheless, during the course of the Civil War and afterward he came to regret even his first letter, and later assured Aguirre that he had concluded that the Basque cause was fully legitimate, and that the nationalists had not violated their religion in supporting it. In private correspondence with Gomá he strongly protested the latter's failure to

condemn fully and openly the execution of Basque priests by the Spanish
Nationalists. The fullest account of *l'affaire* Múgica will be found in
Iturralde, II, 278–368. The bishop published a formal rectification of his
earliest stand under the title "Imperativòs de mi conciencia," in *Euzko-
Deya* (Paris), Dec. 15, 1945. His final clarifying letter to Aguirre, March
19, 1946, is in P. Iñaki de Azpiazu, *El caso del clero vasco* (Buenos Aires,
1957), 29–31.

   An interesting comparison may be made with the only member of the
Spanish church hierarchy to hold resolutely to a completely apolitical and
unmitigatedly Christian position. See Ramon Muntanyola, *Vidal i Barraquer, cardenal de la pau* (Barcelona, 1970).

   41. According to the authoritative study of Antonio Montero Moreno,
Historia de la persecución religiosa en España, 1936-1939 (Madrid,
1961).

   42. Cardinal Isidro Gomá y Tomás, *Pastorales de la Guerra de España*
(Madrid, 1955), 73–93.

   During the next three years a number of polemical works on Basque
nationalism and its relation to Spanish Catholicism and Spanish identity
were published by Spanish Nationalists: R. G. García de Castro, *La
tragedia espiritual de Vizcaya* (Granada, 1938); Sebastián de Romero
Radigales, *El separatismo vasco* (Sofía, 1938); Zacarías de
Vizcarra, *Vizcaya españolísima* (San Sebastián, 1939), and Pedro P.
Altabella Gracia, *El catolicismo de los nacionalistas vascos* (Vitoria,
1939). The best documented was the anonymous *El Clero y los Católicos
vasco-separatistas y el Movimiento Nacional* (Madrid, 1940), published
by the Centro de Información Católica Internactional. One of the first
Basque nationalist replies to this literature from exile was the anonymous
Le Clergé Basque (Paris, 1938). Another nearly twenty years later was
Pedro de Basaldúa's *En defensa de la verdad* (Buenos Aires, 1956).

   During the course of the war there were also several booklets by
leaders of the Catholic political right that criticised the role and position of
nationalism from a primarily political viewpoint, such as José María Gil
Robles's pamphlet, *The Spanish Republic and Basque Independence*, and
the Marquis Merry del Val, *The Spanish Basques and Separatism* (London, 1939).

   43. The correspondence between Aguirre and Gomá has been variously
reprinted by Angel de Zumeta, ed., *Un cardenal español y los católicos
vascos* (Bilbao, 1937) and *La guerra civil en Euzkadi. La teología de la
invasión fascista* (Paris, 1937); Dr. de Azpilikoeta, ed., *The Basque
Problem as seen by Cardinal Gomá and President Aguirre* (New York,
1939); and most recently by Joseph Ma. Llorens, *La Iglesia contra la
República española* (n.p., 1969), 142–51.

44. The text is most easily accessible in Gomá y Tomás, 147–89.

45. According to Aguirre, "Informe," 21. It should be noted that not all these refugees were nationalists and leftists from the other Basque provinces, but also included conservatives fleeing the leftist terror in Santander.

46. Enrique Castro Delgado, *Hombres Made in Moscú* (Barcelona, 1963), 463.

47. Lorenzo, 168. A list of names and political identities of various units in the Basque forces through the spring of 1937 is given in Appendix One.

To what extent the Basques were more genuinely sectarian and exclusive than other Republican elements in the sphere of military unity and cooperation may be questionable, but for an indictment of them from the extreme left, see José M. Arenillas, *Euzkadi, la cuestión nacional y la revolución socialista* (Paris, 1969), 15.

48. In a series of letters to PNV leaders during March and April, Luis de Arana y Goiri complained that they had made of the PNV "a different party," committed to participation in a foreign civil war between Spanish "Reds" and Spanish "Yellows" (a reference to the colors of the Spanish flag and the political connotation of "scab" or antileftist that yellow has in Spanish). These are quoted in Sarrailh, *Vasconia*, 386–94, and Fernández Etxeberria, 111–20.

49. Their composition is given in Sierra Bustamante, 168–71.

50. According to the most complete investigation thus far, approximately five thousand Navarrese were killed on the Franco side in the Civil War, nearly all of them combat casualties. Del Burgo, 106.

51. Col. J. M. Martínez Bande, *Vizcaya* (Madrid, 1971), 224.

52. Ibid., 112.

53. Ibid., 67–68.

54. A list of supplies purported to have been received in Vizcaya down to the beginning of the offensive is given in Sancho de Beurko, pseud., (Luis Ruiz de Aguirre) *Gudaris* (Buenos Aires, 1956), 141–43.

55. Martínez Bande, *Vizcaya*, 84–85.

56. On the aerial aspect of the Vizcayan campaign, see Jesús Salas Larrazábal, *La Guerra de España desde el aire* (Barcelona, 1969), 182–210, 222–66.

When the Republican air command finally admitted to the Republican cabinet in mid-May that it was logistically possible to send planes directly by air to Vizcaya, the anarcho-syndicalist minister García Oliver exclaimed "Then we have been deceiving the Basques!", according to Largo Caballero, 207.

57. These and many other aspects of military supply and organization

are detailed in Salas's account of the Vizcayan campaign (op. cit., II, 1359–1442), the best technical exposition of the struggle with respect to the Vizcayan forces.

58. Guernica was a legitimate military objective insofar as it was a district military command center, a communications hub, and the site of a munitions factory. However, the Condor Legion was apparently ordered by German authorities to make an experimental saturation bombing raid on an urban target—without specific clearance from Franco—and the unlucky target was Guernica. Though Basque casualty claims appear to have been exaggerated, evidence introduced by Spanish Nationalists in support of the latter's contention that Guernica was partially destroyed by its own defenders is rather dubious. The British consul, who certainly could not be accused of pro-Republicanism, visited Guernica two days later and in a dispatch of April 28 indicated little doubt that the city had been destroyed by aerial bombs. (PRO 1937 W 8661/1/41.) There is an excellent recent study by Vicente Talón, *Arde Guernica* (Madrid, 1970), and the analysis by Sales, II, 1384–92, is outstanding. For a different point of view, see Ricardo de la Cierva, *Historia ilustrada de la Guerra civil española* (Madrid, 1970), II, 149–63, and the symposium "Getting at the Guernica Myth," *National Review* 25, no. 35 (Aug. 31, 1973), 936–42.

59. Martínez Bande, *Vizcaya*, 132–33.

60. The fullest account is Manuel Cruells, *Els fets de maig* (Barcelona, 1969).

61. Lorenzo, 169–70.

62. Astigarrabia was eventually expelled from the Communist party several months after the fall of Bilbao. There are references to his role in Castro Delgado, 463–71, and in Ibarruri, 295–97.

63. At one point members of the nationalist Arana-Goiri battalion at the front wrote a collective letter to the editor of the Bilbao Communist paper *Euzkadi Roja*, suggesting that since they already had plenty of picks and shovels and the paper had emphasized that the latter were worth as much or more than aircraft, they would gladly trade 100 picks and 100 shovels for every plane that the Communists brought to the northern front. Fernández Etxeberria, 99.

64. Castro Delgado, 471.

65. Manuel Azaña, *Obras completas* (Mexico City, 1968), IV, 682.

66. A Republican military intelligence (SIM) report of May 12 stated: "The number of Asturian battalions in Vizcaya is now more than ten, and they are continually engaged in pillage. When they passed through Abadiano they shot the parish priest, one municipal councillor of the PNV

and two more of the ANV. They steal cattle from the farms they pass and flaunt their female camp followers from Asturias." Another report of May 18 mentioned the civilians' "terror of the militia from Asturias and Santander, whose lust for destruction is notorious. . . ." Quoted in Martínez Bande, *Vizcaya*, 135.

Resentment of the Asturians among the nationalists was apparently widespread. The radical nationalist Sarrailh (Krutwig) later wrote "their military action consisted of pillage, theft and the murder of Basque priests. More than one Basque patriot was immolated by this Red Spanish rabble. Furthermore, they made no effort to hide their ultimate intentions but clearly stated that 'when we have finished with the others, we will come for you.' " *Vasconia*, 288.

67. Aguirre to Prieto, May 24, 1937, in Ibid., 66.

68. According to Antonio Ramós Oliveira, *Historia de España* (Mexico City, 1952), III, 340.

69. Quoted in Martínez Bande, *Vizcaya*, 134.

70. Ibid.

8

THE CAPITULATION OF SANTOÑA

Efforts to detach the Basque nationalists from their alliance with the wartime Popular Front Republic had never ceased since the beginning of the conflict. These feelers and intermittent contacts seem to have been conducted almost exclusively by Carlists, prominent conservative Catholic laymen, and later by leaders of the church hierarchy itself. The circumstantial Basque alliance was incomprehensible to most other Spanish Catholics, and among the latter there persisted a feeling that only some sort of rational understanding would be needed to break Basque association with the Popular Front.

There appears to have been a momentary lull in such efforts during October and November 1936, when Franco's forces concentrated on an all-out offensive against Madrid to end the war quickly. By early December, however, the prominent Catholic Action leader Francisco Herrera Oria was in St.-Jean-de-Luz to attempt negotiation.[1] This ploy fell through, but a somewhat different approach was taken a month or so later.

Serious consultations directed toward a separate peace with the Basques were begun by Cardinal Gomá very early in 1937, despite the failure of his open letter to Aguirre. In this initiative he had the full approval of the Vatican, to whom he reported on

February 4 that Franco had informed him that the Spanish
Nationalist government "was going to initiate negotiations with the
Basque nationalists to put an end to the war in the north."[2] This
effort failed, partially because the Basque nationalist leaders had
no faith in a private arrangement with Franco. In March Gomá tried
to open more direct discussions with the Basques by means of
Padre Alberto Onaindía, an adviser of Aguirre's who happened to
be in St.-Jean-de-Luz. Gomá proposed to offer the personal integrity of his office as a guarantee that any terms arrived at would
be honored[3] but later related that Onaindía refused to discuss
surrender, alleging that the whole initiative "revealed the weakness
of the Spanish Nationalists, who were being obliged to sue for
peace."[4]

Consequently Gomá sought the good offices of the Italian
government, as an outside power involved in the war and friendly
to both the Vatican and the Franco regime. On March 21 he made
contact with the new Italian consul in San Sebastián, the Marchese
di Cavaletti, to seek his assistance. Shortly afterward a Spanish
Jesuit, Padre Pereda, who had just left Vizcaya, informed Cavaletti
of the growing pessimism there and responded enthusiastically to
the suggestion that Basque nationalists might be willing to surrender to Italian forces under proper guarantees. Cavaletti was encouraged in this effort by the Italian ambassador, Roberto Cantalupo,
who traveled to San Sebastián for discussion of the matter at the
beginning of April. Cantalupo was then recalled to Rome almost
immediately afterward due to general dissatisfaction with his work
by his superiors, but in conversations with Ciano and others he
defended the proposition that Italy might play a useful role in
mediation with Franco's opponents.[5] On April 12 the Italian em-
bassy informed Cavaletti that, while not enthusiastic about the
maneuver, the Italian government was willing to serve as potential
guarantor for terms of surrender by the Basque nationalists.[6]

On April 21 General Mario Roatta ("Mancini"), commander
of Italian forces in Spain, talked with the German ambassador von
Faupel at Franco's military capital, Salamanca. He told Faupel that
he understood the Basques had been negotiating with Franco, but
that the discussions were unlikely to succeed because "the Basques
desired the guaranty of a neutral nation." According to Faupel's
report to Berlin, Roatta suggested that he and Faupel

could propose to Franco, in case he did not grant the guaranties of a neutral government, that the safety of the Basque population be assured by having the conquered territory, in particular Bilbao, occupied first of all by the Italian and German troops which were on the northern front. Mancini [Roatta] added that since the Nationalist troops had shot a large number of people after the capture of Málaga, the desire of the Basques for such a guaranty was very understandable.[7]

Faupel replied that this was very awkward and doubted that it would win Franco's approval.

On April 25 the Spanish generalissimo's brother and political aide, Nicolás Franco, informed the Italian government that the Spanish regime had already offered the following terms to the Basques:

1) Lives and property of all who surrender and are not guilty of personal crimes will be respected.
2) Only those charged with personal crimes will be prosecuted.
3) Leaders will be permitted to go into exile.
4) Those who do not surrender will have their goods confiscated and will be tried for rebellion.
5) No special privileges will be recognized for the Basque provinces, but in his declaration of October 1, 1936, when assuming the powers of Chief of State, Franco promised some degree of administrative decentralization and this would also apply to the Basques.[8]

The channel by which these terms were transmitted to the Basques was not specified, nor was it made clear at what time they had been made.

At this point the devastation of Guernica and the Spanish Nationalist advance into eastern Vizcaya raised fears in Bilbao that the Basque front might soon collapse. The government began to grasp at straws, and on April 28 Aguirre inquired of the British consul R. C. Henderson "whether . . . there was a possibility of the British and French Governments intervening."[9] Henderson replied that he "could not conceive it on any other basis other than surrender" to the Spanish Nationalists. Even his suggestion that at most British ships might evacuate the Basque government was quickly disavowed by the Foreign Office.[10]

The initiative was then resumed by the Vatican, which sent Gomá a coded telegram on May 6 asking him to try to negotiate favorable terms for a Basque surrender with the Spanish Nationalist command. On the following afternoon Gomá worked out a set of terms with General Mola in Vitoria that were similar to those earlier offered by Franco's headquarters. Mola then telephoned directly to Franco in Salamanca, and the insurgent generalissimo softened the terms even more, pledging to respect the "lives and property" of Basque military commanders who "surrender in good faith," offering Vizcaya "administrative decentralization in a form analogous to other favored regions" (presumably referring to Navarra and Alava), and offering "in the social order progressive justice within the possibilities of the national economy, according to the spirit of the encyclical Rerum Novarum."[11] Gomá appeared in St.-Jean-de-Luz to transmit the new terms by way of Padre Onaindía, but was unable to make contact with the latter.[12] The contents of the surrender offer were subsequently made known through a number of leaflets dropped by air behind the Basque lines in Vizcaya.[13]

Some days later, apparently between May 10 and 15, the Vatican secretary of state Cardinal Pacelli sent an uncoded telegram to President Aguirre by way of Republican Barcelona that presumably repeated the terms of this proposal of conditional surrender. The message was naturally intercepted by Republican authorities. Largo Caballero, to whom it was referred, ordered that this telegram and another that followed be suppressed and their contents kept fully secret. Aguirre was never informed.[14] Nevertheless, rumors were flying thick and fast, and the Basque nationalist delegation at Republican government headquarters in Valencia officially denied reports being published abroad about Basque negotiations with the Vatican.[15]

Meanwhile, the Italian consul in San Sebastián, Cavaletti, managed to establish contact with Padre Onaindía in St.-Jean-de-Luz on May 11. Cavaletti urged that Aguirre send a telegram directly to Mussolini asking the Duce's intervention. Onaindía then flew to Bilbao on the following day aboard the single flight of *Air*

Pyrénées operating between the Vizcaya capital and southwestern France, promptly returning with a five-point note from Aguirre, which emphasized that "there can be no dialogue about a 'surrender.' "[16]

At that point conversations were suspended for several weeks while Vizcayan military resistance stiffened and, with a series of straightahead counterattacks, slowed somewhat the pace of the Spanish Nationalist advance. Nevertheless, this continued to go forward and by the end of May had reached the outer limits of the so-called Iron Belt that defended the greater Bilbao area.

The approaching collapse was not due, with certain exceptions, to a lack of determination or fighting spirit among the Vizcayans. Spanish Nationalists have recognized the frequent tenacity of front-line resistance in Vizcaya, which bore the brunt of Franco's elite units for three and a half months before being conquered. By contrast, semimountainous Málaga province in the south, whose geographic situation was not dissimilar, had collapsed within a few days during the preceding February. Whereas the conquest of Vizcaya took months of hard fighting, occupation of the remaining northern sectors during the summer and autumn was a comparatively simple operation. No sector of the Spanish Republican forces proved more determined and tenacious than the Vizcayans in combat. Their inevitable military defeat was due to poor organization and leadership, to overwhelming inferiority in tactical airpower and finally to the complete ineptitude of the main Spanish Republican army in its failure to engage Franco's secondary units elsewhere with enough vigor to relieve the pressure in the north.

Concern about the ability of a semi-isolated Vizcaya to resist further was a major factor in the downfall of the Largo Caballero Popular Front government in mid-May 1937 and its replacement by a new Communist-dominated "win-the-war" government under the Socialist Juan Negrín. Prieto, minister of war in the new cabinet, encouraged Aguirre to cede military command at the end of May to a professional officer, Mariano Gámir Ulibarri. Gámir was a Basque, a qualified professional commander, and a genuine nonpolitical officer not identified with any of the leftist parties. He flew to Bilbao to do what he could to reorganize Basque resistance, but the outlook remained pessimistic. The Republican president, Azaña, noted gloomily in his diary on May 31 that

> The Basque nationalists do not fight for the cause of the Republic or that of Spain, which they abhor, but for their autonomy and semi-independence. With such a state of morale it is to be feared that, once Bilbao is lost, together with their territory and their autonomous government, they will think that their reason for fighting has ended.[17]

This prophecy proved largely though not entirely correct.

When Gámir took over direction of the Basque forces at the beginning of June, they amounted to a nominal eighty-five understrength battalions that altogether apparently totaled scarcely 40,000 organized troops.[18] Total casualties since the first records of the army had been formed amounted to approximately 35,000 men,[19] and for the first time since the start of the offensive Franco's forces began to enjoy a numerical as well as technological superiority. The assault on the main positions of the "Iron Belt," begun on June 11, made deep penetration through a weak spot in the line in thirty-six hours at the cost of only a few hundred casualties. This breakthrough paralyzed much of the Basque defense and sowed consternation in Bilbao, which was then only ten kilometers behind the front. It provoked renewed political dissidence and rumor-mongering.

> One rumor was that the Communist party proposed that it be given the chancellory of war in return for guaranteeing the shipment of aircraft within 48 hours. Another was that the Bilbao district would be turned into a British protectorate before it could fall in the hands of Franco. . . . And finally supporters of surrender emerged. . . .[20]

The first serious effort at arranging a separate peace for Basque nationalism was made by Anacleto de Ortueta, the intellectual who had played the principal role in founding and leading *Acción Nacionalista Vasca*. Ortueta's policy had always been what he conceived to be practical politics in association with the major forces in Spanish affairs. Under the Republic he had believed that a nationalist strategy that failed to align itself with the governmentally dominant Republican left was doomed to failure, and amid the wreckage of civil war and the imminence of total defeat he had reached the not dissimilar conclusion that some accommodation with Franco was the nationalists' only means of survival. During the last phase of the Vizcayan campaign he established contact with Franquist representatives (probably Carlist) and also attempted to employ the good offices of a group of Navarrese monks. Ortueta then got in touch with the commanders of nearly all Basque nationalist military battalions and apparently tried to call a meeting of these chiefs to agree on putting an end to the struggle. The slender evidence that exists concerning this maneuver suggests that several commanders may have been interested in the plan, but one of them eventually betrayed the negotiations to the Basque government. It quashed the whole effort but took no punitive action because Ortueta's tack reflected a growing mood that made punishment scarcely feasible under the circumstances.[21]

The fall of Bilbao was only a matter of days. Among the leadership of the PNV there had spread a mood of bitter disillusionment with the Spanish Popular Front regime, above all due to its failure to send air support and artillery. Though nationalists have sometimes recognized that the military defense of Vizcaya was strategically poorly organized and that some of the heterogeneous units of the Basque army failed to maintain their positions even under slight pressure, the feeling grew that the bargain with the left had been a bad one, leading to the loss of Vizcaya and the temporary eclipse of the nationalist movement. On June 13 the national council of the PNV sent the following message to Manuel Irujo, the Basque minister in Valencia:

> The *Euzkadi-Buru-Batzar* has agreed that you are to resign your ministerial position today on the following terms: In view of the state of defenselessness in which *Euzkadi* has been left by the government of the Republic, which has neither provided absolutely indispensable means for its defense nor generated offensives elsewhere to relieve the pressure on the Basques, the Basque Nationalist Party united declares that from this moment Manuel de Irujo y Ollo ceases to represent it in the government of the Republic. In order for the Basque Nationalist Party to resume governmental collaboration it will be necessary for the government of the Repub-

lic to send immediately to *Euzkadi* the aviation and other
means of war that it needs. The official resignation will be
presented immediately; it will not be announced for 48 hours,
after which it will be made public in the terms explained
above, calling attention to the fact that our defense and
counterattacks during a period of 64 days have been more
than sufficient to permit the Republican forces to develop
adequate offensive plans.[22]

The outcome of this maneuver has not been clarified. Whatever
took place, the decision was changed, and Irujo remained in the
Republican government, having become minister of justice a
month earlier.

The nationalists were further upset by information that Gámir
had orders from Valencia to destroy the industrial facilities of
Bilbao if and when it proved impossible to defend the city.[23]
Anarchists and other revolutionaries had already carried out minor
scorched-earth operations at several intervals in the retreat, and the
nationalists had earlier intervened to defend San Sebastián and
other points in Guipúzcoa from destruction. The nationalist leaders
made clear their determination to avert destruction; those in charge
of the evacuation, headed by Jesús María de Leizaola (and assisted
by the cooperative Basque Communist chief Manuel Astigarrabia—later drummed out of the Spanish Communist party for his
pains) almost completely thwarted incendiarism and also released
the two thousand remaining rightist prisoners from jail.[24] A Republican staff report noted one instance in which PNV battalions fired
on Asturian units attempting to start fires and explosions in the
suburb of Deusto.[25] The city fell on June 19, leaving nearly all
Vizcaya in the hands of the Spanish Nationalists. The campaign
had cost the Basque forces 14,000 prisoners and 8,100 deserters,
according to one incomplete Spanish Nationalist report,[26] in addition to more than 7,000 combat casualties.

From that point the war was over for most Basque nationalists.
Though approximately twenty thousand troops in nationalist battalions withdrew westward to the border of Santander province, they
had lost their homeland and the purpose of the conflict. Santander
itself, a basically conservative province that had voted for the right
in the 1936 elections, was demoralized. According to the last

Republican commander in the north, Colonel Prada, 85 percent of the troops there had been raised by forced draft, and the rear-guard was strongly anti-Republican. He declared that in Santander "the soldiers (both Basques and *santanderinos*) no longer knew what they were fighting for."[27]

Throughout the collapse of Vizcaya the Italian consul had maintained contact with Onaindía in St.-Jean-de-Luz. On May 27 he urged once more that Aguirre "send a telegram to Mussolini, not as Duce but simply as a person who can influence the course of the war,"[28] and on June 3 suggested that it might "deal with any humanitarian theme, though containing a political design."[29] On that occasion Onaindía decided to feel out the potential Italian position further by suggesting

> that the Basque who aspires to political liberty might be more willing to be under Italy than under Franco. Cavaletti replied that it 'might not be impossible,' that this was a matter for study.[30]

Cavaletti picked up the theme five days later, speaking vaguely "of Italian protection for a period of years, together with the regular entry of [Italian] troops and guarantees, if *Euzkadi* surrendered to the Italian command."[31]

Aguirre never showed any personal interest in pursuing negotiations with the Italians, but on June 16, with the fall of Bilbao imminent, the direction of discussions was taken over by Juan Ajuriaguerra, president of the Vizcayan provincial committee (BBB) of the PNV. Recalling that on May 12 Aguirre had told him that Basque forces would not fight beyond the Vizcayan frontier, Onaindía went to Paris on June 22 to inform himself about the position of the top nationalist leadership. There Antonio Irala, secretary general of the presidency of the Basque government, stressed that the Basques must avoid being completely detached from the Popular Front alliance by the Italians because, despite the loss of Vizcaya, the international situation dictated that ultimately the Republic would win.[32]

However that might have seemed to government officials, Vizcayan nationalist leaders were not willing to continue resistance in Santander and were eager to limit the suffering of troops and

civilian refugees. Through Onaindía, the Vizcayan leader Ajuriaguerra arranged a secret nocturnal interview with the Italian military attaché, Da Cunto, in the "Old Port" district of Algorta
(Vizcaya) on June 25.[33] The outcome was to arrange a trip by
Onaindía to Rome, which was officially authorized by Aguirre on
July 3 in order to "expound the Basque national problem and the
current situation of *Euzkadi* before Italy's chief and government."[34]

Accompanied only by the editor of the former newspaper
Euzkadi, Onaindía arrived in Rome on July 6. He found the Italian
foreign minister Ciano to be totally ignorant of the nature of the
Basque problem, but that same day Mussolini—whom Onaindía
never saw—dispatched a personal telegram to Franco. In it the
Italian Duce proposed that he arrange separate surrender of the
remaining Basque forces to Italian troops.[35] In return for promising
that there would be no reprisals and that Basque prisoners would
remain under Italian protection, the Republican forces could be
reduced bloodlessly, diplomatic advantage gained, and the war
shortened.

On the following morning, José Ma. Lasarte, the special PNV
representative sent to Bayonne to assist in the negotiations, wired
in code:

> Onaindía. Telegram Duce to Franco gives impression that
> Euzkadi surrenders diplomatically stop Necessary specifi-
> cally prevent appearance of diplomatic combat that would
> leave us bad position with everyone stop Agreement with
> Rome and arrangement by Euzkadi must all be made form of
> military operation without anyone suspecting anything.[36]

These distinctions were then made clear to Ciano.

Franco's reply was read to Onaindía by Ciano on July 8. The
generalissimo accepted Mussolini's proposal but doubted that a
Basque surrender would bring the immediate collapse of the whole
northern front, since the leftist forces were not likely to participate.[37] Onaindía then left Rome on July 10 with the understanding
that the details of a Basque surrender to the Italian forces on the
northern front under the guise of military operations would be
worked out by their respective military representatives.

This proved the most difficult part of the whole operation. In the meantime the difference of opinion between Aguirre and the regular PNV leaders became more marked. Aguirre had no confidence in a deal with the Italians, whom he detested. He wanted to remain faithful to the Popular Front alliance while playing for time to evacuate as many Basque troops as possible to France and back to the main Republican zone. For most of the PNV leaders, however, the war was over, and they expected to obtain better treatment through Italian intercession than through surrender to Franco,[38] although they realized the potentially harmful consequences of an overt desertion of the Popular Front alliance. The need for great delicacy in the arrangements, together with the technical details of concentrating nationalist battalions and establishing means for evacuating civilians, made it hard to establish concrete terms with the Italian command. A note from the Italian consul and military attaché, dispatched in Biarritz on July 13, accused the Basques of dragging their feet and demanded the arrival of a Basque military plenipotentiary before midnight on July 14 to establish concrete arrangements.[39] The Basque leadership failed to comply, but did radio on July 16 to specify that the Basque battalions would be concentrated between Castro Urdiales and Carranza and that care would be taken to protect the lives of twenty-five hundred rightist prisoners held in the Santoña (Santander) jail. At the same time the Basque authorities insisted that the Italians must guarantee the safe evacuation by sea of fifteen shiploads of the "civilian population" that they were arranging.[40] The Italian representatives in Biarritz replied immediately and with some disgust that nothing had yet been done to establish the concrete terms of surrender and that the Basques were now putting up new demands.[41] They returned to Nationalist Spain to consult with Italian military and diplomatic authorities.

Franco's forces had stopped to regroup throughout July and early August, and the Basques still played for time. Despite the reluctance of most Basque troops to continue fighting outside their territory, one battalion was even transferred to serve in Asturias. On July 20 the Italian delegates complained that it seemed to be Santander and Asturian battalions, rather than Basques, that were concentrating between Castro Urdiales and Carranza.[42] Three days later they repeated this charge, adding that Basque units seemed to be increasingly subdivided and mixed with leftist battalions rather than concentrating. The Italian attaché also observed that the evacuation of civilians seemed to proceed with extreme slowness and that there was at least equal attention in the Bay of Biscay to running in more military supplies for Republicans.[43] Basque representatives protested that civilian evacuation was proceeding as rapidly as possible, two boatloads having just arrived in France, and that Basque battalions were being concentrated as agreed upon.[44] That same day (July 23), the nationalist deputy Julio Jáuregui met in Hendaye with a Spanish Nationalist representative, who suggested very much the same arrangements. In return for a separate Basque surrender, Franco would permit all nationalist leaders to emigrate and would guarantee no reprisals against ordinary Basque troops who surrendered.[45]

The Franquist initiative surprised the Italian delegates, who again expressed their disgust on July 29 with Basque footdragging.[46] In an effort to placate them, Basque negotiators on the following day gave them a list of the boats currently en route to Santander to evacuate civilians.[47] Having learned that Aguirre was currently in Paris, Cavaletti and Da Cunto insisted that the Basque representatives obtain his agreement to meet in France with either the Italian ambassador to Paris or General Roatta. Onaindía traveled to Paris with this message on August 1, but Aguirre refused to deal directly with the Italians.[48] With the military front still quiet, negotiations were temporarily suspended as the Basques continued to play for time. It is not clear whether many troops actually deserted to Franco's forces, but by mid-August the sixteen all-Basque battalions remaining in Santander amounted to little more than six thousand men. It proved impossible to evacuate more than a small number of civilians and a few key personnel because of the Spanish Nationalist naval blockade.

Franco's Santander offensive began on August 13. The main thrust was directed toward pinching off the large Republican salient in the southern part of the province, with the Italian CTV playing a major role, suffering 12 percent casaulties in fourteen days of fighting.[49] The Basque battalions were concentrated in the northeast (the Laredo-Santoña sector) and in reserve. The only Italian force in that region was the mixed Italo-Spanish *Freccie Nere* brigade, operating along the coast together with one of the crack Navarrese brigades.

There was no longer any time for the Basques to lose. On August 17, as Franco's pincers were snapping shut in southern Santander and shattered Republican units were fleeing in disorder, Ajuriaguerra personally met with Italian delegates in Biarritz. It was agreed that the final evacuation by sea and the surrender of Basque troops on land would occur between midnight August 21 and midnight August 24.[50] The Basques would surrender to the *Freccie Nere* advancing along the coast, which would then be the first enemy unit to enter Santander. Final details were arranged between August 19 and 22. On the latter date, an Italian note formally confirmed the terms of surrender: all Basques who laid down their arms would be considered prisoners of the Italians and protected from reprisals, leaders and officers would be allowed to leave by sea, and boats carrying Basque civilians would be given free passage on August 23 with the Spanish Nationalist navy forewarned and requested not to interfere.[51]

Just as the Republican command was ordering final withdrawal toward Asturias, the Basque battalions in the Laredo-Santoña district came out in revolt on August 23. While twenty-five hundred rightist prisoners were being freed from jail in Santoña, the local Basque commander made the gesture of declaring the "Independent Republic of *Euzkadi*." On the following day two Basque officers passed over to Italian lines to negotiate surrender. They found the local Italian commander, General Sandro Piazzoni, chief of the largely Italian *Freccie Nere* division, uncertain how to proceed.[52]

Piazzoni's second-ranking staff officer was Major Bartolomé Barba Hernández, a cofounder of the secret Spanish army officers' association UME and a leading Spanish Nationalist ultra. Barba insisted that a separate surrender was unacceptable because it had not been officially cleared by Franco's headquarters.[53] According to the Spanish *Servicio Histórico Militar*, Barba and the Italian divisional chief of staff, Lieutenant Colonel Farina, then signed a new document with the two Basque captains requiring unconditional surrender.[54]

According to Onaindía, on the evening of the following day (August 25), as Italian troops began to advance into the Basque sector, Ajuriaguerra went to talk with Roatta, the Italian commander-in-chief, behind the enemy front. By August 26 the reamining Basque forces in the Laredo-Santoña area surrendered to Italian units. Spanish Nationalist warships still blocked the evacuation of Basque political and military officials, but Roatta placed the latter under a special Italian guard on August 28 and promised that they would be sent to France on Italian vessels if necessary.[55]

This situation lasted one week, as Franco's forces occupied the remainder of Santander and established Spanish Nationalist authority. On September 4 a Spanish Nationalist unit replaced the Italian guard, seizing Ajuriaguerra and all other Basque leaders and officers who remained as prisoners. Spanish forces had already taken possession of the other Basque prisoners. Roatta was furious, feeling that he had been betrayed and his word of honor besmirched. He spoke of resigning and not long afterward was replaced as commander of Italian military forces in Spain.

Franco's position seems to have been that he agreed to Mussolini's proposal of July 10 on the grounds that the surrender would be speedily arranged and would spare the need for a full-scale assault on Santander province. This had not proven to be the case. The Basques had played for time, their reserve brigade (officially termed a "division") had provided the "only serious resistance" encountered by Franco's forces in pinching off the Reinosa salient,[56] both the Spanish Nationalists and Italians had suffered further casualties and expense, more time had been won for the central Republican zone, and the Basques had only surrendered when objectively all was lost and they had little alternative. Whatever Roatta and other Italian officials in Spain thought, Salamanca and Rome eventually agreed on this policy.[57] All Basques in Santander province became prisoners of Franco.

Basque nationalism had been crushed militarily. Vizcaya lay under occupation, and a relentless purge was carried out there[58] and in Guipúzcoa. A not inconsiderable part of the population nonetheless welcomed Franco's triumph for having defeated the forces of revolution. In the aftermath, hundreds—perhaps several thousand—soldiers of the former Basque army served in Franco's forces during 1938.

From the beginning of the conflict, other thousands of Basques had fled Spain altogether, mostly to France. Conservatives had fled in three directions: to Nationalist Spain, to France, and to the more orderly sectors of Vizcaya. Beginning with the fall of Irún, nationalists and leftists began to flee to France, and sizable evacuations occurred during the spring of 1937. Basque Nationalist sources have calculated that the total exodus amounted to 150,000,[59] though this may well be an exaggeration. That figure includes 20,000 children evacuated from Vizcaya during the bombing, mainly to England, though 1,500 offspring of leftist parents were shipped to the Soviet Union.[60]

Though Ajuriaguerra and other top Vizcayan leaders were imprisoned by Franco, headquarters of both the government of *Euzkadi* and the PNV were transferred to the Republican zone in eastern Spain. Several thousand Basque volunteers, either cut off originally from the northern zone or—in a few cases—escapees by way of France, served in the Republican army for the remainder of the war. Despite the original decision to have him resign, Irujo remained in the Republican cabinet until 1939 and played the leading role in new measures to restore a degree of protection to Catholic religious activities in the Republican zone during 1937–38.[61]

Nonetheless, relations with the Republican government were never fully satisfactory. Though Republican leaders had no idea of the extent of Basque negotiations with the Italians, there remained a strong sense that the Basque nationalists were much more concerned about their separate ambitions than the common defense of the Popular Front Republic. In that, of course, they were no different from most of the other factions making up the wartime Republican coalition.

Aguirre had never believed in the negotiations with the Italians, had refused to participate in them and had never been informed of the full details. After the fall of Bilbao, he and several other Basque leaders threw all their support behind a plan to evacuate all Basque forces in the north—and if possible the entire one hundred thousand Republican troops in the northern zone—through France to the main Republican territory, where he believed that they could contribute much more effectively to the Republican war effort.

This was first officially proposed to the Republican cabinet at a special meeting in Valenica on June 29, 1937, when representatives of each of the three sectors of the northern zone rendered reports. Jesús María de Leizaola spoke for the Basques. Though he had no specific instructions from Aguirre, Leizaola recommended evacuation en masse,[62] but the government quickly decided that this was a military and logistical impossibility. From that time forward, the idea spread in Republican government circles that, at the worst, some Basque leaders favored a deal with Franco[63] and that, at best, the Basques would work in conjunction with Catalanists to form a separate bloc in the Republican coalition.[64]

The Republican government was officially moved to Barcelona in October 1937, and during the last year and a half of the civil war the PNV and Catalan *Esquerra* closely supported each other.[65] Late in 1938 the Catalanist representative walked out of the Republican cabinet temporarily in protest against the Republican government's takeover of central authority in many aspects of Catalan administration. He was accompanied by Irujo. Despite such contretemps, the Basque leaders did stand by the Republican government to the end. Aguirre told President Azaña on October 11, 1937, "that his loyalty to the Republic would be unshakeable so long as the war lasted. After that we shall see what happens."[66] In the final Republican political crisis of February-March 1939, when even Azaña had refused further service to the Republican cause, Aguirre was willing to cooperate with the CNT in forming a broad last-ditch Republican coalition government to end the war honorably.[67] Though Basque nationalism at that point remained little more than a symbol, the Basques were perhaps the only political group to conduct themselves with dignity and discipline during the mass evacuation of Catalonia, caring for their refugees efficiently and with their own resources.[68]

NOTES

1. On December 4, 1936, Chilton reported a conversation that he had had with Herrera Oria as the latter was en route to St.-Jean-de-Luz. PRO 1936 W17612/62/41.

2. Anastasio Granados, *El Cardenal Gomá* (Madrid, 1969), 156.

3. According to an undated "Nota Informativa" in the *Servicio Histórico Militar* (Madrid), quoted in Martínez Bande, *Vizcaya*, 61–62.

4. Granados, 164.

5. Roberto Cantalupo, *Embajada en España* (Barcelona, 1951), 185–218.

6. This paragraph is based on notes from research in the Italian diplomatic archives of the period by Prof. John Coverdale of Princeton University, courtesy of Professor Coverdale. For the background of Italo-Spanish relations and Italian intervention in the conflict, see his book *Mussolini and Franco: Italian Intervention in the Spanish Civil War* (Princeton, 1975).

7. *Documents on German Foreign Policy*, Series D (London, 1961), III, 276.

8. Coverdale notes. Parenthetically, it may be noted that a "Sergeant Yoldi" of the Basque army has written that when a Basque counterattack on May 1–2 pinned down and partially cut off the "Freccie Nere" brigade (nearly half the members of whom at that point were Italian troops) along the coast, "the Basque government refused to let us go in for the kill." Robert Payne, ed., *The Civil War in Spain* (London, 1963), 230. This is very possibly an exaggeration, but may also indicate that the Basque government was concerned to avoid offense to Rome, in the expectation that the latter might be of assistance to it.

9. PRO 1937 W8661/1/41.

10. Marginal note to ibid.

11. Granados, 158–59.

12. Granados, 159; Iturralde, III, 207.

13. Granados, 161. This is apparently the offer referred to in the pro-Spanish Nationalist pamphlet by the moderate Catalanist Juan Estelrich, *La cuestión vasca y la guerra civil española*. (Buenos Aires, 1937).

14. Largo Caballero's version is given in *Mis recuerdos*, 207. Aguirre subsequently wrote that he only learned of this communication some three years later, as he relates in his *De Guernica a Nueva York*, 33–39. This version is corroborated by Padre Alberto Onaindía, quoted in Indalecio Prieto, *Palabras al viento* (Mexico City, 1969), 213–15. According to the Basque account, Largo Caballero made the matter the subject of a special cabinet meeting to which he did not invite the three Republican ministers identified with the regionalist position: the Catalan Ayguadé, the Basque Irujo, and the Bilbao Socialist Prieto.

A different version was published by Viborg de la Saudée, S. J., in the *Revue des Deux Mondes*, Feb. 10, 1940. Cf. Juan Estelrich, *La cuestión vasca y la guerra civil española* (Buenos Aires, 1937).

On or immediately after May 11, a delegation of Basque nationalist priests left Bilbao for Rome where they spoke with Pacelli and other officials of his secretariat. They protested the correctness and Catholic orthodoxy of Basque nationalism and their right to an independent political position. The Vatican tacitly accepted their protest concerning their religious and moral fidelity, though continuing to disagree sharply with their politics. Iturralde, III, 210−14.

15. *Castilla Libre* (Madrid), May 11, 1937.

16. The fullest account of the Basque-Italian negotiations is given in Onaindía's unpublished memoir, "Antecedentes de la capitulación de Santoña," which through the good offices of Professor Jon Bilbao he has kindly given me permission to consult and to quote.

17. He also claimed, with notable exaggeration, that Vizcaya had been "a bottomless pit" for war material. Manuel Azaña, *Obras completas* (Mexico City, 1968), IV, 608.

18. Gen. Gámir Ulibarri, *De mis memorias: Guerra de España 1936-1939* (Paris, 1939), 22.

19. Ibid.

The casualty list to which Gámir referred is presumably the same one recently published by Salas:

Casualties Suffered by the
Basque Army Corps to June 1, 1937

Date	Total Casualties	Wounded	Sick	Dead
19 July to				
10 Nov. '36	6,042	50.8%	31.1%	8.1%
Dec. '36	6,182	54 %	29.3%	16.7%
Jan. '37	2,345	21.1%	77.3%	1.6%
Feb. '37	3,000	34.7%	58.5%	6.8%
Mar. '37	2,997	25.8%	66.6%	7.6%
Apr. '37	7,344	53.8%	27.4%	18.8%
May '37	8,793	56.5%	26.5%	23 %
Grand total	36,703			

SOURCE: Salas, *Historia del Ejército Popular*, III, 2908.

20. Undated staff report of Lt. Col. Buzón Llanes, in Martínez Bande, *Vizcaya*, 21.

21. The only source is Fernández Etxeberría, 157, 160−63, who talked with several of those involved in this negotiation.

22. Iturralde, III, 259−60.

23. Iturralde, III, 258; Víctor de Frutos, *Los que no perdieron la guerra* (Buenos Aires, 1967), 119ff. Julián Zugazagoitia, *Guerra y vici-*

situdes de los españoles (Paris, 1968), II, 12, reported certain plans for destruction by Prieto himself.

24. Aguirre, *De Guernica a Nueva York*, 57−58; Beurko, 92.
25. Martínez Bande, *Vizcaya*, 192−93.
26. Ibid., 220.

Fully reliable casualty figures are not available, and the real totals may have been higher. For what they are worth, one nationalist source has offered the following statistics:

Gudaris killed in action	10,800
Gudaris killed by Spanish Nationalist aircraft	4,700
Civilians killed by Spanish Nationalist aircraft	10,500
Gudaris missing in action	3,000
Gudaris wounded in action	17,500
Gudaris wounded by aircraft	12,500
Civilians wounded by aircraft	19,500
Basques imprisoned (civilian and military)	86,550
Basques killed by the Franquist repression	21,780

Astilarra, "La guerra en Euzkadi," cited in Fernández Etxeberría, 141. All these figures of Astilarra seem to be crude exaggerations and are included here mainly to give the Basque nationalist self-image of their war losses.

In addition to the monographs of Col. Martínez Bande, the principal Spanish Nationalist accounts of the Basque campaign are Lt. Gen. Rafael García Valiño, "La Campaña del Norte," in *Guerra de Liberación nacional* (Zaragoza, 1961), 259−314; Lt. Gen. Carlos Martínez de Campos, *Dos batallas de la Guerra de Liberación de España* (Madrid, n. d.); Lt. Col. Julio García Fernández, *Diario de operaciones del 3er Batallón de Palencia y 5a Bandera de Navarra* (Burgos, 1939); P. Cía Navascuez, *Memorias del Tercio de Montejurra* (Pamplona, 1941); and Col. M. Ribas de Piña, *El 11° Ligero durante el primer año triunfal* (Santander, 1938).

The major Italian accounts are in Gen. Emilio Faldella, *Venti mesi di guerra in Spagna* (Firenze, 1939); Gen. Sandro Piazzoni, *Las tropas "Flechas Negras" en la guerra de España* (Barcelona, 1941); and Gen. Francesco Belforte, *La Guerra Civile in Spagna* (Milano, 1938−39), III.

27. Azaña, IV, 846.
28. Onaindía to Aguirre, May 27, 1937, in Onaindía, 14.
29. Onaindía to Aguirre, June 4, 1937, in Ibid., 17.
30. Ibid., loc. cit.
31. Onaindía to Aguirre, Ibid., 25.
32. Ibid., 37.
33. Ibid., 43−45.

34. Ibid., 50.

35. Ibid., 58.

36. Ibid., 59.

37. Ibid., 62.

38. Ibid., 79–80.

39. Ibid., 72–73.

40. Ibid., 74–75.

41. Ibid., 76–77.

42. Ibid., 85.

43. Ibid., 86–87.

44. Ibid., 87–88.

45. Ibid., 89–90.

46. Ibid., 94.

47. Ibid., 95–97.

48. Ibid., 98–99.

49. According to Ricardo de la Cierva et al., *Historia ilustrada de la guerra civil española* (Barcelona, 1971), II, 254.

50. Onaindía, 104–6.

51. Ibid., 107–10.

52. Ibid., 112–19.

53. La Cierva, II, 255–56.

54. Martínez Bande, *El final del frente Norte* (Madrid, 1972), 93.

55. This account is based on the documents in Onaindía, 120–42, the most important of which is a three-page letter by Ajuriaguerra explaining the final phase.

56. Manuel Aznar, *Historia militar de la guerra de España* (Madrid, 1940), 456.

57. This was made clear to Onaindía in a brief, unpleasant visit to Rome on September 2 and in a final conversation with Cavaletti on November 19. Op. cit., 147–50.

58. On October 6, 1937, the British consul Henderson reported from Bilbao: "The prisons are filled to overflowing with political offenders. . . . On the other hand, cases are prepared with meticulous care. Evidence is sifted . . . and genuine efforts made to provide justice. Sentences passed on prisoners found guilty, however, are to my mind unduly severe. . . . Estimates of the total shootings effected at Bilbao since its capture by General Franco vary between a minimum of 300 and a maximum of 1,000. Many prisoners, however, still await trial. . . . The confiscation of property from political enemies, following legal investigation, is ruthless." PRO 1937 W19078/1/41. Cavaletti indicated to Onaindía that according to his own calculations 300 death sentences had been officially decreed in Bilbao.

Henderson, who had never before seen a twentieth-century revolutionary civil war, put the killings down to the supposed fact that "every Spaniard, deep down or otherwise, has a Moorish spark in his character, which political strife inevitably fans to flame, and it is an axiom of Spanish politics that the man on top must hit the man underneath. This unhealthy spirit . . . is not a weakness of General Franco's regime but of the inherent Spanish character. . . ."

In reality, the Spanish conflict was perhaps proportionately less bloody than some other twentieth-century revolutionary civil wars. In contrast to the supposedly "Moorish" Spaniards, the presumably "Nordic" or "Turanian" Finns—who are usually praised, and not without reason, for their democracy and progressivism—killed off an approximately equal proportion of their population in a shorter time, according to the figures given in Jaako Paavolainen, *Poliittiset väkivaltaisundet Suomessa 1918* (Helsinki, 1967), 2 vols.

59. Iturralde, III, 272.

60. Ibid., III, 270–71; Pedro de Basaldúa, *En defensa de la verdad* (Buenos Aires, 1956), 94.

61. A. de Lizarra (pseud. of Andrés de Irujo), *Los vascos y la República española* (Buenos Aires, 1944), 92–241.

62. Onaindía, 114; Letter of Leizaola to the author, Aug. 25, 1971.

63. As in the apparently garbled references recorded in Azaña's diary on June 29 and July 1, 1937. *Obras completas*, IV, 637, 641.

64. The Republican ambassador to Paris, Ossorio y Gallardo, bristled at Aguirre's suggestion in Paris on August 2, 1937, that thousands of Basque troops might yet be transferred to Catalonia, suggesting that he suspected an attempt to establish a separatist force there. Onaindía, 134–35.

65. Lizarra, 259–87; Ricard Altabà-Planuc, *Vuit mesos a la delegació del govern d'Euzkadi* (Barcelona, 1938).

66. Azaña, IV, 816.

67. Juan López, *Una misión sin importancia* (Madrid, 1972), 179.

68. The CNT leader López wrote that during the evacuation to Perpignan "only the Basques or those assisted by the Basques were truly well cared for. They were perfectly organized in everything. But as for the rest of the Spanish, everyone did as best he could." Ibid., 123.

Conclusion

NATIONALISM AND THE BASQUE
COUNTRY SINCE 1939

Defeat in the Civil War crushed the nationalist movement as an open political force in the Basque provinces, but it completely failed to eradicate nationalist sentiment. Amid the bitterness of the exiles there was a tendency to criticize the wartime policy of collaborationist autonomy and revive more radical aspirations. This mood had already begun to emerge in the spring of 1937, when an effort was made to achieve greater coordination among all the nationalist groups. Representatives of the ANV, the STV, the *Mendigoitzales*, and the women's and peasant's associations, together with those from smaller groups, discussed the formation of a common council that would have a broader base than that of the PNV organization. This coincided with renewed emphasis on the goal of an essentially independent Basque state merely associated with the Spanish system.[1]

The final collapse of the Spanish Republic in 1939 left Aguirre and the leadership of the PNV free to take a more independent course themselves. From temporary exile headquarters at Paris, the PNV canvassed the other parties that had been allied in the government of *Euzkadi* to obtain agreement "that their conduct and political discipline will remain oriented with independence of any organism that is not limited to *Euzkadi* and its citizens."[2] Though there was apparently no complete commitment by the non-nationalist parties, Aguirre established the office of a Basque government-in-exile and after the start of the Second World War carried on independent contacts with the governments of Britain and France. The fall of France in June 1940 forced the precipitous evacuation of the Paris office, with the loss of most political and historical records that still remained in the hands of the PNV and the *Euzkadi* government. Aguirre eventually escaped to America by way of Berlin,[3] and nationalist activities were transferred to London and the western hemisphere for the next five years. Manuel de Irujo, who as president of the EBB was the titular head of the party, formed a Basque National Council in London of representatives from all the Basque nationalist groups.

The goals of nationalism were explicitly redefined in the autumn of 1940 when the EBB under Irujo, in consultation with the other nationalist groups, produced a new draft project (*anteproyecto*) for a Constitution of the Republic of *Euzkadi*. It declared:

> *Euzkadi*, the Basque nation, constitutes a state under the regime of a democratic Republic. The Republic forms an integral state that is compatible with the autonomy of regions and municipalities.[4]

The proposed Basque Republic was to be an essentially sovereign state, legally bilingual, that would include not merely the four modern provinces but also parts of Huesca, Logroño, and Santander provinces, though no mention was made of the French Basque region.

On January 18, 1941, leaders of the Catalan National Council and Basque National Council in London handed a joint note to the British foreign minister affirming the rights of their respective peoples to "autodetermination" as independent nations and solicited British assistance (albeit with extreme vagueness) to achieve their goals. The British government carefully kept its distance from any plans for the virtual dismemberment of Spain, and the fact that Franco's status of "nonbelligerence" at that point was clearly pro-German only increased the British circumspection. Nonetheless, independence remained the nominal goal of the Basque and

Catalan Councils throughout the war years, even though this drew active opposition from the exiled leftist groups of their region.[5]

Nationalist policy changed once more in 1945, when it appeared that though the Spanish state was not going to be directly overthrown by international pressures, a united Spanish opposition might soon accomplish that task with only indirect help from abroad. The leaders of the PNV participated in the reorganization of a Spanish Republican government-in-exile under the Left Republican José Giral, with an *Euzkadi* government-in-exile under Aguirre reorganized as an autonomous entity in accordance with the 1936 statute.[6] Expectations ran high during the years 1945 to 1947, and an attempt at an opposition general strike was made at Bilbao in May 1947.

All these hopes and plans came to naught. With the crystallization of the Cold War and the beginning of the international rehabilitation of the Franco regime in 1948, such prospects faded away. During the next decade internal opposition in the Basque country, together with nationalist militancy, reached a new low.

The processes of social and economic change that made the Basque country one of the two most modern and distinctive regions of Spain at first accelerated under the Franco regime. Thanks in part to the care taken by the nationalists, the Civil War had not wrecked Basque industry, and the two industrial provinces immediately reassumed their elite role in the Spanish economy.[7] Only marginal residues of foral legislation remained in the legal usages of Vizcaya and Guipúzcoa, and their application has been steadily reduced.[8] The basic exceptions—above all the special tax arrangements—had been swept away in Franco's decree of 1937, but this proved scant economic handicap.

Alava and Navarra alone of the fifty-two Spanish provinces have continued to enjoy certain special rights of autonomous corporative (right-wing) self-government and a special tax regimen under the Franco regime.[9] Advantages from this began to accrue during the general Spanish economic expansion of the 1950s, when both provinces commenced an accelerated program of attracting new industry and soon began to lose their heavily rural character. Moreover, by the 1960s Navarra developed the best provincial road network in Spain and in certain respects enjoyed superior government services, particularly in health facilities.

During the late 1940s and early 1950s the industrial base and technical skills of the economies of Vizcaya and Guipúzcoa—together with certain incentives of the system of Franquist autonomy then in effect—enabled those provinces not merely to sustain their lead but perhaps to widen the gap even further. Precise figures for earlier periods are not available, but the middle years of the twentieth century may have been the time of widest lead in the

TABLE 3

Economic Position of Linguistically Distinct Provinces

Region	Province	Rank in Per Capita Income (among 50 provinces) 1969	1960	Per Capita Income in Thousand Pesetas	Share of Total Income, 1969 (percent)	
Basque	Guipúzcoa	1	1	82.0	2.76	
	Vizcaya	2	2	81.0	4.52	8.15
	Alava	3	11	80.7	0.87	
	Madrid	4	4	76.6	15.10	
Catalonia	Barcelona	5	3	76.1	15.68	
Baleares	Baleares	6	16	71.8	2.12	
Basque	Navarra	7	8	69.7	1.73	
Catalonia	Gerona	8	10	68.8	1.54	
	Tarragona	10	7	64.8	1.50	19.32 incl.
	Lérida	11	15	62.8	1.18	Barcelona
Valencia	Castellón	15	14	58.0	1.21	
	Valencia	18	5	56.5	5.30	9.92
	Alicante	21	19	49.6	2.41	
Galicia	Pontevedra	27	25	43.6	1.79	
	La Coruña	31	33	41.9	2.31	5.63
	Lugo	39	43	37.5	0.88	
	Orense	50	50	28.2	0.65	
National Average				54.7	100	

SOURCE: Banco de Bilbao, *Renta nacional de España y su distribución provincial 1969*, pp. 50–51 and the same publication for 1960, in Juan J. Linz, "Politics in a Multi-Lingual Society with a Dominant World Language: The Case of Spain", in *Les Etats multilingues*, ed. J. G. Savard and R. Vegneault (Québec, 1974).

Basque per capita income over the general Spanish norm. During the 1950s and 1960s productivity and income in Basque industry continued to increase, but at a rate lower than the norm of other developing regions, and proportionate Basque income no longer greatly overshadowed that of other advanced provinces (table 3).

This dramatic change in income balances among several of the more developed regions in the 1960s was due to the industrialization and diversification of the economy of Madrid and several other provinces. State planning was partially responsible, for government investment was systematically shunted away from the three northwestern Basque provinces of Alava, Guipúzcoa, and Vizcaya (*las Vascongadas*). Only in part was this to elevate the most backward regions, for state investment reinforced growth in other developed regions much more than in *las Vascongadas*, as table 4 concerning the place of state industrial investment in various regions shows.

TABLE 4
Number of INI Employees Per 1,000 Active
Employees in Industry and Services by Region (1965)

Murcia	29	Barcelona	15
Coastal Galicia	28	Navarra	12
Madrid	26	Central Spain	10
Aragón	25	*Las Vascongadas*	0.4
West Andalusia	25		

SOURCE: FOESSA, *Informe sociológico 1970*, (Madrid, 1970) Table 4.63, p. 341.

Despite the proportionate change in gross income figures compared with Madrid, *las Vascongadas* continued to enjoy the strongest overall financial and industrial position in Spain. The proportionate number of individual bank and savings accounts was greater than anywhere else, and after corrections were made for taxation and indebtedness, the per capita "disposable" income was still higher than anywhere else, including Madrid, according to a 1967 study of the Banco de Bilbao, shown in table 5.

TABLE 5

Per Capita Disposable Income in Pesetas, 1967

Province	Disposable Income	Rank Order
Guipúzcoa	57,154	1
Vizcaya	54,545	2
Alava	53,028	3
Barcelona	52,377	4
Madrid	51,623	5
Navarra	47,266	6
Spanish Average	39,789	

SOURCE: Banco de Bilbao, *Renta Nacional de España y su distribución provincial* (Bilbao, 1967), 27, in Da Silva, 181.

As late as 1964 Barcelona and the three *Vascongadas* provinces were the only parts of Spain in which the majority of the active population was employed in industry, as indicated in table 6.

TABLE 6

Distribution of the Active Population by Occupation

Region	Percent in Agriculture and Fishing	Percent in Industry	Percent in Services
Madrid	5	40	55
Barcelona	5	56	39
Las Vascongadas	14	55	31
Navarra	35	36	29
Interior Galicia	67	15	18
Extremadura	60	20	20

SOURCE: FOESSA, *Informe*, 172.

By 1971, when the average percentage of agrarian workers in Spain's entire active population was 25, the figures for Vizcaya were 7, Guipuzcoa 1, Alava 15, and Navarra 26.[10] Conversely, in terms of the percentage of the total active population employed by firms with more than a hundred employees, the Spanish average was 12.8, but in Vizcaya 28.2, Guipúzcoa 28.1, Alava 22.7, and Navarra 12.1.[11]

Primarily as a result of steadily advancing industrialization, the population has continued to increase rapidly (table 7).

TABLE 7

Population of the Basque Provinces, 1945–68

| Province | Population | | | Persons Per Square Kilometer |
	1945	1960	1968	
Alava	117,500	138,934	202,891	51
Guipúzcoa	370,114	478,337	660,208	264
Vizcaya	579,978	754,383	1,086,369	375
Navarra	347,369	402,042	443,714	40

SOURCES: Pedro González Blasco, "Modern Nationalism in Old Nations as a Consequence of Earlier State-Building: The Case of Basque-Spain" Table 1, and *Anuario Estadístico* 1970, 477–78.

The Basque percentage of total Spanish population also continued to climb steadily, though not so dramatically as those of the provinces of Madrid and Barcelona, as shown in table 8.

TABLE 8

Population Growth by Regions in Terms of Percentage of Total Spanish Population

	1887	1920	1950	1960	1965	1968	1971
Madrid	3.9	5.0	6.7	8.6	10.0	10.3	11.5
Barcelona	5.1	6.3	8.0	9.5	10.6	11.1	11.6
Las Vascongadas	2.9	3.6	3.8	4.5	5.2	5.3	5.8
Navarra	1.7	1.5	1.4	1.3	1.4	1.3	1.3
Valencian region	8.3	8.2	8.3	8.2	8.7	8.7	8.9
Coastal Galicia	6.0	5.8	5.8	5.5	5.5	5.3	5.2
Inner Galicia	4.8	3.9	3.5	3.1	2.8	2.7	2.5

SOURCE: Amando de Miguel and Juan Salcedo, *Dinámica del desarrollo industrial de las regiones españolas* (Madrid, 1972), 52.

As was true before the Civil War, much of the growth of the "Basque population" is not really Basque but the product of massive immigration, mainly from other provinces of northern Spain (table 9).

TABLE 9

Total Number of Immigrants by Province in Spain, 1901–69

	1901–10	1911–20	1921–30	1931–40	1941–50	1951–60	1961–69
Alava							
	−9,203	−7,293	−5,210	−1,350	203	7,073	32,653
Barcelona							
	57,112	203,174	376,081	95,597	241,906	479,613	458,528
Guipúzcoa							
	6,159	8,173	12,732	3,964	16,567	48,754	59,909
Madrid							
	72,161	158,682	219,650	106,899	275,523	411,697	506,333
Navarra							
	−25,959	−14,485	−21,182	−10,300	−16,836	−20,499	2,655
Vizcaya							
	−2,958	18,997	18,290	−1,350	18,988	96,399	127,821

SOURCE: FOESSA, *Informe*, Table 8.31, 580.

Immigration thus accelerated enormously after 1950. Total immigration into the three *Vascongadas* provinces during the 1950s was 152,226, and reached 220,383 for the years 1961 to 1969.

There has been a notable increase in the proportion of young people in the Basque population during the 1950s and 1960s. In 1940 the percentage of inhabitants of the Basque country less than fifteen years of age was 27.3, compared with 9.9 for all of Spain, and the proportion remained similar in 1950. By 1965 the Basque percentage had climbed to 30.0, compared with a Spanish average of 27.3. The only other regions with more than 30 percent were traditionally backward, high-birthrate areas such as Andalusia and the Canaries. The figures for Barcelona remained consistently 6 to 7 points below the national average, and those for Navarra about 1 percent below.[12]

In general Basque municipalities have maintained and improved upon the superior level of local services that they developed earlier in the century.[13] Nonetheless, rapid urbanization has made it difficult to extend educational facilities at the rate needed, and the same differences by region were noticeable in the 1960s as at the beginning of the century. By 1965 the total percentage of Spanish children between six and thirteen years of age enrolled in school was 82.3. This level was significantly exceeded only in some of the better organized semirural provinces. Madrid, Barcelona, Alava,

Guipúzcoa, and Vizcaya only approximated the Spanish average, while Navarra exceeded it by 5 percent.[14]

The influence of the church has declined in the industrialized provinces, though it has remained little changed in Navarra. Even though their indices of religiosity have fallen well below those of Navarra, Guipúzcoa and Vizcaya remain much more Catholic than other highly urbanized or industrialized regions of Spain, as indicated in table 10.

TABLE 10

Percentage of Population Who Declare Themselves "Practicing Catholics," by Regions

Navarra	95
Inner Galicia	93
Murcia	91
Baleares	89
Old Castilla	87
Catalonia w/Barcelona	86
Aragón	86
León	82
Basque Country	80
Asturias	76
Center	75
West Andalusia	74
East Anadalusia & Extremadura	71
Coastal Galicia	68
Levant	67
Madrid	64
Barcelona	58

SOURCE: FOESSA, *Informe*, 449.

If the figures for the Basque country were broken down to differentiate between inhabitants from native Basque and non-Basque families, the percentage of practicing Catholics among the former would undoubtedly be higher. Over all, the figures are probably somewhat too high, but at least they give some measurement of continuing regional differences.

Navarra is the only province in Spain that maintained the same ratio of total population to priests (273 to 1) between 1915 and

1967. In the other Basque provinces together the ratio rose from 331 to 575, and in Spain as a whole it grew from 535 to 910.[15]

The 1970 FOESSA study constructed a "felicity calculus" to measure the degree of contentment in various regions, results of which are given in table 11.

TABLE 11

Index of Felicity of Housewives by Regions

	1 Index of Felicity	2 Percent Who Consider Selves "Very Happy"	3 Regional Per Capita Income Rank
Navarra	.85	60	8
Baleares	.85	58	4
Rest of Catalonia	.85	55	7
Barcelona	.84	52	2
Las Vascongadas	.81	45	3
Asturias	.80	50	5
Aragón	.78	35	9
Levant	.76	42	6
Castilla	.76	33	11
Central	.76	31	16
Madrid	.75	39	1
Murcia	.72	23	12
Coastal Galicia	.70	27	14
West Andalusia	.69	34	10
East Andalusia	.69	20	17
Inner Galicia	.66	22	15

SOURCE: FOESSA, *Informe*, 623.

Though the Basque provinces have achieved great economic success during the past generation, their future identity as genuinely "Basque" provinces, especially in the industrialized provinces, is open to doubt. The degree of immigration has been so great that by 1966 only 62 percent of the heads of households in the Basque country had been born there,[16] and a small minority of these were not originally of Basque families. Only the provinces of Madrid and Barcelona had a lower proportion of native-born heads of families.

The decline in the use of *Euskera* has been much greater than in other regions with separate languages, as shown in table 12.

TABLE 12

Percentages of Housewives' Familiarity with Regional Languages

Region	Understand	Speak	Read	Write
Galicia	96	92	43	24
Balearic Islands	94	91	51	10
Catalonia	90	77	62	38 .
Valencia	88	69	46	16
Basque country	49	46	25	12

SOURCE: FOESSA, *Informe*, 1305.

Urbanization is perhaps as important as immigration in the decline in the use of *Euskera*. The FOESSA study found that 82 percent of rural housewives could speak the language, but only 51 percent of those in cities between 10,000 and 100,000 inhabitants, and only 19 percent in the large cities.

Whereas Galician, Catalan, and the Catalan provincial dialects are functional Romance languages easily adapted to contemporary cultural and technological requirements, *Euskera* is extremely hard either to learn or adapt. Non-Catalan-speaking immigrants to Catalonia not infrequently achieve some degree of familiarity with Catalan and tend culturally and psychologically to become "Catalanized," at least in part.[17] This process is encouraged by the fact that Catalan attitudes are broader and encourage assimilation, whereas Basque loyalties have always been more exclusive and particularistic. Moreover, immigrants into the Basque country come predominantly from the more literate provinces of northern Spain and possess a stronger Castilian culture than do the semiliterate immigrants from the less developed provinces of southeastern Spain who have composed the bulk of immigrants into Catalonia during the past two or three generations. Conversely, though the rate of marriage of Basques with non-Basques has been somewhat higher than that of Catalans with non-Catalans, the consequence may be to discourage rather than encourage assimilation and lead to further loss of Basque identity, given the linguistic and cultural problems involved.[18]

Another marked difference is that in Catalonia the use of Catalan tends to be associated with upward mobility, and knowledge of the regional language increases according to income and social status. The situation is almost the reverse in the Basque country, where knowledge of *Euskera* is highest among sectors of the lower and middle classes and lowest among the wealthiest and best educated.[19] This serves further to explain why no more than 12 percent of the Basque population is actually able to write in Basque.

Catalan and also Galician have remained more functional languages, useful in current affairs. By contrast, most Basque mothers consider it desirable but not really necessary for their children to learn *Euskera* in order to function in contemporary society, as illustrated in table 13.

TABLE 13

Attitudes of Housewives Toward Their
Children Speaking the Regional Language

Region	Would Like	Believe it Necessary	Difference
Catalonia	97	87	10
Balearic Islands	91	75	16
Valencian Region	78	50	28
Galicia	73	49	24
Basque Country	69	31	38

SOURCE: FOESSA, *Informe*, 1306.

The centralized, Castilian-language educational system of modern Spain has steadily discouraged regional identity, and the trend became much more severe under the Franco regime. During the first years after the Civil War publication in the regional languages was prohibited almost altogether, and no form of pedagogy in any language other than Castilian was permitted. In Barcelona street signs at first insisted that Catalans "Speak the Language of the Empire!"

This situation changed slowly with the relaxation of government restrictions during the 1950s, and regional cultural activity enjoyed a considerable degree of official tolerance after the Gali-

cian Manuel Fraga Iribarne became Spanish minister of information in 1962. During the 1960s Catalan cultural activity expanded
enormously,[20] and there were marked revivals in Valencia and
Galicia. Basque cultural work also increased notably, though distinctly less than in the case of Catalonia. Whereas nearly all new
Catalan cultural publications appeared in Catalan, most new material on Basque history and culture was published in Castilian.

Even under conditions of partial tolerance, cultural proselyti-
zation was handicapped by the fact that, except in Guipúzcoa, most
schoolteachers in the Basque country were ignorant of *Euskera*.
This was as true of educationally autonomous Alava and Navarra as
of centralized Vizcaya,[21] for in the former provinces use of the
regional language seemed in danger of vanishing altogether.
Therefore a drive emerged in the 1960s to open *ikastolas*, part-time
Euskera-language schools that could give an hour or two of instruction daily. By 1970 more *ikastolas* were in operation than at any
previous time in Basque history, but they reached less than twenty
thousand students[22] and because of their limited function their
long-range influence is problematic. Potentially the most far-
reaching step was taken by the *Diputación de Navarra* in 1967
when it approved a plan to have *Euskera* taught half an hour per day
within its autonomous provincial educational system.[23]

During the 1950s and 1960s nationalist sentiment in the
Basque country remained strong among the same elements that had
supported it most directly in the 1930s: farmers and white collar
workers of the lower-middle class, shopkeepers and smaller entrepreneurs, and minority elements of skilled workers and/or native
Basque Catholics among the urban lower classes. The upper
Basque bourgeoisie, on the other hand, had if anything become
even more closely associated with the Spanish system and their
Madrid connections than before the civil war. The conservative
Basque elite has enjoyed preferential treatment from the structure
of economics in Franquist Spain, and the protected position of
established Basque industry has produced stronger autarchist/
Spanish nationalist feelings among wealthy Basque entrepreneurs
than among Spanish businessmen as a whole. In a study of Spanish
businessmen published in 1963, Juan Linz and Amando de Miguel
found that 71 percent of the industrial elite in Valencia and Cádiz

favored economic integration in Europe, compared with 62 percent of that of Madrid but only 45 percent of that of Vizcaya. Compared with businessmen elsewhere, it was found that the leaders of Vizcayan heavy industry were more dependent on the Spanish national market, had more links with the central Spanish financial elite, and as a group were more elderly.

Industrial workers have remained dissatisfied and dissident, though in Guipúzcoa and Vizcaya they constitute one of the best-paid sectors of the Spanish labor force. Their tradition of strong union organization and opposition activity have made workers in the Basque country one of the three or four significant foci of worker unrest in Franco Spain, but amid the depoliticized environment of the past generation their discontent, like that of most Spanish workers, has been focused on economic rather than politico-ideological issues. In fact, in Spain as a whole, the suppressed political section of the 1970 FOESSA study found that skilled workers were the least politicized sector of the general Spanish urban population (see table 14).

TABLE 14
Index of Political Inertia

High School Students	.34
University Graduate Students	.19
Lawyers	.16
Doctors	.25
High-Level Employees	.26
Low-Level Employees	.36
Skilled Workers	.41
Unskilled Workers	.29

The same study found that half the population preferred some form of continuation of the Franquist system (table 15).

TABLE 15
Political System Preferred after Franco

	Number	Percentage
As now	149	29.8 } 50.6
Monarchy	104	20.8
Republic	247	49.4 49.4

Workers were found to be the sector that most preferred political continuity (table 16).

TABLE 16

Political System Preferred after Franco According to Vocations[24]

	Students (percent)	Lawyers (percent)	Employees (percent)	Doctors (percent)	Workers (percent)
Present Regime	1	8	37	20	55
Regency	4	5	6	9	4
Bourbon Monarchy	11	23	5	8	5
Carlist Monarchy	3	—	1	1	—
Monarchy	5	10	7	19	6
Republic	76	53	45	43	30

Nevertheless, such findings must be treated with considerable caution, for it is very difficult to judge the possible effect of fears of reprisal that may have conditioned artificially conformist responses. It is doubtful that such results are representative of common attitudes in Vizcaya and Guipúzcoa, where most indicators have consistently indicated a greater degree of dissidence than in other parts of Spain. In the first postwar plebiscite of 1947 on the Law of Succession, for example, there was a high level of abstentions and void or negative votes compared with most of the rest of Spain.

During the past two decades, the discontented and proto-revolutionary class has, as is normally the case, not been primarily the industrial workers but rather the radical intelligentsia, including in this case the ultraliberal sector of the younger clergy. That the Basque radical intelligentsia became during the 1960s the most dissident element in Spain has been due to a complex combination of factors: the greater conflict between problems of values and identities in the Basque country compared with other regions, the continuing sense of particularism (and of nationalism among a minority), the declining status of *Euskera*, and the slow but at least noticeable growth of secularism in what had been a strongly religious environment. In the 1950s sociologists and political scientists assumed that strong particularism and regional identities were well on their way to elimination or homogenization in advanced European societies under the pressures of mass society, centralization,

economic coordination, and modern communications. The suc-
ceeding decade showed that this was far from the case, for the same
pressures of modernization led to growing anomie and crises of
personality, identity, values, and self-definition for which
regionalist/nationalist alternatives seemed to offer alleviation.

The Basque Nationalist party (PNV) during the past decade
has reinforced its own stance as a party of middle-class, parliamen-
tarian Christian democracy.[25] It has continued to define itself
exclusively within the Spanish context and continues to postulate
the goal of full autonomy in association within the Spanish state.[26]
For example, it completely disassociated itself from nationalist
feeling in the French or "continental" Basque country, which had
begun to flicker once more in 1945[27] and finally began to rally
modest support in the 1960s.[28]

Thus it was not surprising that the PNV was after mid-century
outflanked to the left by a new and violent nationalist group based
on radical youth politics named *Euzkadi ta Azkatasuna* (ETA;
Basque Land and Liberty). The origins of ETA apparently lay in a
small group of nationalist student radicals in the Jesuit university at
Deusto (Bilbao) who founded a clandestine journal called *Ekin*
(Action) in 1953–54. It was originally to some extent associated
with EGI, the PNV's clandestine youth group, though the members
of *Ekin* did not share the moderate, evolutionary orientation of
most of the EGI organization. Small radical elements of EGI,
especially the latter's leader, José Luiz Alvarez Emparanza, became increasingly identified with *Ekin*. Alvarez Emparanza was
eventually deposed as EGI leader and worked full time with *Ekin*,
which was officially reorganized as ETA in 1959–60.

There are three basic differences between ETA and the PNV.
ETA postulates federation of all seven Basque provinces on both
sides of the Pyrenees (on the basis of municipal and district autonomy in a federal Europe) after breaking up of the existing
structure of the Spanish and French states. It rejects the moderate,
parliamentary-oriented tactics of the PNV[29] in favor of revolutionary violence. Whereas the PNV is middle-class reformist and
does not go beyond the concept of worker participation in management and a vaguely specified expansion of the public sector of
the economy, ETA is social-revolutionary and aims at radical

syndical organization to achieve some not well defined form of Basque socialism.[30]

The great majority of nationalists in the Basque country have remained loyal to the PNV,[31] and the hard-core membership of ETA has probably never been more than a few hundred. ETA originally concentrated on syndical propaganda among industrial workers in Vizcaya and Guipúzcoa, but its top leaders were soon arrested. All were released within less than a year and moved to France in 1961. ETA's first major proclamation occurred in the following year, differentiating the group from the PNV by pledging to use any means to gain Basque independence and affirming that "violence is necessary," while calling for social democracy and the avoidance of dictatorship whether fascist or communist, and indicating willingness to work with other nationalist groups. Jesús María de Leizaola, the new president of the *Euzkadi* government-in-exile, responded on the occasion of the 1963 Aberri-Eguna celebration in Paris by denouncing ETA and its new journal *Zutik* (Arise) for their radicalism and calls to violence. During 1963 a new program of activities was attempted in Vizcaya and Guipúzcoa with a cadre of some fifty activisits, but their labors were quickly broken up by police.[32]

From approximately that point the ideology and program of the group moved increasingly toward a sort of Marxism or pseudo-Marxism. ETA had originated as a radical, social-oriented outgrowth of the PNV youth movement, and the predecessors of the organization of the 1950s had still been somewhat influenced by Catholic residues. In 1963, however, ETA activists cooperated with Basque Communists in setting up the first clandestine opposition *comisión obrera* among workers in Bilbao. The dominant cadre began to espouse Marxist rhetoric, rejecting any association with religion in favor of determinist materialism and adopting Basque socialism as the goal of a "war of liberation," though there is no indication that the Communist party has actually exercised any direct control over the ETA organization.[33]

The fifth assembly of ETA leaders and delegates, held clandestinely in Guipúzcoa at the beginning of 1967, declared the organization to be a "Basque Socialist Movement of National Liberation," establishing the complete victory of the Marxist

"ETA-*berri*" elements over the "ETA-*zarra*" old guard. The latter were much more nationalist than socialist and still retained Aranist residues. Several of the original leaders then left the party and published a pamphlet, *Por qué salimos de ETA*. The Marxist José María Escubi Larraz became the top leader of ETA in mid-1968 and established closer contact with international Communist groups. This led to a reaction even among the Marxist elements. Escubi was denounced by rivals as an *españolazo* and his rather arbitrary leadership overthrown in 1970. However, at the sixth assembly held that same year, ETA's identity as a "class movement" was firmly asserted. In this it followed the Leninist precedent of a movement of the radical middle- and upper-class intelligentsia arrogating for itself the identity of the working classes.[34]

The key sector of ETA, however, was not the propagandists and ideologues, but the *milis*—the direct-action squads led by Juan José Echave Orobengoa. Though some of the ultra-Marxist elements tended to denounce them as petit-bourgeois nationalist terrorists, the *milis* carried out the deeds in the late 1960s that made ETA the most notorious of Spanish political groups.

The increased agitation in the Basque country from the mid-1960s stemmed from a growing mood of particularist dissatisfaction among middle-class youths that adopted a nationalist form, from the militancy of the younger clergy, from the active economic discontent of workers, and most spectacularly from the terrorist blows of ETA. Spanish church leadership first moved to differentiate its position from the Franco regime in 1960, but the only militant clergy were some of the younger priests of Vizcaya and Guipúzcoa. Most Basque priests are of Basque birth, and their sympathies with the affirmation of local identity and values has in general diminished little since the Civil War. In the Basque country the growing social conscience of younger Spanish priests became identified with the cause of local rights and freedoms, all the more attractive because of the high degree of Catholic practice among Basques. In 1960 339 Basque priests signed a document requesting an independent investigation by the Vatican of the situation in the Basque country.

Meanwhile the activities of EGI among the more "respectable" pronationalist middle-class youth were accelerated in an effort to avoid being outdistanced by ETA. In the more relaxed atmosphere of the 1960s, muted *Aberri-Eguna* celebrations were once again being held. In 1966 the EGI celebrated the occasion at Vitoria, while a separate rally was held by ETA at Irún, where twenty-three were arrested. During the year that followed, activity by both sectors of nationalists stepped up, accompanied by protests from younger priests and an accelerated tempo of industrial strikes. By the eve of the *Aberri-Eguna* celebrations in April 1967, the situation in Vizcaya and Guipúzcoa was the most volatile in any part of Spain for the past twenty years. At that point, under pressure from hard-liners, the Spanish regime reversed the trend of two decades of slow relaxation by suspending the three principal civil guarantees in the Spanish Bill of Rights (Articles 14, 15, and 18) for the province of Vizcaya during the next three months, reestablishing de jure martial law. During the first week approximately one hundred persons, mostly connected with labor agitation, were arrested. One year later, two thousand special police were moved into San Sebastián to forestall *Aberri-Eguna* demonstrations.[35]

Though dissident clergy were occasionally arrested, police repression was primarily concentrated against leftist activists, some of whom were treated with great brutality, as had been more or less customary for Spanish police since 1936. Despite numerous protests over arbitrary and violent procedures, the only rectification won by the opposition was an order by the Spanish supreme court in April 1968 that removed from office the civil governor of Guipúzcoa, Manuel Valencia Remón, indicting him for arbitrary and illegal acts. Valencia Remón was rescued by the government, which awarded him a safe seat in Cortes that carried immunity from such prosecution.[36]

In this atmosphere ETA terrorists struck their most resounding blow on August 2, 1968, when they assassinated Melitón Manzanas, a leading official of the *brigada social* (political police) in San Sebastián. This was their third killing, but the first that was a significant premeditated assassination, and constituted a major exception to the tacit rules by which both police and opposition had operated in recent years.

The regime responded two days later by declaring a state of emergency in Guipúzcoa, where civil guarantees were once more suspended for three months. Within a week approximately two hundred people were arrested, including a score of priests. On August 14 the regime reimposed selective martial law for repression of subversive acts and public disturbances.

Direct political opposition at that point was primarily expressed not through strikes—which had become fairly frequent in industrial centers and had even received a degree of legal sanction under new regulations in 1966—but by the clerical and student intelligentsia. It was calculated that of the 700 clergy in the province of Vizcaya, the liberals numbered from 200 to 300. There were two sit-ins by liberal priests at the diocesan seminary in San Sebastián, and 40 were eventually suspended. On November 4, 1968, a group of liberal priests in Bilbao sent a letter directly to Pope Paul VI calling attention to the grievances of the Basques and urging that the church no longer promote "Castilianization."

Student demonstrations, primarily at the universities of Madrid and Barcelona, were more provocative and violent. They were the most immediate incentive to the regime's hard-liners in leading the government to declare a two-month state of emergency in February 1969. Opposition outbursts temporarily diminished, but agitation among the Basque clergy continued. Some five hundred Basque priests addressed a collective letter to the Spanish Episcopal Conference of 1969, and in a pastoral letter of May 1969 the bishop of Bilbao, José María Cirarda, drew attention to the persistent violation of the terms of the existing church-state concordat by the government's arrest of priests. On June 6, more than two hundred fifty priests in Bilbao signed a statement in support of five of their fellows currently conducting a hunger strike in the diocesan chancery in protest against the repression.[37]

Though assassinations were not repeated, ETA militants sustained a high incidence of direct action in 1969−70, concentrating mainly on acts of public sabotage.[38] Scores of nationalists, not all of them from ETA, were arrested and prosecuted by the government in the late 1960s.[39] The repression was climaxed by the trial of sixteen nationalists accused of terrorism, among them several ETA leaders and two priests, before a military tribunal in Burgos in December 1970.

The "Burgos trial" quickly mushroomed into the nearest thing to a political crisis that the Franco regime had seen since the 1940s. It was accompanied by a massive mobilization of liberal and leftist opinion abroad that in some ways resembled the *ferrerada* of 1909. In earlier years most of the nationalist militants would have been quickly prosecuted under court-martial with only minimal public hearing and probably executed. In 1970 considerable care was given the rights of the accused as far as technical courtroom procedure was concerned. Proregime elements in the bureaucracy and military responded to foreign opinion and continued public protests from workers and intelligentsia at home by mobilizing a massive rally in support of the government at Madrid, echoed by smaller gatherings in some provincial capitals.

The resonance attained by the Burgos trial was due to the convergence of many factors. ETA terrorism, though not usually sanguinary, marked the first revival of violent methods by the leftist opposition in twenty years. Its sharp repression, together with the intermittent imposition of a state of emergency in Vizcaya and Guipúzcoa and briefly in Spain as a whole, marked a halt or at least a distinct slowdown in the gradual process of moderation and liberalization in Spain. The trial occurred after a decade of increasingly aggressive initiative by the leftist intelligentsia throughout the western world, and by 1970 the Spanish intelligentsia as a whole, especially the young, were more thoroughly leftist-oriented than in 1935. Worker dissidence, though frequent, was not much of a political problem, but the intelligentsia was as usual harder to deal with. That one of the twin foci of ETA militancy was Basque nationalism also presented a serious challenge, for the broader and more diffuse sentiments of regionalism and nationalism proved in some ways more resistant than the old myth of class loyalties. The successful kidnapping of the West German consul in San Sebastián as a form of ransom indicated that the Spanish police were no longer fully in control of the situation. Finally, the recrudescence of an extreme form of regionalist rebellion coming in the final phase of Franco's life posed a severe question for the unity and continuity of the Spanish regime in the future.

Six of the fifteen accused were found guilty of major acts of "military rebellion," but all were reprieved and given lesser prison terms.[40] In the aftermath, measures were taken to improve the behavior of some sections of the Spanish police and try to embellish their public image.

Economic protest by workers and political protest by university students continued in the early 1970s, but the spotlight was increasingly held by the opposition clergy. At one point late in 1970 at least twenty-six priests were in jail. In April 1971 the bishop of Pamplona publicly protested the infliction of torture by the police, results of which he claimed to have seen personally. At the end of that year, the conservative Antonio Añoveros was named bishop of Bilbao, leading to new protest in which 196 priests participated. To a considerable extent the Vatican discreetly supported moderate liberalization in the Spanish hierarchy and as new bishoprics fell vacant tended to appoint only auxiliary prelates so as to avoid having to obtain the regime's approval for a regular nomination as stipulated in the 1953 Concordat. Appointment of Monsignor José María Setien, a respected moderate liberal and intellectual, as auxiliary bishop of San Sebastián particularly drew the ire of the Spanish state, for it seemed a gesture in clear support of the liberal Basque clergy.

The continuing dynamism generated by Basque nationalism has been graphically illustrated by the dramatic events of late 1973 and early 1974. On December 20, 1973, Admiral Luis Carrero Blanco, the first man to serve as prime minister (president of government) aside from Franco himself and the latter's chosen political successor, was killed by ETA activists in one of the most technically expert assassinations in modern history. Though in the aftermath Spain remained perfectly calm and orderly, the deed did change the course of regime politics. Carrero's successor was Carlos Arias Navarro, a leading *Movimiento* administrator and bureaucrat, accompanied by a new cabinet that reversed much of the apolitical "technocrat" policy of the preceding cabinet and eliminated all the major *Opus Dei* figures from government.[41] The result has been to chart a more liberal course that is moving in the direction of slightly freer political associations.

Within two years, Bishop Añoveros came to espouse some of the more moderate requests of his Vizcayan parishioners. Rather vague remarks about regional rights that he made in a sermon in the late winter of 1974 led to an abrupt political clash with the regime, which failed in an effort to expel him informally from Spain, though the church hierarchy intervened to remove him temporarily from the scene. These two dramatic developments, coming within a few months' time, graphically demonstrate the central role of Basque dissidence in internal political conflict within Spain.

To most Spaniards the persistence and regrowth of regional sentiment in the distinct peripheries of the north and east is as inexplicable as until recently it would have been to most contemporary political science theorists. During the late 1940s and 1950s it was generally held that the process of "modernization" produced increasing atomization and homogeneity and generated an ever more inclusive network of social communications that formed common identities and values. Modern society was supposed to promote a natural *gleichschaltung* based on economic interests, education and entertainment, all of which broke down parochialism while promoting secularization and cosmopolitanism.

During the past decade, however, it has become clear that the dominant political passion of the second half of the twentieth century is nationalism, not any form of social, class, or ideological revolt per se. Nationalism has returned to the center of attention even among totalitarian systems theoretically based on class-conscious internationalism. Regional nationalism among small ethnic groups has gained new momentum all over western Europe.

Modernization, rather than diluting and erasing national consciousness among small ethnic groups, may actually exacerbate it. In the case of Spain, modernization occurred first and most rapidly in regions of distinct identity and local culture, so that the process led to dissociation rather than homogenization. Urbanization sharpened cultural tensions rather than merely transforming them, and the formation of political parties tended to reproduce rather than cut across regional differences. In the Basque country modernization has not even produced the vaunted secularization that is supposedly its inevitable concomitant, and Basque religiosity to a considerable extent has fueled Basque nationalism. The modernization process has led to a combination of feelings of superiority and exploitation that have undermined the concept of a Spanish nation-state.[42] Thus Basque nationalists have sometimes accepted

the Franco regime as a not illogical expression of Spanish civic
consciousness as a whole and insisted that Castilian "backward-
ness" and authoritarianism will also drag the Basque people down,
whose moral and civic consciousness is held to be of an altogether
higher order.[43]

Another paradox of Basque nationalism is that its recent
virulence has been due probably more to the severeness of the
threat to Basque identity than to the basic strength of Basque
nationalism itself. All evidence indicates that a broad sense of
Catalanism is, for example, more deeply rooted in Catalonia than
Basque political and linguistic identity is in the Basque country.
The very shrinkage of the Basque proportion of the population has
encouraged a stronger reaction, and the intensity of radical
nationalists is perhaps not unrelated to the fact that the clergy have
always played such an active role in association with the movement. Catalanism, both more secular and more secure, has largely
been limited to clandestine assemblies that call for the restoration
of the autonomy statute of 1932. Catalanism was always more
collaborationist and less extreme in its demands, and after the
frustrations of exaggerated ultra-Catalanism between 1934 and
1937 many Catalanists no longer have such interest in the extremes
of political self-assertion.

It seems undeniable that most political opinion in Vizcaya and
Guipúzcoa is opposed to the Franquist regime. Opposition attitudes
are probably more diffuse and widespread there than anywhere else
in Spain save Barcelona province. Opposition to and alienation
from the Franco regime are one thing,[44] however, and positive
support for Basque nationalism is another. Without free elections it
is impossible to determine the exact extent of the latter, but it seems
doubtful that after the unassimilated immigration of recent decades
it is any more widespread than in 1936, when nationalism
mobilized scarcely half the vote in Vizcaya and Guipúzcoa, and
less than one-third that of the population of the Spanish Basque
region as a whole. Shrinkage of the language base and the rapid
decline of the rural population[45] steadily diminish the traditionally
and incontestably Basque proportion of society. There is no indication that the great majority of the industrial workers, more numerous than ever before, have any allegiance to nationalism, especially

since so many of them are of non-Basque origin. Nor will economic conditions necessarily encourage nationalism in the future. All the Basque provinces have continued to benefit from the structure of the Spanish economic system, though in different ways. Navarra and Alava, particularly Alava, have sometimes gotten slightly more than they have received from the Spanish state (as shown in table 17), which has promoted their industrialization. Finally, in a semi-industrial Spain, the preeminence of Vizcaya and Guipúzcoa is no longer so secure. Though they still rank at or near the top in productivity and income, their growth, as in many mature industrial systems, has begun to level off, and the concentration on the metallurgical industry may ultimately create new problems of imbalance.[46]

TABLE 17

Government Revenue and Direct Expenditures
in Catalonia and the Basque Country as
Percentages of the Totals for Spain

	Government Revenue			Government Expenditures		
	1962	*1967*	*1970*	*1962*	*1967*	*1970*
Catalonia	23.9	27.4	30.97	10.4	12.20	12.80
Barcelona province	18.9	22.0	26.25	7.3	8.79	9.38
Other Catalan provinces	5.0	5.4	4.72	3.0	3.41	3.42
Basque Country	15.6	14.7	12.84	4.6	5.41	5.39
Vizcaya	9.5	7.8	8.25	2.6	2.98	2.92
Guipúzcoa	5.7	6.6	3.96	1.5	1.69	1.85
Alava	0.3	0.3	0.63	0.5	0.54	0.62
Navarra	—	—	1.03	—	—	1.05

SOURCE: Juan J. Linz, "Early State-Building and Late Peripheral Nationalisms against the State," in *Building States and Nations*, ed. S. N. Eisenstadt and S. Rokkan (Beverly Hills, 1974).

Nevertheless, if the nationalists per se are probably likely to remain a minority within the greater Basque region, they are conversely not likely to fade away or lose their own vigor.[47] With no more than a plurality, nationalism can well reassert itself within a more liberal Spanish system as the leading single factor in the Basque country, resting on the middle classes, the nationalist intelligentsia, and the remaining rural population of Vizcaya and Guipúzcoa. If the opportunity for direct political representation is finally regained, it will not be necessary for nationalism to enroll the bulk of the population in order to regain a broad Basque autonomy. The principle of autonomy is accepted by all the Spanish left and by much of the Spanish center. Nearly all political groups in the Basque region support some form or degree of autonomy. Some form of serious accommodation of regional feeling is virtually assured if anything approaching liberal or democratic government returns to Spain.[48]

Nationalism in the Basque country and Catalonia was born of the contradictions, imbalances, and frustrations in the organization of a modern polity, economy, and culture in Spain. During the past generation these imbalances have been somewhat reduced in the economic sector, but the political and cultural frustrations that gave rise to Basque nationalism remain and are likely to persist for some time to come. The twentieth century bears witness that the spirit and consciousness of small peoples do not easily die.

NOTES

1. Sarrailh de Ihartza, *Vasconia*, 289–90.

2. According to the text of the circular cited in the pamphlet *Los socialistas vascos frente a la actitud del gobierno provisional de su región* (Mexico City, 1945), in Madariaga, 75–77.

3. A bizarre odyssey that Aguirre has recounted in his *De Guernica a Nueva York pasando por Berlín* (Buenos Aires, 1944).

4. The full text of this *anteproyecto*, dated Nov. 30, 1940, is given in *Vasconia*, 488–503.

5. The Socialists made public their opposition in the pamphlet cited in footnote 2.

On the Catalanist stance of autodetermination, whose tone was more federalist, see Juan Cuatrecasas, "La Generalitat de Cataluña en el exilio," *Cuadernos Americanos*, Jan.-Feb. 1966, and Fidel Miró, *Cataluña, los trabajadores y el problema de las nacionalidades* (Mexico City, 1967), 282–99.

6. The Basque government later published a white paper that also covered the postwar period, *La Gestión del Gobierno de Euzkadi desde 1936 a 1956* (Paris, 1956).

7. This occurred most dramatically in Vizcayan iron ore production. The latter had averaged 130,000 tons a month before the Civil War, but fell

off to only 25,000 tons a month under the autonomous regime during the first year of the conflict. By December 1937, six months after the fall of Bilbao, it had shot back up to 138,000 tons.

8. See Adrián Celaya Ibarra, *El Derecho foral de Vizcaya en la actualidad* (Bilbao, 1970).

9. For Alava, there is a brief exposition by José Badía La Calle, *El Concierto Económico con Alava* (Bilbao, 1965). The *Diputación de Navarra* has issued numerous publications on aspects of that province's institutions.

10. Amando de Miguel and Juan Salcedo, *Dinámica del desarrollo industrial de las regiones españolas* (Madrid, 1972), 160.

11. Ibid., 235.

12. Ibid., 35.

13. Juan J. Linz and Amando de Miguel, "Within-Nation Differences and Comparisons: The Eight Spains," in R. L. Merritt and S. Rokkan, eds., *Comparing Nations* (New Haven, 1966), 307−9, and the *Anuario Estadístico de las Corporaciones locales* (Madrid, 1964−65), cited in Kenneth Medhurst's booklet, *The Basques* (London, 1972), 24.

14. De Miguel and Salcedo, 288.

15. FOESSA, *Informe*, 470.

16. Ibid., 546.

17. See Francesc Candel, *Els altres catalans* (Barcelona, 1966).

18. These last two points have been made by Juan Linz, "The Party System of Spain: Past and Future," in S. Lipset and S. Rokkan, *Party Systems and Voter Alignments* (New York, 1967), 272.

19. FOESSA, *Informe*, 1305, 1307.

20. On the present extent of Catalan usage and Catalan-language culture, see Josep Melià, *Informe sobre la lengua catalana* (Madrid, 1970).

21. According to one survey of unspecified date (presumably from the 1960s), *Euskera* was unknown by 85 percent of the schoolteachers of Alava, 76 percent of those in Vizcaya, 74 percent of those in Navarra, and 19 percent of those in Guipúzcoa. Arteaga, 31.

22. The following figures have been given as of about 1970:

	Number of ikastolas	Pupils
Guipúzcoa	75	11,000
Vizcaya	40	6,000
Alava	13	350
Navarra	10	?

Ibid., 32−34.

23. *Diccionario de Legislación Administrativa y Fiscal de Navarra* (Pamplona, 1969), 1118−19, in Da Silva, 156.

24. The same study found that indicated party preferences, by percentages and number of those questioned were:

Movimiento-Falange	21	126
Christian Democracy } Social Democracy }	52.4	314
Socialist	16.3	98
Carlist	2	12
Nationalist	2	12
Others	7.3	43

25. The most coherent ideologist for Basque nationalist Christian democracy among the senior leaders is the former Alavese Cortes deputy, Francisco Javier de Landaburu.

26. Some elements of the old guard remained and their most vocal spokesmen were among the Basque colony in Caracas. On October 25, 1960, the latter issued a "Manifiesto de Caracas," demanding a Basque state composed of all seven provinces with its capital in Pamplona. *Vasconia*, 292, 587. This was disavowed by the PNV.

27. The first faint signs of Basque nationalism in the French Basque country had appeared in the 1890s, but a modest organizational effort was only begun in 1933 and then revived at the end of the war. At that time the most prominent spokesman was Marc Legasse, a somewhat quixotic figure whose position might be described as that of lower-middle-class anarchism or libertarian nationalism that aimed at the confederation of all seven districts. Legasse was harassed by French authorities and repudiated by Aguirre's government of *Euzkadi* in exile, which assured Paris that they were only interested in the autonomy of the Spanish Basque provinces. This brought a sharp letter from Legasse to Aguirre that among other things charged the PNV with having accepted the old Carlist program of regional autonomy in an antiquated and repressive Spanish system. The text of this letter, dated March 25, 1946, is given in *Vasconia*, 533–37.

28. There are only about 90,000 *Euskera*-speaking people in the exiguous French Basque country, compared with possibly as many as 600,000 on the Spanish side, according to Manuel de Lecuona, *Literatura oral vasca* (San Sebastián, 1964), 8. The only notable nationalist group in the French district is Enbata, which emerged in 1960 and was formally organized in 1963. It advocates the unified autonomy of the three French Basque provinces and ultimately the confederation of all seven Basque provinces within the framework of a federal western Europe. Enbata advocates parliamentary democracy and emphasizes technocratic economic administration and planning. It blames the French government for purposeful neglect of the nonindustrial French Basque region. Enbata

received 5 percent of the vote in the French Basque country during the French general elections of 1967, but this dropped to 3 percent under the pressure of resurgent Gaullism in 1968.

In recent years the French government has placed increasing restrictions on some aspects of the Basque and Breton movements within France. It has tried to prevent radical Spanish Basque nationalists from taking up residence in the French Basque country, and in 1971 several Enbata leaders were sentenced to a month's imprisonment for "inflammatory" and "subversive" activities in connection with the celebration of the *Aberri Eguna*.

Enbata has published a good deal of propaganda defining its position, and there is a sketch in J. P. Mogui, *La Révolte des Basques* (Paris, 1970), 53–62. On the regionalist problem in France as a whole, see Paul Sérant, *La France des minorités* (Paris, 1965); Thiébaut Flory, *Le Mouvement régionaliste français* (Paris, 1966); Robert Lafont, *La Révolution régionaliste* (Paris, 1967).

29. In a completely apolitical vein a new nationalist cultural movement called GERO emerged in 1962, devoted to building a spirit of unity and cooperation among all Basques, expanding the knowledge and use of *Euskera* and developing Basque culture in all seven provinces. The full text of the 1962 GERO program is given in *Vasconia*, 589–602.

30. Two tiny Basque socialist groups have appeared during recent years, but neither has been able to mobilize support.

The first was named ELNAS (standing for Basque Workers and Peasants Socialist Party) and stood for an independent Basque republic based on the communal *biltzar*. It called for the "communalization" of land and industry and required that all its members either know Euskera or learn it within two years of joining. (See *Vasconia*, 619–20). After ELNAS faded, a group called ESBA was formed, but did only slightly better.

31. Compared with ETA, the PNV has received scant attention in recent years. There is a limited sketch in Sergio Vilar, *Protagonistas de la España democrática* (Paris, 1968), 527–34.

32. There are sketches of the origins of ETA in Arteaga, 239–41; Juan Pérez del Corral in *Arriba* (Madrid), Aug. 4, 1968; and in Mogui, 62–75. There is a chronology in Patxi Isaba, *Euzkadi socialiste* (Paris, 1971), 17–20, 158–59.

33. By the 1960s the Communist party of Spain was calling for a "plurinational" rather than federal system to replace Franquism, with special statutes for Catalonia, Galicia and the Basque country and lesser autonomies for ordinary provinces. Guy Hermet, *Les Communistes en Espagne* (Paris, 1971), 170.

34. This account follows Arteaga, 242−55.

35. These developments have been primarily through the accounts appearing in the *New York Times*. One of the more unique incidents was the arrest of seven Basque mountaineers in November 1967 after their return from an expedition to the Andes. They were charged with having planted the Basque nationalist flag atop one of the mountains they had conquered.

36. Kepa Salaberri, *El proceso de Euskadi en Burgos* (Paris, 1971), 66−67.

37. The foregoing was gleaned from reports in the *New York Times* and *Alderdi* (a PNV bimonthly), and Da Silva, 149−51.

38. A list of terrorist and sabotage activities attributed to ETA down to the close of 1970 is given in Arteaga, 379−84.

39. In addition, two hundred young Basques were arrested at Guernica in April 1970 after a protest commemorating the thirty-third anniversary of the bombing.

40. For a full account of the trial and attendant events from the opposition viewpoint, see Salaberri and also G. Halemi, *Le Procès de Burgos* (Paris, 1971). The official Spanish version is in Arteaga, 273−94.

41. For a chronicle of the assassination and its immediate political aftermath, see Joaquín Bardavío, *La crisis: Historia de quince días* (Madrid, 1974).

42. There is an excellent discussion of the ways in which Basque nationalism and other contemporary movements have confounded the older political science theories in Da Silva, 211−16 and passim.

43. The correspondent Richard Eder quoted one young nationalist in 1968: "We cannot carry Spain on our backs indefinitely. The Castilians, the Andalusians are uneducated and primitive and they are not really ready for democracy. As long as we are tied to Spain, we shall have to endure their dictatorship." *New York Times*, Dec. 3, 1968.

44. Participation by heads of families in the 1971 Cortes elections was only 26 percent in Guipúzcoa and 33 prrcent in Vizcaya. *La Gaceta del Norte* (Bilbao), Sept. 31, 1971, in Medhurst. This was the lowest in Spain, whereas under the Republic the Basque provinces had registered the highest electoral participation figures in Spain.

45. A recent unpublished study by Davydd Greenwood has shown that in part of Guipúzcoa the flight from the land is due mainly to cultural not economic factors. The lure of urban industrial society is even strong enough to outweigh pure income considerations among some of the more affluent farmers, and has evidently become irreversible. Certain aspects of contemporary Basque village mores have been studied by William A. Douglass, *Death in Murélaga* (Seattle, 1969).

46. Cf. Gonzalo Sáenz de Buruaga, *Ordenación del territorio. El caso del País Vasco y su zona de influencia* (Madrid, 1969), 274–80. In the 1960s Asturias surpassed Vizcaya as the leading steel-producing province, though the entire Basque complex as a whole still produces 50 percent of the steel in Spain.

In a similar vein, Víctor Alba has argued in *Catalunya sense cap ni peus* (Barcelona, 1971) that, due to recent social and economic changes in Catalonia, Spain, and western Europe the terms of the old Catalan problem have been transcended and that contemporary Catalanism must adjust accordingly. A succinct recent overview of the Catalan economy from the Catalan point of view has been given by Ramon Trías Fargas, *Introducció a l'economia de Catalunya* (Barcelona, 1972).

The most ambitious current attempt to survey the entire Basque problem and recommend solutions within the Spanish context is José Miguel de Azaola's projected three-volume *Vasconia y su destino*. The first volume, *La regionalización de España*, appeared in 1972.

47. Recent summaries of the persistence of regional-national identities have been given by Oriol Pi-Sunyer, "The Maintenance of Ethnic Identity in Catalonia," and W.A. Douglass and Milton da Silva, "Basque Nationalism," in Pi-Sunyer, ed., *The Limits of Integration: Ethnicity and Nationalism in Modern Europe* (University of Massachusetts Dept. of Anthropology Research Report No. 9, Oct., 1971).

48. Nonetheless, the continuing resistance to autonomy even in a fully representative polity can remain significant. For an overview of the regional autonomy issue in Italian politics, there is a study by L. B. Weinberg, "The *Senz' Altro* Tradition in Italian Politics: The Regions and the Parties" (Ph.D. diss., Syracuse University, 1968).

Appendix One

PRINCIPAL POLITICAL

ORGANIZATIONS

ANV (*Acción Nacionalista Vasca*). Basque Nationalist Action party, organized in 1930 to represent the more liberal, pro-Republican, and somewhat anticlerical minority in the movement.

BBB (*Bizkai-Buru-Batzar*). Vizcayan provincial committee of the Basque Nationalist party.

CEDA (*Confederación Española de Derechas Autónomas*). The major party of all-Spanish political Catholicism under the Second Republic, organized in 1932.

CNT (*Confederación Nacional del Trabajo*). The anarcho-syndicalist movement of Spain, which was first organized in 1910 and became a mass movement after 1917.

CNV (*Comunión Nacionalista Vasca*). Basque Nationalist Communion, a temporary transformation of a major portion of the PNV between 1917 and 1930 that sought greater compromise and cooperation with the Spanish political system. The CNV and branch PNV were reunited in 1930.

CT (*Comunión Tradicionalista*). Traditionalist Communion, reorganized movement of the Spanish Carlists, formed in 1931.

EBB (*Euzkadi-Buru-Batzar*). *Euzkadi* national committee of the PNV.

Esquerra Catalana. Catalan Left, a coalition of lower-middle-class radical and/or progressive Catalan nationalist groups, which was organized in 1930 and became the dominant political force in Catalonia under the Republic.

Estat Català. Catalan State, a radical Catalanist group based on middle-class youth organized in the 1920s.

ETA (*Euzkadi ta Azkatasuna*). Basque Land and Liberty, a clandestine, terrorist Basque nationalist group organized in 1959 that adopted the adjective of "Marxist" and propounds the fusion of Basque nationalism and "revolutionary socialism."

FAI (*Federación Anarquista Ibérica*). Iberian Anarchist Federation, dominant organizational nucleus of Spanish anarchism, first organized in 1926 and seizing predominant influence within the CNT in 1931–32.

Lliga Regionalista (Regionalist League), reorganized in 1931 as the *Lliga Catalana*. From the beginning of the century to 1936 the party of moderate (and often conservative) middle-class Catalanism.

PNV (*Partido Nacionalista Vasco*). The principal standard-bearer of Basque nationalism, organized in 1895, temporarily split in two between 1917 and 1930. Has remained the core Basque nationalist party.

POUM (*Partido Obrero de Unificación Marxista*). A small "revolutionary Marxist-Leninist" party organized in 1935, representing the extreme left wing of organized Spanish politics, quite sympathetic to left Catalanism, and to progressive regionalism generally.

SIM (*Servicio de Inteligencia Militar*). Chief military intelligence organ of the Spanish Republican army during the Civil War.

STV (*Solidaridad de Trabajadores Vascos*). Basque nationalist trade union movement organized in 1911. Associated with the PNV, it espoused the principles of Rerum Novarum and of social Catholicism.

UGT (*Unión General de Trabajadores*). The Spanish Socialist trade union movement, organized in 1879 and later particularly strong in Vizcaya.

Appendix Two

NAMES OF BATTALIONS IN
THE *EJERCITO DE EUZKADI* [1]

Official Number and Name	*Origin and Meaning of Name*
PNV battalions:	
13 Itxas-Alde	"By the seashore," composed of men from the coast.
14 Araba	"Alava," composed of men from that province.
15 Ibaizábal	A river in Vizcaya.
16 Gordexola	Site of a military victory against Castilian forces in 1355.
17 Itxarkundia	"Awakening."
18 Loyola	Apparently named after the town where the unit was raised.
19 Amayur	A mountain in Navarra.
37 Otxandiano	A town in Vizcaya where forces of the Castilian crown were defeated in 1355.
38 Avellaneda	The assembly place of the Vizcayan *Encartaciones*.
39 Arana Goiri	The founder of the party.
40 Mungia	Site of a military victory in 1470.

[1] For this list I am indebted to Mr. Michael Alpert of the Polytechnic Institute of Central London, who is preparing a general study of the Spanish Republican army.

Official Number and Name	*Origin and Meaning of Name*
41 Padura	Site of a military victory against Leonese forces in 888.
49 Larrazábal	A rural *finca* where Arana met with supporters.
50 San Andrés	Patron saint of the STV.
53 Saseta	One of the organizers of the Basque units, later killed in action.
54 Malato	Site where a famous tree marked the boundary of Vizcaya.
55 Kirikiño	"Hedgehog"—A Basque writer whose real name was Evaristo de Bustintza.
56 Martiatu	Place near Algorta at the mouth of the Bilbao estuary.
57 Muñatones	A castle in the Basque country.
59 Rebelión de la Sal	Commemorated Basque refusal to pay a salt tax imposed by the Castilian crown in the fourteenth century.
62 Ariztimuño	The Guipuzcoan priest and party leader executed by the Spanish Nationalists.
69 Sukarrieta	The Arana Goiri family home.
70 Simón Bolíbar	The Liberator of northern South America, whose family was of Basque origin.
71 Aralar	Site of shrine of San Miguel, the patron saint of Basque nationalism.
77 Irrintzi	Cry signifying euphoria.
79 Alkartzeak	"Signals and liaison."

Jagi-Jagi battalions:

31 Zabalbide	A town in Vizcaya.
33 Lenago-il	⎰ Titles of songs by Arana Goiri meaning
66 Zergaitik-ez	⎱ "Death before surrender" and "Why not?"

ANV battalions:

6

23

68

Leftist battalions:

1

2 Meabe	A Socialist leader.
3 MAOC	Initials of the Communist party militia.

Official Number and Name		*Origin and Meaning of Name*
4	Rosa Lux- emburgo	A prominent Polish Social Democrat.
5	UHP	Abbreviation for slogan, "Unite, Proletarian Brothers!"
7	Azaña	
8	Rusia	
9	Mateos	A Socialist leader.
10	Facundo Perezagua	An early Communist leader in the Basque country.
20	Azaña	
22	Dragones	
24	Prieto	Socialist leader in Bilbao.
25	UGT	Initials of the Socialist trade union organization.
26	Karl Liebknecht	A German Spartacist leader.
27	Casilla	A district in Bilbao.
28	Martínez de Aragón	A Communist regular army officer.
29	Leandro Carro	A Communist leader.
30	Celta	Perhaps the name of a football club.
32	Madrid	
34	Carlos Marx	
35	Amuátegui	A Socialist leader from Eibar.
36	Malatesta	Famous Italian anarchist.
42	Pablo Iglesias	Founder of the Spanish Socialist party.
43	Cultura y Deporte	Perhaps named after a sports group.
44	Salsamendi	Unknown.
46	Octubre	After the insurrection of October 1934.
47		
48	UGT	
52	Capitán Casero	Perhaps named after Félix Casero, who led a group of Asturians in the defense of Irún in August 1936.

Official Number and Name		*Origin and Meaning of Name*
58	Lenin	
60	MAOC	
61		
63		
67	Guillermo Torrijos	A Socialist leader in Guipúzcoa.

CNT battalions included 11, 12, 61 and 65. Regular army units incorporated into the Basque forces were numbered 1, 64, and 72 to 78. Most of the information in this list was derived from *Gudari*, an émigré journal of Basque nationalists, and Martínez Bande, *Vizcaya*, 131.

Works Cited

I. Official Publications and Archival Collections

Documents on German Foreign Policy, 1918-1945. Series D, III. Washington, D.C., 1950.

Jefatura de Servicios Documentales, Salamanca. Legajos Bilbao.

Public Record Office of Great Britain. British Diplomatic Correspondence from and concerning the Basque Country, 1935−37.

II. Unpublished Reports and Memoirs

Aguirre y Lecube, José Antonio de. "Informe" to the Spanish Republican Government-in-exile, Oct. 15, 1950. Bolloten Collection, Hoover Institution. Stanford, California.

Irujo, Manuel de. "La Guerra Civil en Euzkadi antes del Estatuto." Bayonne, Jan. 6, 1938. Bolloten Collection, Hoover Institution. Stanford, California.

Onaindía, P. Alberto. "Antecedentes de la capitulación de Santoña."

III. Unpublished Studies

Bard, R. R. "The Medieval Fueros of Navarre." Master's thesis, University of Washington, 1971.

Bilbao, Jon. "Raíces del nacionalismo vasco en el siglo XIX." Paper presented at the meeting of the Society for Spanish and Portuguese Historical Studies, April, 1972.

Blinkhorn, R .M. "The Carlist Movement in Spain 1931−1937." Ph.D. dissertation, Oxford University, 1970.

Reece, J. E. "Anti-France: The Search for the Breton Nation (1898−1948)." Ph.D. dissertation, Stanford University, 1971.

Silva, Milton da. "The Basque Nationalist Movement." Ph.D. dissertation, University of Massachusetts, 1972.

Tusell Gómez, J., and G. García Queipo de Llano. "Introducción a una Sociología Electoral del País Vasco durante la Segunda República." 1973.

Weinberg, L. B. "The *Senz' Altro* Tradition in Italian Politics: The Regions and the Parties." Ph.D. dissertation, Syracuse University, 1968.

IV. Books and Pamphlets

A Reply to the Anglo-Christino Pamphlet entitled "The Policy of England towards Spain." London, 1837.

Adán, Joaquín. *Obra póstuma.* Bilbao, 1938.

Aguado Sánchez, Francisco. *La revolución de octubre de 1934.* Madrid, 1972.

Aguirre y Lecube, José Antonio de. *De Guernica a Nueva York pasando por Berlín.* Buenos Aires, 1943.

————. *Entre la libertad y la revolución. 1930-1935.* Bilbao, 1935.

Alba, Víctor. *Catalunya sense cap ni peus.* Barcelona, 1971.

Altabà-Planuc, Ricard. *Vuit mesos a la delegació del govern d' Euzkadi.* Barcelona, 1938.

Altabella Gracia, Pedro P. *El catolicismo de los nacionalistas vascos.* Madrid, 1939.

Alzola y Minondo, Benito de. *Estudio relativo a los recursos de que la industria naval dispone para las construcciones y armamentos navales.* Madrid, 1886.

Alzola y Minondo, Pablo de. *Informe relativo al estado de la industria siderúrgica en España.* Bilbao, 1904.

Ametlla, Claudi. *Memòries polítiques 1890-1917.* Barcelona, 1963.

Aralar, José de. *Los adversarios de la libertad vasca 1794-1829.* Buenos Aires, 1944.

Arana y Goiri, Luis de. *Formulario de los principios esenciales o básicos del primitivo Nacionalismo Vasco contenidos en el lema "Jaungoikua-eta-lagizarra."* Bilbao, 1932.

Arana y Goiri, Sabino de. *Obras completas.* Buenos Aires, 1965.

Aranzadi, Engracio de ("Kizkitza"). *Ereintza (Siembra de Nacionalismo Vasco).* Zarauz, 1935.

————. *La nación vasca.* Bilbao, 1918.

Arbeloa, Joaquín. *Los orígenes del Reino de Navarra,* 3 vols. San Sebastián, 1969.

Ardit, Manuel. *Els valencians de les Corts de Cadis.* Barcelona, 1968.

Areitio y Mediolea, Darío de. *Temas históricos vascos.* Bilbao, 1969.

————. *Los vascos en la historia de España.* Bilbao, 1959.

Arenillas, José Ma. *Euzkadi, la cuestión nacional y la revolución socialista*. Paris, 1969.

Ariztimuño, José de. *La democracia en Euzkadi*. San Sebastián, 1934.

Arocena, Fausto de. *Guipúzcoa en la historia*. Madrid, 1964.

Arocena, Ignacio. *Oñacinos y gamboínos*. Pamplona, 1959.

Aróstegui Sánchez, Julio. *El carlismo alavés y la guerra civil de 1870-1876*. Vitoria, 1970.

Arquer, Jordi. *Los comunistas ante el problema de las nacionalidades ibéricas*. Barcelona, 1936.

Arrarás, Joaquín, ed. *Historia de la Cruzada española*. 8 vols. Madrid, 1940-43.

————. *Historia de la segunda República española*. 4 vols. Madrid, 1956-68.

Arrese, Domingo de. *Bajo la Ley de Defensa de la República*. Madrid, 1933.

————. *El País Vasco y las Constituyentes de la Segunda República*. Madrid, 1931.

Arteaga, Federico. *E. T. A. y el proceso de Burgos*. Madrid, 1971.

Artíñano y Zuricalday, Arístides. *El Señorío de Bizcaya, histórico y foral*. Barcelona, 1885.

Aunós, Eduardo. *Discurso de la vida*. Madrid, 1951.

Azaña, Manuel. *Obras completas*. 4 vols. Mexico City, 1968.

Azaola, José Miguel de. *Vasconia y su destino*. Madrid, 1972.

Azcoitia, Xavier. *Defensa de la obra de los vascos. ¡Cavernícolas, cavernícolas!* Bilbao, 1931.

Azcona y Díaz, J. *Zumalacárregui*. Madrid, 1946.

Aznar, Manuel. *Historia militar de la guerra de España*. Madrid, 1940.

Azpiazu, P. Iñaki de. *El caso del clero vasco*. Buenos Aires, 1957.

Azpilikoeta, Dr. de, ed. *The Basque Problem as seen by Cardinal Gomá and President Aguirre*. New York, 1939.

Badía La Calle, José. *El Concierto Económico con Alava*. Bilbao, 1965.

Balcells, Albert. *El problema agrari a Catalunya 1890-1936*. Barcelona, 1968.

Balparda, Gregorio de. *La crisis de la nacionalidad y la tradición vascongada*. Bilbao, 1932.

————. *Errores del nacionalismo vasco*. Bilbao, 1919.

————. *¿Federalismo? ¡Feudalismo!*. Bilbao, 1931.

————. *Historia crítica de Vizcaya y de sus Fueros*. 3 vols. Madrid, 1924-25.

————. *Relaciones entre el Estado y la Iglesia en Vizcaya*. Bilbao, 1908.

El Banco de Vizcaya y su aportación a la economía española. Bilbao, 1955.

Barthe, Roger. *L'idée latine*. 2 vols. Toulouse, 1951–52.

Basaldúa, Pedro de. *En defensa de la verdad*. Buenos Aires, 1956.

———. *El libertador vasco*. Buenos Aires, 1953.

Belforte, Gen. Francesco. *La Guerra Civile in Spagna*. 4 vols. Milan, 1938–39.

Bernoville, G., Etcheverry, M., Veyrin, P., and Ithurriague, J., *Pays Basque*. Strasbourg, 1964.

Beurko, Sancho de (pseud. of Ruiz de Aguirre). *Gudaris*. Buenos Aires, 1956.

Bilbao, Jon, *Eusko Bibliographia*. 3 vols. San Sebastián, 1970.

Borrow, George. *The Bible in Spain*. London, 1906.

Boussard, Léon. *L'Irrintzina, ou le destin des Basques*. Paris, 1969.

Burgo, Jaime del. *Bibliografía de las guerras carlistas y de las luchas políticas del siglo XIX*. 5 vols. Pamplona, 1966.

———. *Conspiración y guerra civil*. Madrid, 1970.

———. *Requetés en Navarra antes del alzamiento*. Pamplona, 1954.

Burgo, Jaime Ignacio del. *Ciento veinticinco años de vigencia del Pacto-Ley de 16 de agosto de 1841*. Pamplona, 1966.

———. *Origen y fundamento del régimen foral de Navarra*. Pamplona, 1968.

———. *El Paco Foral de Navarra*. Pamplona, 1966.

———. *Régimen fiscal de Navarra*. Pamplona, 1971.

Calatrava, Francisco. *La abolición de los fueros vasco-navarros*. Madrid, 1876.

Calvo Sotelo, José. *Mis servicios al Estado*. Madrid, 1931.

Cambó, Francesc. *Vuit mesos al Ministeri de Foment*. Barcelona, 1919.

Campión, Arturo. *Discursos políticos y literarios*. Pamplona, 1907.

Camps i Arboix, J. de. *Història de l' agricultura catalana*. Barcelona, 1969.

———. *Història de la Solidaritat Catalana*. Barcelona, 1970.

———. *El Memorial de Greuges*. Barcelona, 1968.

Candel, Francesc. *Els altres catalans*. Barcelona, 1966.

Cantalupo, Roberto. *Embajada en España*. Barcelona, 1951.

Carballo Calero, Ricardo. *Historia da literatura galega contemporánea*. Vol. 1. Vigo, 1963.

Carmona, Angel. *Dues Catalunyes*. Barcelona, 1967.

Caro Baroja, Julio. *La hora navarra del siglo XVIII*. Pamplona, 1969.

———. *Vasconiana*. Madrid, 1957.

———. *Los Vascos*. Madrid, 1958.

Carretero, Felipe. *Crítica del nacionalismo vasco*. Bilbao, n. d. (ca. 1918).

Carretero y Nieva, Luis. *Las nacionalidades españolas*. Mexico City, 1952.

Castro Delgado, Enrique. *Hombres Made in Moscú*. Barcelona, 1963.

Celaya Ibarra, Adrián. *El Derecho foral de Vizcaya en la actualidad*. Bilbao, 1970.

Centro de Información Católica Internacional. *El clero y los católicos vasco-separatistas y el Movimiento Nacional*. Madrid, 1940.

Chalbaud y Errazquin, Luis. *La familia como forma típica y trascendental de la constitución social vasca*. Bilbao, 1919.

Chilcote, Ronald H. *Spain's Iron and Steel Industry*. Austin, 1968.

Cía Navascuez, P. *Memorias del Tercio de Montejurra*. Pamplona, 1941.

Cierva, Ricardo de la. *Historia de la Guerra Civil española*. Vol. I. Madrid, 1969.

――――. *Historia ilustrada de la Guerra Civil española*. 2 vols. Barcelona, 1971.

Le Clergé Basque. Paris, 1938.

El Clero vasco frente a la Cruzada franquista. Toulouse, 1966.

Contestación de la Excelentísima Diputación de Vizcaya a la Memoria que la Excelentísima Diputación de Guipúzcoa proponía se elevase al Directorio Militar sobre el régimen de las Provincias Vascongadas. Bilbao, 1924.

Cordero, Juan Luis. *Regionalismo (Problemas de la provincia de Cáceres)*. Barcelona, 1917.

Cortada, E. *Catalunya i la Gran Guerra*. Barcelona, 1969.

Coverdale, John F. *Mussolini and Franco. Italian Intervention in the Spanish Civil War*. Princeton, 1975.

Cruells, Manuel. *Els fets de maig*. Barcelona, 1972.

――――. *El 6 d'octubre a Catalunya*. Barcelona, 1970.

Cucó, Alfons. *Aspectes de la política valenciana en el segle XIX*. Barcelona, 1965.

――――. *El valencianisme polític 1874-1936*. Valencia, 1971.

Cucurull, Fèlix. *Orígens i evolució del federalisme català*. Barcelona, 1970.

Délégation Basque. *La Question Basque*. Lausanne, 1917.

Díaz, José. *Por la unidad, hacia la victoria*. Valencia, 1937.

Douglass, William A. *Death in Murélaga*. Seattle, 1969.

Echave-Sustaeta, E. *El partido carlista y los fueros*. Pamplona, 1914.

Echeandía, Dr. José. *La persecución roja en el País Vasco*. Barcelona, 1945.

Echegaray, Carmelo de. *Compendio de las instituciones forales de Guipúzcoa*. San Sebastián, 1924.

————. *Las provincias vascongadas a fines de la Edad Media*. San Sebastián, 1895.

Elías de Tejada, Francisco. *La Provincia de Guipúzcoa*. Madrid, 1965.

————. *El Reino de Galicia hasta 1700*. Vigo, 1966.

————. *El Señorío de Vizcaya (hasta 1812)*. Madrid, 1963.

————. *La tradición gallega*. Madrid, 1944.

Escarra, Edouard. *El desarrollo industrial de Cataluña (1900-1908)*. Barcelona, 1970.

Escarzaga, P. Eduardo de. *Avellaneda y la Junta General de las Encartaciones*. Bilbao, 1927.

Estecha y Martínez, José Ma. *Régimen político y administrativo de las provincias vasconavarras*. Bilbao, 1920.

Estelrich, Juan. *La cuestión vasca y la guerra civil española*. Buenos Aires, 1937.

Estella, P. Bernardino de. *Historia vasca*. Bilbao, 1931.

Estornés Lasa, B. and M. *¿Cómo son los vascos?* San Sebastián, 1967.

"Evangelista de Ibero," P. (pseud. of Goicoechea Oroquieta). *Ami vasco*. 3rd ed. Buenos Aires, 1957.

Faldella, Emilio. *Venti mesi di guerra in Spagna*. Florence, 1939.

Farré Moregó, José Ma. *Los atentados sociales en España*. Madrid, 1922.

Fernández Etxeberría, M. *Euzkadi, patria de los vascos*. Caracas, 1969.

Ferrer, Melchor, et al. *Historia del Tradicionalismo español*. 30 vols. Seville, 1930–59.

Figuerola, Laureano. *Estadística de Barcelona en 1849*. Barcelona, 1968.

Flory, Thiébaut. *Le Mouvement régionaliste français*. Paris, 1966.

Frutos, Víctor de. *Los que no perdieron la guerra*. Buenos Aires, 1967.

Fundación FOESSA. *Informe sociológico sobre la situación social de España 1970*. Madrid, 1970.

Galíndez, Jesús. *Los vascos en el Madrid sitiado*. Buenos Aires, 1945.

Gallastegui, Elías de. *Por la libertad vasca*. Bilbao, 1935.

García de Castro, R. G. *La tragedia espiritual de Vizcaya*. Granada, 1938.

García de Cortázar, J. A. *Vizcaya en el siglo XV*. Bilbao, 1966.

García de Salazar, Lope. *Las bienandanzas e fortunas*. Bilbao, 1955.

García Fernández, Lt. Col. Julio. *Diario de operaciones del 3er Batallón de Palencia y 5a Bandera de Navarra*. Burgos, 1939.

García Venero, Maximiano. *Historia del nacionalismo catalán*. 2 vols. Madrid, 1967.

————. *Historia del nacionalismo vasco*. Madrid, 1968.

García Villada, Z. *Organización y fisionomía de la Iglesia española*. 2 vols. Madrid, 1935.

Gil Cremades, J. J. *El reformismo español*. Barcelona, 1969.

Gil Robles, José Ma. *No fue posible la paz*. Barcelona, 1969.

————. *The Spanish Republic and Basque Independence*. London, 1937.

Gomá y Tomás, Isidro Cardenal. *Pastorales de la guerra de España*. Madrid, 1955.

González Echegaray, Joaquín. *Los cántabros*. Santander, 1966.

González Sugrañes, Miguel. *La República en Barcelona*. Barcelona, 1896.

Graell, Guillermo. *La cuestión catalana*. Barcelona, 1902.

La Gran Enciclopedia Vasca. 7 vols. Bilbao, 1962– .

Granados, Anastasio. *El cardenal Gomá*. Madrid, 1969.

Guerra, Juan Carlos de. *Oñacinos y gamboínos*. San Sebastián, 1930.

Guerra de Liberación Nacional. Zaragoza, 1961.

Guiard y Larrauri, Teófilo. *La industria naval vizcaina*. Bilbao, 1968.

Halemi, G. *Le Procès de Burgos*. Paris, 1971.

Hayes, C. J. H. *The Historical Evolution of Modern Nationalism*. New York, 1932.

Hermet, Guy. *Les Communistes en Espagne*. Paris, 1971.

Hernández, Jesús. *Yo, ministro de Stalin en España*. Madrid, 1954.

Hurtado, Amadeu. *Quaranta anys d'advocat*. 2 vols. Barcelona, 1967–69.

Ibarruri, Dolores. *They Shall Not Pass*. New York, 1966.

Informe sobre la situación de las provincias vascongadas bajo el dominio rojo-separatista. Valladolid, 1938.

Iradier, Manuel. *Africa: Viajes y trabajos de la Asociación Euzkara "La Exploradora."* 2nd ed. 2 vols. Vitoria, 1958.

Iribarren, José Ma. *Mola*. Zaragoza, 1938.

Irujo, Daniel de. *Inocencia de un patriota*. Buenos Aires, 1913.

Irujo, Manuel de. *Inglaterra y los vascos*. Buenos Aires, 1946.

————. *Instituciones jurídicas vascas*. Buenos Aires, 1945.

Isaba, Patxi. *Euzkadi socialiste*. Paris, 1971.

Iturralde, Juan de (pseud. of P. Usabiaga). *El Catolicismo y la cruzada de Franco*. 3 vols. Vienne-Toulouse, 1955–65.

Jamar, Benito. *La cuestión vascongada*. San Sebastián, 1891.

Jemein, Ceferino de. *Biografía de Arana Goiri 'tar e Historia gráfica del Nacionalismo*. Bilbao, 1935.

Joaniquet, Aurelio. *Calvo Sotelo*. Madrid, 1939.

Jústiz, Martín de. *En defensa del Concierto Económico del País Vasco*. San Sebastián, 1936.

Jutglar, Antonio. *Federalismo y revolución*. Barcelona, 1966.

Labayru, E. J. de. *Historia general del Señorío de Bizcaya*. 6 vols. Bilbao, 1895–1903.

Lacarra, José Ma. *Estudios de historia navarra*. Pamplona, 1971.

————. *Historia política del Reino de Navarra desde sus orígenes hasta su incorporación a Castilla*. Pamplona, 1972.

Lafarga, Adolfo. *Aportación a la historia social y política de Vizcaya (Siglos XVI a XIX)*. Bilbao, 1971.

Lafarga Lozano, A. *Los vascos en el descubrimiento y colonización de América*. Bilbao, 1973.

Lafont, Robert. *La Révolution régionaliste*. Paris, 1967.

Largo Caballero, Francisco. *Mis recuerdos*. Mexico City, 1954.

Larrañaga, Jesús. *¡Por la libertad de Euzkadi, dentro de las libertades de España!* Barcelona, 1937.

Lasala y Collado, Fermín. *La separación de Guipúzcoa y la Paz de Basilea*. Madrid, 1895.

————. *La última etapa de la unidad nacional. Los fueros vascongados en 1876*. Madrid, 1924.

Lazúrtegui, Julio de. *Una nueva Vizcaya a crear en el Bierzo*. Bilbao, 1918.

Lecuona, Manuel de. *Literatura oral vasca*. San Sebastián, 1964.

Lequerica, José Félix de. *La actividad económica de Vizcaya en la vida nacional*. Madrid, 1956.

Libro del Aberri-Eguna. Bilbao, 1932.

Lizarra, A. de (pseud. of Andrés de Irujo). *Los vascos y la República española*. Buenos Aires, 1944.

Llorens, Josep M. *La Iglesia contra la República española*. N. p., 1968.

Llorens, Rodolf. *Com han estat i com som els catalans*. Barcelona, 1968.

López, Juan. *Una misión sin importancia*. Madrid, 1972.

Lorenzo, César M. *Les Anarchistes espagnols et le pouvoir*. Paris, 1969.

Madariaga, Ramón de. *El derecho foral de Vizcaya en relación con la organización familiar*. Bilbao, 1932.

Madariaga, Salvador de. *Memorias de un federalista*. Buenos Aires, 1967.

Mañaricúa, Andrés E. de. *Historiografía de Vizcaya*. Bilbao, 1971.

Mañé y Flaquer, Juan. *El oasis. Viaje al país de los fueros*. 3 vols. Barcelona, 1878−80.

————. *La paz y los fueros*. Barcelona, 1876.

Mar, Ramón de la. *El separatismo vasco-catalán favorece a España*. Bilbao, 1933.

Maravall, José Antonio. *El concepto de España en la Edad Media*. Madrid, 1954.

Martínez Bande, Col. J. M. (Servicio Histórico Militar.) *El final del frente Norte*. Madrid, 1972.

————. *La guerra en el Norte*. Madrid, 1969.

————. *Vizcaya*. Madrid, 1971.

Martínez de Campos, Lt. Gen. Carlos. *Dos batallas de la Guerra de Liberación de España*. Madrid, n. d.

Medhurst, Kenneth. *The Basques*. London, 1972.

Melià, Josep. *Informe sobre la lengua catalana*. Madrid, 1970.

Merry del Val, Marquis. *The Spanish Basques and Separatism*. London, 1939.

Michelena, Luis de. *Historia de la literatura vasca*. Madrid, 1960.

————. *D. Resurrección Ma. de Azkue*. Bilbao, 1966.

Miguel, Amando de and Juan Salcedo. *Dinámica del desarrollo industrial de las regiones españolas*. Madrid, 1972.

Miró, Fidel. *Cataluña, los trabajadores y el problema de las nacionalidades*. Mexico City, 1967.

Mogui, J. P. *La Révolte des Basques*. Paris, 1970.

Molas, Isidre. *Lliga Catalana*. 2 vols. Barcelona, 1972.

————. *El sistema de partits polítics a Catalunya (1931-1936)*. Barcelona, 1972.

Montero Moreno, Antonio. *Historia de la persecución religiosa en España*. Madrid, 1961.

Muntanyola, Ramon. *Vidal i Barraquer, cardenal de la pau*. Barcelona, 1970.

Nogaret, Joseph. *Petite histoire du Pays Basque français*. Bayonne, 1928.

Olívar Bertrand, Rafael. *Prat de la Riba*. Barcelona, 1966.

Ortiz de Zárate, Ramón. *Jamás los romanos conquistaron completamente a los vascongados y nunca estos belicosos pueblos formaron parte integrante del imperio de los Césares*. Vitoria, 1866.

Ortueta, Anacleto. *Nabarra y la unidad política vasca*. Barcelona, 1931.

————. *Sancho el Mayor, rey de los vascos*. 2 vols. Buenos Aires, 1963.

Orueta, José de. *Fueros y autonomía*. San Sebastián, 1934.

Ossa Echaburu, Rafael. *Riqueza y poder de la ría 1900-1923*. Bilbao, 1969.

Oyarzun, Román. *Historia del carlismo*. Madrid, 1940.

Paavolainen, Jaako. *Poliittiset väkivaltaisundet Suomessa 1918*. 2 vols. Helsinki, 1967.

Pabón, Jesús. *Cambó*. 3 vols. Barcelona, 1952−68.

Partido Nacionalista Vasco. *La labor del Partido Nacionalista Vasco en materia religiosa y social*. Bilbao, 1936.

Payne, Robert, ed. *The Civil War in Spain*. London, 1963.

Peiró, Juan. *Problemas y cintarazos*. Rennes, 1946.

Pi-Sunyer, Oriol, ed. *The Limits of Integration: Ethnicity and Nationalism in Modern Europe*. Univ. of Massachusetts Dept. of Anthropology Research Report No. 9, Oct., 1971.

Piazzoni, Sandro. *Las tropas "Flechas Negras" en la guerra de España*. Barcelona, 1941.

Pinilla de las Heras, E. *L'empresari català*. Barcelona, 1967.

Pirala, Antonio. *Historia contemporánea*. 6 vols. Madrid, 1879.

Pla, Josep. *Cambó*. 3 vols. Barcelona, 1930.

Poblet, Josep M. *El moviment autonomista a Catalunya dels anys 1918-1919*. Barcelona, 1971.

————. *Els precursors de la renaixença*. Barcelona, 1968.

Posada, Adolfo. *La evolución legislativa del régimen local*. Madrid, 1910.

Prieto, Indalecio. *Palabras al viento*. Mexico City, 1969.

Primer Congreso de Estudios Vascos. Bilbao, 1919.

Primo de Rivera, Miguel. *Intervenciones en la Asamblea Nacional del General Primo de Rivera*. Madrid, 1930.

El Pueblo Vasco frente a la cruzada franquista. Toulouse, 1966.

Puget, H. *Le Gouvernement local en Espagne*. Paris, 1920.

Ramos Oliveira, Antonio. *Historia de España*. 3 vols. Mexico City, 1952.

Redondo, Gen. Luis and Maj. Juan de Zavala. *El Requeté*. Barcelona, 1957.

Ribas de Piña, Col. M. *El 11° Ligero durante el Primer Año Triunfal*. Santander, 1938.

Roca, F. León. *Blasco Ibáñez*. Barcelona, 1970.

Rodríguez Garraza, Rodrigo. *Navarra de Reino a provincia (1828-1841)*. Pamplona, 1968.

Romero Radigales, Sebastián de. *El separatismo vasco*. Sofia, 1938?

Rovira Virgili, Antoni. *Els polítics catalans*. Barcelona, 1929.

————. *Prat de la Riba*. Barcelona, 1968.

————. *Resum d'història del catalanisme*. Barcelona, 1936.

————. *Valentín Almirall*. Barcelona, 1936.

Royo Villanova, Antonio. *El problema catalán*. Madrid, 1908.

Sabaté, Modest. *Història de la "Lliga."* Barcelona, 1968.

Sacz, M. *Bayonne et le Pays Basque*. Bayonne, 1968.

Sáenz de Buruaga, Gonzalo. *Ordenación del territorio. El caso del País Vasco y su zona de influencia*. Madrid, 1969.

Sagarmínaga, Fidel de. *El gobierno y el régimen foral de Vizcaya*. 8 vols. Bilbao, 1892.

Salaberri, Kepa. *El proceso de Euskadi en Burgos*. Paris, 1971.

Salas Larrazábal, Jesús. *La guerra de España desde el aire*. Barcelona, 1969.

Salas, Ramón. *Historia del Ejército Popular de la República*. Madrid, 1974. 4 vols.

Salaverría, José M. *Iparraguirre, el último bardo*. Madrid, 1932.

Sanabre, Josep. *Resistencia del Rosselló a incorporarse a França*. Barcelona, 1970.

Sánchez Ramos, F. *La economía siderúrgica española*. Madrid, 1945.

Sanchis Guarner, M. *Renaixença al País Valencià*. Barcelona, 1968.

Sarrailh de Ihartza, Fernando (pseud. of Federico Krutwig Sagredo). *Vasconia*. Buenos Aires, 1962.

Sarraill, F. (pseud. of ibid.). *La cuestión vasca*. N. p., n. d., (ca. 1967).

Sérant, Paul. *La France des minorités*. Paris, 1965.

Shafer, Boyd. *Faces of Nationalism*. New York, 1972.

———. *Nationalism: Myth and Reality*. New York, 1955.

Sierra Bustamante, Ramón. *Euzkadi*. San Sebastián, 1941.

Smith, Anthony D. *Theories of Nationalism*. New York, 1971.

Los socialistas vascos frente a la actitud del gobierno provisional de su región. Mexico City, 1945.

Solá, Lluís. *¡Cu-cut! (1902-1912)*. Barcelona, 1967.

Solé Tura, Jordi. *Catalanisme i revolució burgesa*. Barcelona, 1967.

Soraluze, Andoni de. *Riqueza y economía del País Vasco*. Buenos Aires, 1945.

Steer, G. L. *The Tree of Gernika*. London, 1938.

Talón, Vicente. *Arde Guernica*. Madrid, 1970.

Tasis, Rafael. *La renaixença catalana*. Barcelona, 1967.

Torras Elías, Jaime. *La guerra de los Agraviados*. Barcelona, 1967.

Torras i Bages, Josep. *La Iglesia y el regionalismo*. Barcelona, 1887.

———. *La tradició catalana*. Barcelona, 1892.

Tortella Casares, Gabriel. *Los orígenes del capitalismo en España*. Madrid, 1972.

Tovar, Antonio. *The Basque Language*. Philadelphia, 1957.

Trainin, I. P. *Baski v borbe za svoiu natsionalnuiu nezavisimost*. Moscow, 1937.

Trías Fargas, Ramon. *Introducció a l'economia de Catalunya*. Barcelona, 1972.

Trueba, Antonio de. *Bosquejo de la organización social de Vizcaya*. Bilbao, 1870.

Tusell Gómez, Javier, et al. *Las elecciones del Frente Popular*. 2 vols. Madrid, 1971.

Ubieto Arteta, Antonio. *Ciclos económicos en la Edad Media española*. Valencia, 1969.

Ulibarri, Gen. Gámir. *De mis memorias: Guerra de España 1936-1939*. Paris, 1939.

276 BASQUE NATIONALISM

Unamuno y Jugo, Miguel de. *Obras completas*. 16 vols. Madrid, 1959—64.

Urkina, J. de. *La democracia en Euzkadi*. San Sebastián, 1935.

Varela, José Luis. *Poesía y restauración cultural de Galicia en el siglo XIX*. Madrid, 1958.

Veyrin, Philippe. *Les Basques de Labourd, Soule et Basse-Navarre*. Paris, 1955.

Vicens Vives, Jaime. *An Economic History of Spain*. Princeton, 1969.

———. *Cataluña en el siglo XIX*. Madrid, 1961.

———. *Noticia de Cataluña*. Barcelona, 1954.

Vilar, Pierre. *La Catalogne dans l'Espagne moderne*. 3 vols. Paris, 1963.

Vilar, Sergio. *Protagonistas de la España democrática*. Paris, 1968.

Vizcarra, P. Zacarías de. *Vizcaya españolísima*. San Sebastián, 1938.

Walton, W. *The Revolutions of Spain from 1808 to the End of 1836*. 2 vols. London, 1837.

Ximénez de Embrun, T. *Ensayo histórico acerca de los orígenes de Aragón y Navarra*. Zaragoza, 1878.

Yanguas y Miranda, José de. *Diccionario de antigüedades del Reino de Navarra*. 3 vols. Pamplona, 1840—43.

Ybarra, Javier de. *Política nacional en Vizcaya*. Madrid, 1948.

Zabala, Federico de. *Historia del Pueblo Vasco*. 2 vols. San Sebastián, 1971.

Zabala y Allende, Federico. *El Concierto Económico*. Bilbao, 1927.

Zariátegui, J. A. *Vida y hechos de D. Tomás Zumalacárregui*. San Sebastián, 1946.

Zugazagoitia, Julián. *Guerra y vicisitudes de los españoles*. 2 vols. Paris, 1968.

Zumeta, Angel de, ed. *Un cardenal español y los católicos vascos*. Bilbao, 1937.

———. *La guerra civil en Euzkadi. La teología de la invasión*. Paris, 1937.

V. Articles

Areilza, José Ma. de. "Otro centenario: Sabino de Arana y Goiri." *Vizcaya*, no. 24 (1965).

Burgo, Jaime Ignacio del. "Descentralización foral." *El Europeo* (Madrid-Barcelona), Mar. 24, 1972.

García Venero, M. "La Solidaridad de Obreros Vascos (1911—1937)." *Revista de Trabajo*, no. 8, 3—21.

"Getting at the Guernica Myth." *National Review*, XXV:35 (Aug. 31, 1973), 936—42.

González Blasco, Pedro. "Modern Nationalism in Old Nations as a Consequence of Earlier State-Building: The Case of Basque-Spain," in W. Bell and W. E. Freeman, eds., *Ethnicity and Nation-Building* (Forthcoming).

Levine, Morton. "The Basques." *Natural History*, 76, no. 4 (April, 1967), 44–51.

Linz, Juan J. "Early State-Building and Late Peripheral Nationalisms against the State," in S. N. Eisenstadt and S. Rokkan, eds., *Building States and Nations* (Beverly Hills, 1974).

———. "Politics in a Multi-Lingual Society with a Dominant World Language: The Case of Spain," in J. G. Savard and R. Vegneault, eds., *Les Etats multilingues: Problèmes et solutions* (Quebec, 1974).

——— and Amando de Miguel. "Within-Nation Differences and Comparisons: The Eight Spains," in R. L. Merritt and S. Rokkan, eds., *Comparing Nations* (New Haven, 1966).

Lluch, Ernest. "La Catalunya del segle XVIII i la lluita contra l'absolutisme centralista." *Recerques* (Barcelona, 1970), 1, 33–50.

Martínez Esparza, Gen. José. "El sitio de Villarreal de Alava." *Ejército*, no. 111 (April 1946).

Moral Sandoval, E. "El nacionalismo catalán: esquema de su evolución." *Boletín Informativo de Ciencia Política*, no. 7 (Aug. 1971).

Muñatones, Isidro. "El Partido Nacionalista Vasco: Su desarrollo." *Alderdi*, no. 262 (April, 1971), 28–32.

Torras, Jaume. "Societat rural i moviments absolutistes." *Recerques*, 1 (1970), 123–30.

VI. Newspapers

ABC (Madrid), 1933–34.

Aberri (Bilbao), 1921–23.

Arriba (Madrid), 1968–72.

Euzkadi (Bilbao), 1914–23, 1931–37.

Euzkadi Roja (Bilbao), 1937.

La Gaceta Regional (Salamanca), 1936–37.

El Heraldo Alavés (Vitoria), 1931–32.

La Libertad (Bilbao), 1931.

New York Times, 1968–72.

El Pensamiento Navarro (Pamplona), 1936–37.

Index